Modern HOME PLUMBING

Modern HOME PLUMBING
REPAIRS, IMPROVEMENTS AND PROJECTS

by Mort Schultz

CREATIVE HOMEOWNER PRESS®

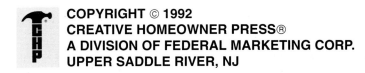
Editor: Kimberly Kerrigone
Illustrations: James Randolph
Additional Illustrations: Norman Nuding
Production Assistants: Mindy Circelli
                        Carolyn Anderson-Feighner

Cover Design: Warren Ramezzana
Cover photograph: Decorage, Ltd./George Kopp
                   Products courtesy of American Standard, Inc.

Illustrations found on the following pages are reprinted with permission from *The Family Handyman:* 32 (Figs. 1 and 2), 33 (Fig. 4), 35 (Figs. 2 and 3), 71 (Figs. 2 and 4), 75 (Fig. 5).

Technical Review: Patrick J. Higgins,
                     P.J. Higgins and Associates

                     Milton Snyder,
                     Maryland State Board
                     of Plumbing Commissioners

Electronic Prepress: M.E. Aslett Corporation
Printer: Webcrafters, Inc.

Current Printing (last digit)
10 9 8 7 6 5

LC: 91-76827
ISBN: 1-880029-01-4 (paper), 1-880029-11-1 (hardcover)

CREATIVE HOMEOWNER PRESS®
A DIVISION OF FEDERAL MARKETING CORP.
24 PARK WAY,
UPPER SADDLE RIVER, NJ 07458

HOW TO USE THIS BOOK

An understanding of how your home's plumbing system works will be a big help as you tackle projects involving plumbing fixtures and appliances. It also will help you pinpoint what is going wrong when a plumbing-related problem arises.

Chapter I provides you with a clear, simplified description so you can understand how your home's plumbing system works. In Chapter II, you'll find a list of tools for doing home plumbing. The function of each tool is described to help you make any necessary purchases. In addition, each project in the book lists the tools and materials required to complete the job. Those you actually may need depend on what you encounter.

Each of the four chapters that follow Chapter II is devoted to projects involving a plumbing fixture. Chapter III is "All About Sinks" (the term "sink" includes those in bathrooms, which in plumbing parlance are called lavatories). The 20 projects included in this chapter cover repairs and improvements a homeowner might need to make to a sink or lavatory.

Included are repairing all the various types of faucets, relieving clogs in the drainage network, temporary and permanent repairs to

the various kinds of water pipes, installing water shutoff valves, replacing a faucet, repairing damage to the surface of a sink and installing a larger sink.

The same concept developed in

CAUTION

Use caution, care, and good judgment when following the procedures described in this book. To prevent injury, observe precautions. We urge you to wear goggles and the appropriate gloves (work or rubber) at all times, as even a sliver of material in the eye or hand can be serious. To prevent electric shock, use a battery-operated light or flashlight when working near or with water. All projects and repairs in this book conform to "The National Standard Plumbing Code" and "The National Electric Code" that is current at the time of publication. Always obey local codes and laws and follow manufacturers' operating instructions when available.

Chapter III is carried through in Chapters IV, V and VI for toilets, bathtubs and showers and water heaters, respectively. Notice that each of these chapters begins with a section entitled "Anatomy of a . . . (sink, toilet, bathtub and shower, or water heater)" and a section entitled "Troubleshooting Guide."

The anatomy sections describe in

layman's terms the design of the particular plumbing fixture. The Troubleshooting Guide gives you a step-by-step approach to resolving plumbing problems. Suppose, for example, a toilet in your house is making noise. Consult that part of the Toilet Troubleshooting Guide that describes the reasons and cures for a noisy toilet. By going down that list and making the called-for inspections, you'll be able to pinpoint the cause of your problem and the recommended repair.

The final chapter in this book, Chapter VII, is a catchall chapter that, with one exception, guides you in making major improvements in your plumbing system. The exception is the project on handling and avoiding emergencies, which is more in the realm of repair than improvement.

For the most part, the various projects described in Chapter VII involve extension of the home's existing plumbing system. Therefore, the first three sections of the chapter cover what you should know about that system before you begin any of the jobs. Many of the projects in this chapter involve carpentry and electrical skills, as well as plumbing.

Difficulty Scale

There is a difficulty scale rating presented for each project: one hammer if we consider the job an easy one to do, two hammers if it's moderately difficult, and three hammers if it's difficult.

EASY

MODERATELY DIFFICULT

DIFFICULT

Admittedly, ratings are the author's opinion and are subjective. You may or may not agree with them. In either case, the instructions and illustrations will show and tell you in a clear and concise way how to tackle a particular project. They also will help you decide if a particular project is one you should undertake or leave for a professional.

CONTENTS

ALL ABOUT SINKS

ALL ABOUT TOILETS

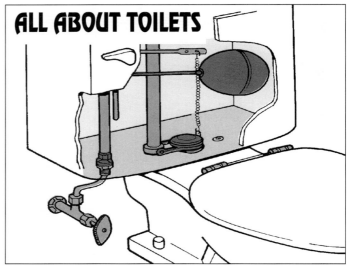

ALL ABOUT TUBS AND SHOWERS

ALL ABOUT WATER HEATERS

MAKING PLUMBING IMPROVEMENTS

Anatomy of the Modern Home Plumbing System

The plumbing system in your home delivers potable (drinking) water and carries away waste and sewage. Waste is liquid. Sewage is waste containing animal or vegetable matter in suspension or solution.

Potable water is defined by the National Standard Plumbing Code (NSPC) as "Water free from impurities present in amounts sufficient to cause disease or harmful physiological effects and conforming in bacteriological and chemical quality to the requirements of the Public Health Service Drinking Water Standards or the regulations of the public health authority having jurisdiction."

Potable water is pumped from reservoirs by companies that comply with government regulations. If your water doesn't come from this municipal source, it comes from your own private well, in which case you're responsible for its quality. For example, if it contains a high level of sulfur, it's up to you to get an effective filtration system installed.

If you reside in an urban or suburban area, the plumbing system in your home is probably connected to a municipal sewer that carries waste and sewage to a treatment plant. If you reside in a rural area, you probably have a septic tank to handle sewage and a distribution box to dispense waste. In time, a septic tank, which is buried on your property, has to be emptied by trained service personnel who haul matter to treatment facilities.

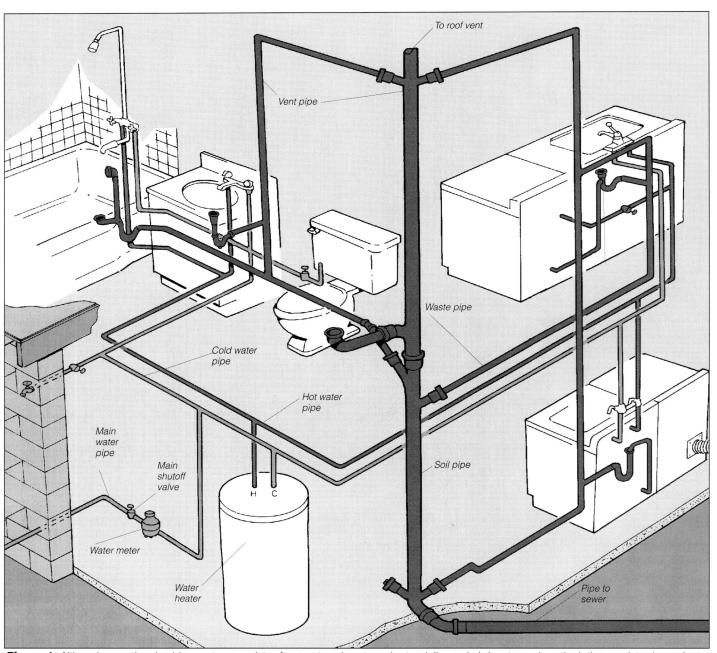

Figure 1. Although an entire plumbing system consists of separate subsystems (water delivery, drain/waste, and venting), they are interdependent.

Water Delivery

The illustrations on this page (Figures 2 and 3) show the parts of a typical home plumbing system via the hot and cold water systems. The delivery of potable water is done through pipes or lines that transport it to plumbing fixtures, plumbing appliances, and to outside-the-house spigots. Water enters the home from the municipal or private source through a main pipe, which parcels it into branch lines. Branch lines carry water to fixtures, appliances, and points outside the house.

Plumbing fixtures are sinks (this book uses sink and lavatory interchangeably), toilets, bathtubs, shower stalls, and bidets. Plumbing appliances are washing machines, dishwashers, garbage disposers, water heaters and boilers of heating systems. Points outside the house include faucets, in-the-ground lawn sprinklers and swimming pools.

Every pipe transporting potable water in a modern home plumbing system should have a water shutoff valve so if it becomes necessary to turn off water on a particular pipe you won't have to shut down the entire system. The valve on the main pipe, when closed, stops the flow of water throughout the house. It is usually located on the inlet side of the water meter. Shutoff valves on each pipe should be near the fixture or appliance the pipe serves. There should be a shutoff valve on the interior side of a pipe where it penetrates the wall to the outside. Turning off water becomes necessary when making a repair and at other times as a precaution.

For example, when a washing machine isn't in use, it's a good idea to keep the shutoff valves on the hot and cold water branch pipes serving the machine turned off to prevent flooding if a hose connecting a branch pipe to the machine's water-intake valve disintegrates and splits.

If your home is served by a well, the pump (probably of the submersible type) and holding tank are parts of the water delivery setup. Potable water pumped into the house from the well flows into the holding tank and is held there until it's needed. When you turn on a faucet or flush a toilet, a diaphragm inside the holding tank reacts to differences in air and water pressure to drive the water from the tank to the fixture or appliance.

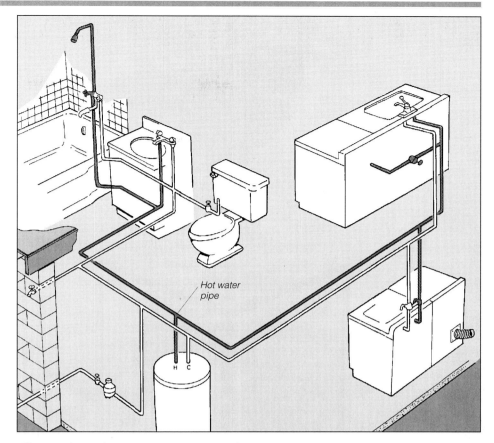

Hot water pipe

Figure 2 *(above) shows how hot water gets from a municipal water supply into the water heater and then to fixtures and appliances while* **Figure 3** *(below) shows the route for cold water from a municipal water supply to inside the home.*

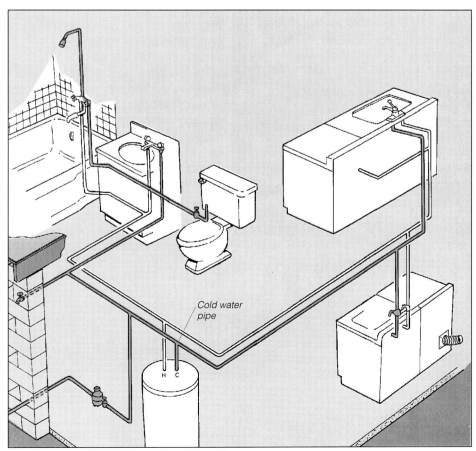

Cold water pipe

Anatomy of the Modern Home Plumbing System

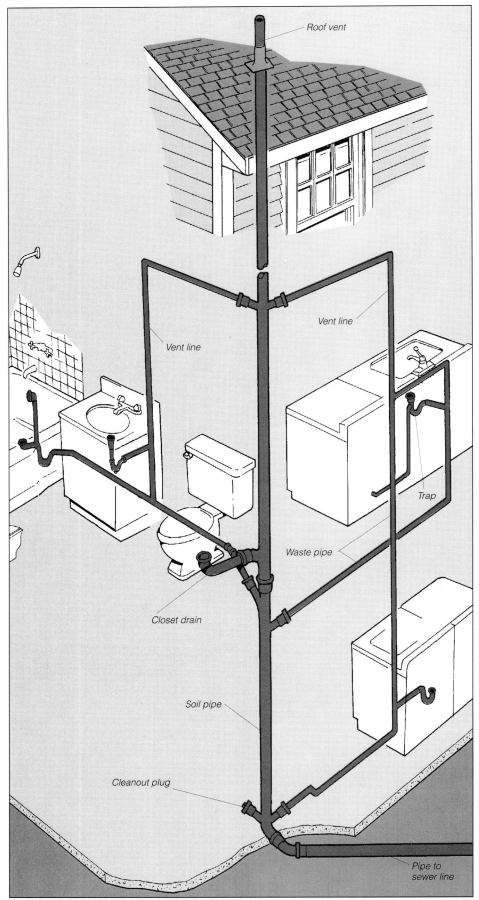

Figure 4. The drain, waste, vent (DWV) system transports waste and sewage from fixtures and appliances to the sewer or septic tank.

Drainage and Venting

Drainage of waste and sewage is done through a network of various size pipes that transport waste and sewage from fixtures and appliances to the sewer or septic tank/distribution box network (Figure 4). The largest pipe is the soil pipe. It's the one into which all others drain. The soil pipe transports waste and sewage outside the house to the sewer or septic tank/distribution box network.

Toilets utilize soil pipes that are as large as the main soil pipe into which they empty. The water in a toilet bowl serves two purposes: (l) to carry away sewage and waste; (2) to block sewage gas from permeating the house.

Each sink, bathtub, stall shower, bidet, washing machine and dishwasher is outfitted with the smallest diameter pipes of the drainage network. (Note: The term sink includes lavatories.) They're called waste pipes. Each waste pipe has a curved section that remains filled with water. This acts as a trap to block sewer gases. In fact, this section is called a trap.

With a sink, the trap is usually right beneath the sink and in view. With other fixtures and appliances, the trap is exposed below the floor in the basement. If the home doesn't have a basement, the trap may be embedded in the floor with a removable cover often provided over an opening so there's access to the trap.

The soil pipe and waste pipes of a modern plumbing system should be outfitted with a cleanout plug that can be removed to gain access into the pipe when it becomes clogged. Closet drains do not have cleanout plugs.

Extensions from the soil pipe project through the roof of the house for venting. Each fixture and appliance is connected to an extension via a vent line. Venting is necessary to maintain an equalization of air and/or water pressure throughout the drainage network so traps and toilet bowls won't have water pulled out of them. This siphoning action would leave the house exposed to sewage gases.

One or more venting methods may be employed. They include continuous venting, dry venting, wet venting, individual venting (or reventing), loop venting, relief venting and side venting. The positioning of vents is established by the National Standard Plumbing Code or the municipal plumbing code.

TOOLS FOR EVERY JOB

This section provides a general reference guide to tools used in repairing and modernizing a home plumbing system. It supplements the lists titled "Tools & Materials" that accompany the step-by-step directions before each project described in this book. The information will help you identify tools and review their recommended uses.

Even though the tools illustrated and described below are classified as plumbing tools, some have nonplumbing uses. They include the hacksaw, adjustable pliers, vise-grip pliers, offset screwdriver, deep socket and ratchet, and propane torch.

Each tool described below is placed into one of six categories (1) general purpose tools that don't fit any of the other categories; (2) cutting tools; (3) holding and/or turning tools; (4) forming tools; (5) appliance repair tools; and (6) common tools.

General Purpose Tools

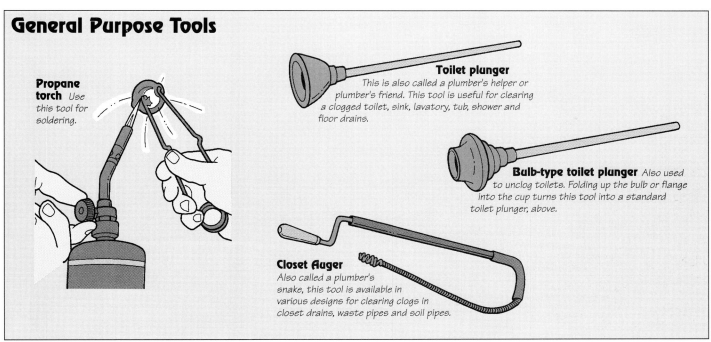

Propane torch Use this tool for soldering.

Toilet plunger
This is also called a plumber's helper or plumber's friend. This tool is useful for clearing a clogged toilet, sink, lavatory, tub, shower and floor drains.

Bulb-type toilet plunger Also used to unclog toilets. Folding up the bulb or flange into the cup turns this tool into a standard toilet plunger, above.

Closet Auger
Also called a plumber's snake, this tool is available in various designs for clearing clogs in closet drains, waste pipes and soil pipes.

Cutting Tools

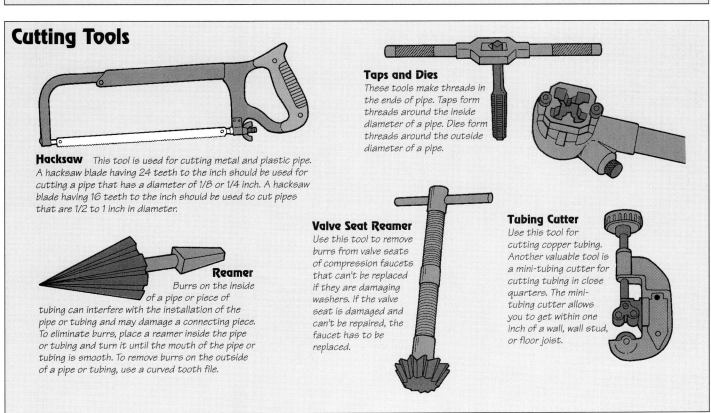

Hacksaw This tool is used for cutting metal and plastic pipe. A hacksaw blade having 24 teeth to the inch should be used for cutting a pipe that has a diameter of 1/8 or 1/4 inch. A hacksaw blade having 16 teeth to the inch should be used to cut pipes that are 1/2 to 1 inch in diameter.

Reamer
Burrs on the inside of a pipe or piece of tubing can interfere with the installation of the pipe or tubing and may damage a connecting piece. To eliminate burrs, place a reamer inside the pipe or tubing and turn it until the mouth of the pipe or tubing is smooth. To remove burrs on the outside of a pipe or tubing, use a curved tooth file.

Taps and Dies
These tools make threads in the ends of pipe. Taps form threads around the inside diameter of a pipe. Dies form threads around the outside diameter of a pipe.

Valve Seat Reamer
Use this tool to remove burrs from valve seats of compression faucets that can't be replaced if they are damaging washers. If the valve seat is damaged and can't be repaired, the faucet has to be replaced.

Tubing Cutter
Use this tool for cutting copper tubing. Another valuable tool is a mini-tubing cutter for cutting tubing in close quarters. The mini-tubing cutter allows you to get within one inch of a wall, wall stud, or floor joist.

Holding and/or Turning Tools

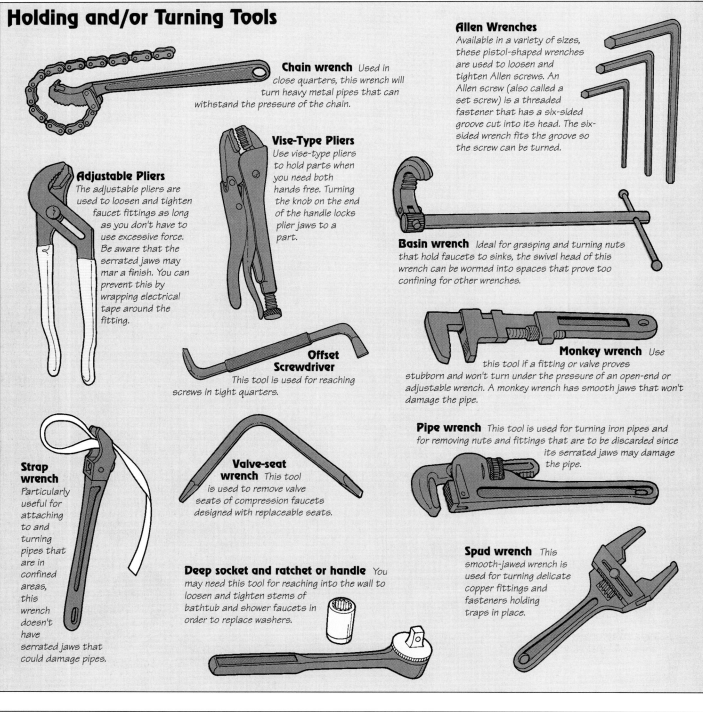

Chain wrench Used in close quarters, this wrench will turn heavy metal pipes that can withstand the pressure of the chain.

Allen Wrenches Available in a variety of sizes, these pistol-shaped wrenches are used to loosen and tighten Allen screws. An Allen screw (also called a set screw) is a threaded fastener that has a six-sided groove cut into its head. The six-sided wrench fits the groove so the screw can be turned.

Adjustable Pliers The adjustable pliers are used to loosen and tighten faucet fittings as long as you don't have to use excessive force. Be aware that the serrated jaws may mar a finish. You can prevent this by wrapping electrical tape around the fitting.

Vise-Type Pliers Use vise-type pliers to hold parts when you need both hands free. Turning the knob on the end of the handle locks plier jaws to a part.

Basin wrench Ideal for grasping and turning nuts that hold faucets to sinks, the swivel head of this wrench can be wormed into spaces that prove too confining for other wrenches.

Offset Screwdriver This tool is used for reaching screws in tight quarters.

Monkey wrench Use this tool if a fitting or valve proves stubborn and won't turn under the pressure of an open-end or adjustable wrench. A monkey wrench has smooth jaws that won't damage the pipe.

Strap wrench Particularly useful for attaching to and turning pipes that are in confined areas, this wrench doesn't have serrated jaws that could damage pipes.

Valve-seat wrench This tool is used to remove valve seats of compression faucets designed with replaceable seats.

Pipe wrench This tool is used for turning iron pipes and for removing nuts and fittings that are to be discarded since its serrated jaws may damage the pipe.

Deep socket and ratchet or handle You may need this tool for reaching into the wall to loosen and tighten stems of bathtub and shower faucets in order to replace washers.

Spud wrench This smooth-jawed wrench is used for turning delicate copper fittings and fasteners holding traps in place.

Forming Tools

One or both of the following tools is used when installing copper tubing:

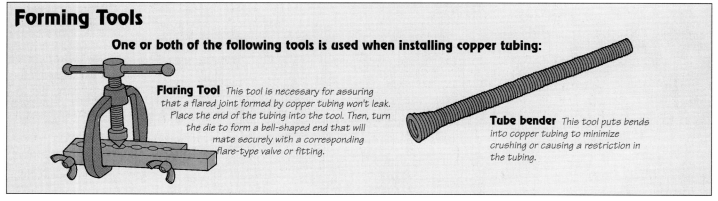

Flaring Tool This tool is necessary for assuring that a flared joint formed by copper tubing won't leak. Place the end of the tubing into the tool. Then, turn the die to form a bell-shaped end that will mate securely with a corresponding flare-type valve or fitting.

Tube bender This tool puts bends into copper tubing to minimize crushing or causing a restriction in the tubing.

Appliance Repair Tools

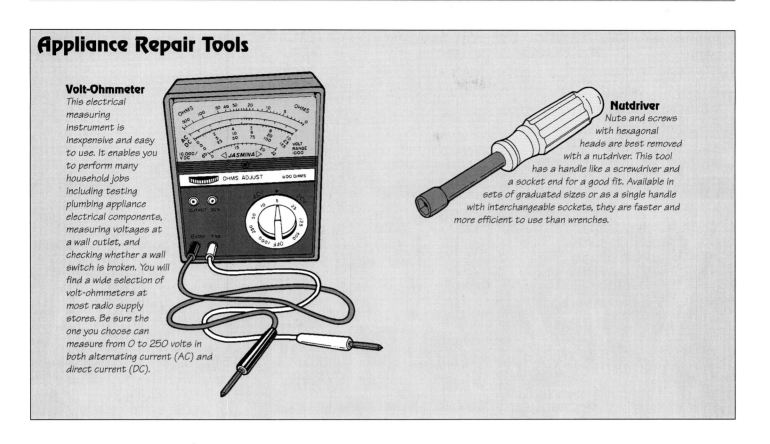

Volt-Ohmmeter
This electrical measuring instrument is inexpensive and easy to use. It enables you to perform many household jobs including testing plumbing appliance electrical components, measuring voltages at a wall outlet, and checking whether a wall switch is broken. You will find a wide selection of volt-ohmmeters at most radio supply stores. Be sure the one you choose can measure from 0 to 250 volts in both alternating current (AC) and direct current (DC).

Nutdriver
Nuts and screws with hexagonal heads are best removed with a nutdriver. This tool has a handle like a screwdriver and a socket end for a good fit. Available in sets of graduated sizes or as a single handle with interchangeable sockets, they are faster and more efficient to use than wrenches.

Common Tools

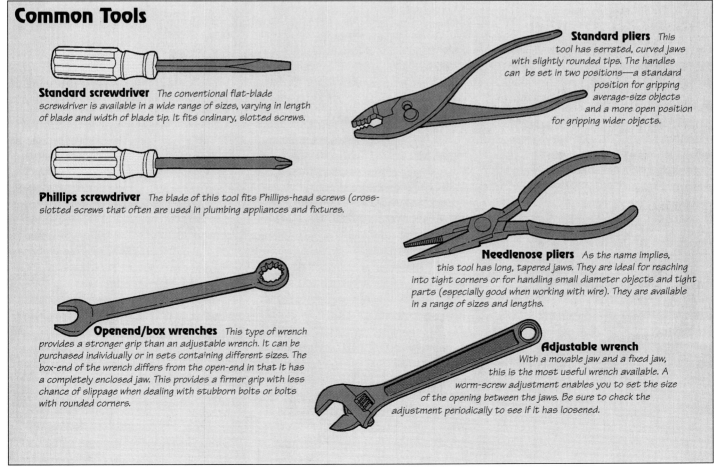

Standard screwdriver The conventional flat-blade screwdriver is available in a wide range of sizes, varying in length of blade and width of blade tip. It fits ordinary, slotted screws.

Phillips screwdriver The blade of this tool fits Phillips-head screws (cross-slotted screws that often are used in plumbing appliances and fixtures.

Openend/box wrenches This type of wrench provides a stronger grip than an adjustable wrench. It can be purchased individually or in sets containing different sizes. The box-end of the wrench differs from the open-end in that it has a completely enclosed jaw. This provides a firmer grip with less chance of slippage when dealing with stubborn bolts or bolts with rounded corners.

Standard pliers This tool has serrated, curved jaws with slightly rounded tips. The handles can be set in two positions—a standard position for gripping average-size objects and a more open position for gripping wider objects.

Needlenose pliers As the name implies, this tool has long, tapered jaws. They are ideal for reaching into tight corners or for handling small diameter objects and tight parts (especially good when working with wire). They are available in a range of sizes and lengths.

Adjustable wrench With a movable jaw and a fixed jaw, this is the most useful wrench available. A worm-screw adjustment enables you to set the size of the opening between the jaws. Be sure to check the adjustment periodically to see if it has loosened.

THE ANATOMY OF A SINK

A sink is called a sink unless it's in a bathroom. Then it's called a lavatory. Sink or lavatory, the job it does is the same—to provide a basin to receive potable water, to retain water for as long as you want and to allow water to drain when you're done with it.

Note: Throughout this section and in this book, the terms "sink" and "lavatory" are often used interchangeably.

Stopping and Straining

They may not look like much, but sinks and lavatories are carefully engineered pieces of equipment. According to the National Standard Plumbing Code, sinks and lavatories must have a device to retain water in the basin and to trap matter floating in the water so it can't flow into the waste pipe, causing a clog. The exception to this is a kitchen sink that supports a food waste disposer. It has a stopper—not a strainer—since you want food scraps to flow down the drain hole into the disposer.

Most lavatories have pop-up stoppers that are controlled by lift-rods. The height that a stopper can be raised can be limited so any large-size matter will be stopped from flowing through the drain hole into the waste pipe. Unfortunately, this does not include hair, which tangles around the stem part of the stopper. When enough hair gets entwined, it clogs the drain hole and restricts the flow. This is the main cause of a lavatory stoppage.

Older lavatories and utility room sinks use plain rubber or metal stoppers that you insert into and remove from drain holes by hand. Have you ever noticed, however, that the drain holes of these lavatories and sinks are outfitted with cross bars that will trap much of the debris floating in the water so it can't run into the waste pipe?

Holes

Everyone who's ever used a sink and lavatory knows what a drain hole looks like. But not everyone realizes that these holes are drilled to precise measurements. A drain hole of a kitchen sink is at least 1 1/2 inches in diameter unless the sink is outfitted with a food waste disposer (Figure 1); then, the drain hole must be no less than 3 1/2 inches in diameter. The drain hole of a sink in a utility room must also be at least 1 1/2 inches in diameter.

The drain holes of lavatories are drilled so they're at least 1 1/4 inches in diameter (Figure 2). Although not required by the National Standard Plumbing Code, lavatories also may have one or more holes called overflow ports. This hole (or holes) is located approximately three quarters of the way up on one wall of the basin. It allows water to drain so it doesn't overflow onto the floor if someone carelessly lets too much water flow into the lavatory when the stopper is closed or there's a clog.

There are other holes that become important when you buy a sink or lavatory and a faucet for it. The distance from the center of the hole in the sink or lavatory for the hot water side of the faucet to the center of the hole for the cold water side of the faucet is commonly 4 or 8 inches. Thus, distance between the hot and cold water sides of the faucet must match the distance between the holes in the sink or lavatory. This assumes that you're selecting a faucet with two handles. What about a one-handle faucet? Distance between holes is still critical. The mounts holding the faucet to the sink or lavatory fit into the holes. These mounts are commonly 4 or 8 inches apart as well.

Surface

You can install a sink or lavatory anywhere as long as potable water and a waste pipe are accessible. You can mount it on a wall. You can let it stand on legs or a pedestal, or you can insert it into a countertop. Lavatories also come as part of a countertop; that is, the

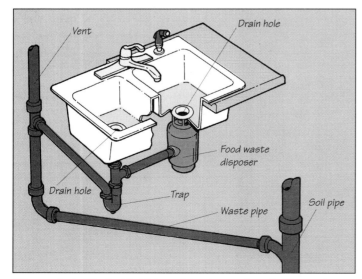

Figure 1. *In this double kitchen sink setup equipped with a garbage disposer, notice that only one side of the unit has a trap. The National Standard Plumbing Code permits this if the distance between sink drain openings is 30 inches or less.*

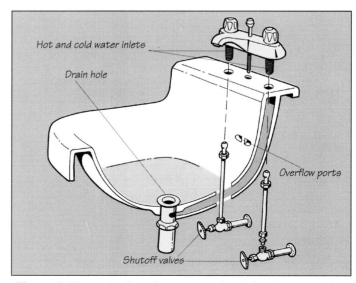

Figure 2. *When selecting a faucet to match a sink or lavatory, make sure that the hot and cold water inlets match the holes in the sink or lavatory.*

lavatory and countertop are formed as a one-piece unit.

Sinks and lavatories are made from a variety of materials, including enameled cast iron and steel, vitreous china, stainless steel, cultured marble, and plastic. The only qualification is that the surface be smooth and non-absorbent and meet standards established by the American Society of Mechanical Engineers. The surface may stain or chip. You can often repair minor imperfections (see page 56). You can't, however, fix a sink that cracks and leaks. It has to be replaced.

Myth Exploded. You <u>can</u> install a food waste disposer in a kitchen sink if your home is served by a septic system. The National Standard Plumbing Code does not prohibit this, and research done by food waste disposer manufacturers shows that there is no adverse effect on the septic system.

FAUCET AND DRAIN TROUBLESHOOTING

The following chart summarizes causes of and solutions for problems with faucets and drains.

PART INVOLVED	PROBLEM	CAUSE	SOLUTION
Two-Handle Faucets	Drip from spout	• Faucet open	• Close
		• Worn washer	• Replace (page 17)
		• Damaged washer seat	• Repair or replace (page 17), or replace faucet (page 17)
		• Impeded or worn cartridge (washerless faucet)	• Clean or Replace (page 17)
	Drip from around handle	• Loose packing nut	• Tighten (page 17)
		• Worn packing, packing washer, or O-ring	• Restore packing (page 17) or replace packing washer or O-ring (page 17)
One-Handle Faucets	Drip from spout or handle	• Faucet open	• Close
		• Deposits on ceramic disc	• Clean (page 19)
		• Worn water-inlet seals (ceramic disc type)	• Replace (page 19)
		• Loose tension ring (ball type)	• Tighten (page 20)
		• Corroded or damaged ball	• Replace (page 20)
		• Worn or damaged water port springs and seals (ball type)	• Replace (page 20)
		• Dirty tipping valve seat	• Flush (page 22)
		• Damaged seat or tipping valve	• Replace (page 22)
All Faucets	Leak from around spout Leak from around faucet base	• Damaged O-ring	• Replace (page 27)
		• Disintegrated caulk or gasket	• Seal with caulk (page 54)
Sink/Lavatory Drain	Water flow sluggish or stopped altogether	• Buildup of grease, hair or other matter in drain	• Remove & clean pop-up stopper (lavatory)(page 32)
			• Use plumber's helper (page 32)
			• Use chemical drain cleaner (page 32)
			• Remove & clean trap (page 33-34)
			• Use auger to clear matter from waste pipe (page 35)

REPAIRING FAUCETS
WASHER-STYLE TWO-HANDLE

Tools & Materials:
- ❑ conventional or Phillips screwdriver
- ❑ utility knife
- ❑ plastic-headed hammer
- ❑ adjustable wrench or pliers
- ❑ handle puller
- ❑ valve seat reamer
- ❑ valve seat wrench
- ❑ electrical tape
- ❑ washers and brass screws
- ❑ rope-type packing, packing washer or stem O-ring(s)
- ❑ petroleum jelly or heatproof grease

Remember: *Turn off the water shutoff valves or the main valve (see Figure 1, page 8) before beginning work.*

If you aren't sure whether your two-handle faucet is equipped with washers (Figure 1) or plastic cartridges, you'll find out when you disassemble the unit.

Disassembly

Remove the screw holding the handle to the stem and take off the handle. If the handle is outfitted with a cap, slip a utility knife under the cap and pry it off (Figure 2) to get at the screw holding the handle. A handle that is stubborn can often be loosened by tapping it from beneath with the handle of your screwdriver or a plastic-headed hammer. Easy does it. You don't want to crack the cap.

If there is no handle screw, the handle is pressed onto the stem. Wrap electrical tape around the tip of a screwdriver, slide the tip under the handle, and pry using moderate pressure. Move the position of the screwdriver and again apply pressure. Keep repeating the procedure, moving the screwdriver around the entire circumference, until the handle loosens. This method should also be used if a handle is stuck in place because of corrosion. If a handle is stubborn, you may have to use a handle puller (Figure 3).

When the handle is off, place an adjustable wrench on the stem retaining nut (often called the packing nut), and turn the wrench counterclockwise to loosen (Figure 4). You can use adjustable pliers, but protect the nut by wrapping electrical tape around the jaws of the pliers. Turn the stem out of the faucet by hand. If the stem is tight, re-attach the handle and use that for leverage.

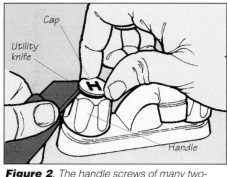

Figure 2. *The handle screws of many two-handle washer-style faucets are hidden under caps. They can be removed by placing the tip of a utility knife under the cap and prying up. If a faucet doesn't have caps or visible screws, look for Allen screws in the base of the handles.*

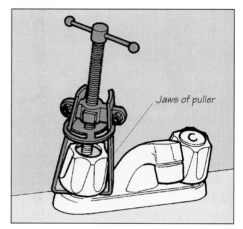

Figure 3. *If using excessive force would cause damage to a handle that is frozen tightly to a stem, then a special puller will be needed.*

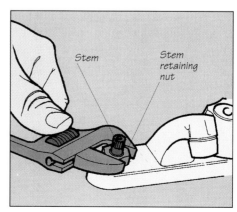

Figure 4. *With the handle removed, use a wrench or adjustable pliers to loosen the stem retaining nut. Remove the part by hand.*

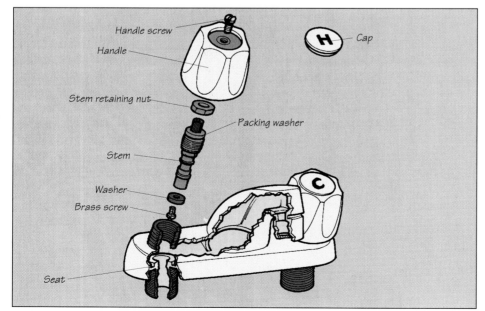

Figure 1. *Although styles have changed over the years, the internal parts of the compression or washer-style faucet have remained relatively the same.*

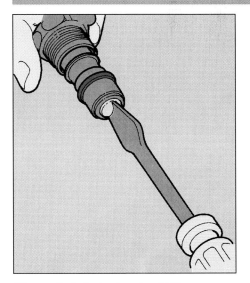

Figure 5. A single slotted or Phillips screw holds the worn washer to the stem. Use a conventional or Phillips screwdriver, respectively, to undo the screw.

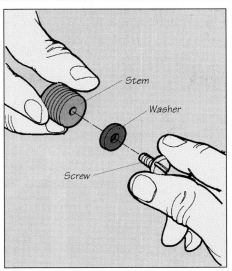

Figure 6. Replace both the washer with one that fits the stem and the brass screw that holds the washer to the stem.

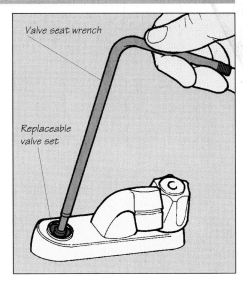

Figure 7. Seat damage occurs when faucets are overtightened. If this is causing washers to fail often, replace the seat (if possible).

Note: If the base of the stem doesn't have a washer, the faucet is the plastic cartridge design. Turn to page 24.

Leak from Spout

1. Remove the brass screw holding the washer to the stem (Figure 5). Take the old washer and brass screw with you when shopping for replacements to ensure the same sizes (Figure 6).

2. Attach the new washer to the stem with the new brass screw, tightening just enough to hold the washer securely.

3. If you've been experiencing frequent washer failure, the seat in the faucet against which the washer sits is probably damaged. You may be able to feel roughness by inserting your finger into the hole and moving it against the seat. Roughness can often be eliminated by rotating a valve seat reamer against the seat a few revolutions. If this doesn't help, use a valve seat wrench to replace a replaceable seat (Figure 7). A faucet that doesn't have replaceable seats will probably have to be replaced.

➡PLUMBER'S TIP:
If stems are equipped with neoprene caps instead of washers, you may not be able to find replacements. The design wasn't popular. Take the stem with you to see if you can find new stems of the same configuration that use washers. If this fails, replace the faucet.

Leak from Around Handle

If tightening the stem retaining nut doesn't stop a leak (see reassembly below), the seal around the stem needs to be replaced. Depending upon the age of your faucet, the seal is either a graphite-impregnated, rope-like material called packing (Figure 8) that's wrapped around the top of the stem, a packing washer that fits inside the stem retaining nut, or one or more small O-rings that fit into grooves in the stem (Figure 9). When purchasing replacements, take the stem with you to be certain you get what you need. If your stem uses O-rings, spread a thin coating of petroleum jelly or heatproof grease on them before putting them on the stem.

Reassembly

1. Remove any corrosive deposits from the metal or plastic part of the stem. If necessary, rub them off gently with fine (No. 000) steel wool. Place the stem back into the faucet, turning it clockwise by hand until it's tight.

2. Attach the handle and turn on the water. If there's a chatter, the washer is loose. Remove the stem to tighten the washer a bit more. If water seeps out from around the handle, the stem retaining nut may not be tight enough. Remove the handle and turn it another one-quarter turn.

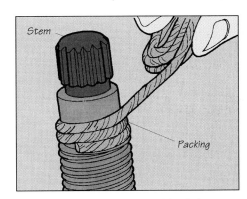

Figure 8. If the faucet is an old unit, it probably will require a winding of rope-type packing on the stem to prevent a leak from around the handle.

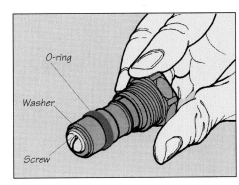

Figure 9. Instead of rope-type packing or a packing washer, modern faucets use O-rings to prevent leaks around handles. If there is a leak at a handle, the O-ring is worn. Lift it off using the tip of an awl and replace the part with a new one of the same size. However, before you do, coat the new O-ring with a thin layer of petroleum jelly.

REPAIRING FAUCETS
CERAMIC-DISC ONE-HANDLE

Tools & Materials:
❑ conventional or Phillips screwdriver
❑ Allen wrench
❑ pliers
❑ utility knife
❑ awl
❑ replacement assembly (if needed)

Remember: *Turn off the water shutoff valves or the main valve (see Figure 1, page 8) before beginning work.*

A ceramic-disc one-handle faucet consists of a cylinder in which there is a movable disc that rotates against a stationary disc to control the temperature of the water mixture.

➡**PLUMBER'S TIP:**
If you don't know whether you have a ceramic-disc (Figure 1) or ball-style one-handle faucet, you'll find out as soon as you remove the handle. You don't have to remove the handle to identify the tipping valve design (page 22).

Remove the Handle
Remove the handle by undoing the screw holding the handle (Figure 2) and then the cap, if there is one (Figure 3). The screw may be concealed under a cover or button.

Disassembly
If the problem is a leak around the handle, tightening the screws holding the ceramic-disc assembly should stop it.

To fix a leak from the spout, unscrew and remove the ceramic-disc assembly

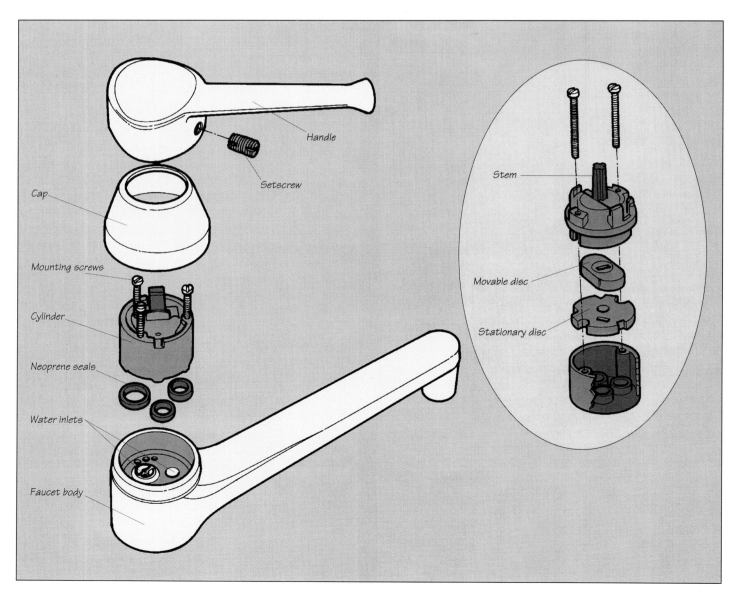

Handle

Setscrew

Cap

Mounting screws

Cylinder

Neoprene seals

Water inlets

Faucet body

Stem

Movable disc

Stationary disc

Figure 1. *The ceramic-disc one-handle faucet consists of a cylinder with seals that fit into openings in its base. These are the weakest link of this otherwise reliable unit.*

(Figure 4). Turning the cylinder upside down to remove the seals (Figure 5).

Clean both the base of the cylinder and the seats in which the seals sit (Figure 6). Flush with water to remove deposits that might be the reason for the leak.

Reassembly

Reinsert and secure the ceramic-disc assembly. Avoid overtightening screws. Turn on the water to see if the leak has been fixed. If not, disassemble the faucet again and replace seals (Figure 7).

To ensure proper fit, make sure you buy seals that fit your particular make of faucet.

If seals don't resolve the problem, replace the ceramic-disc assembly. When replacing the handle, place it in a partially open position and slowly turn on the water shutoff valves. When water flows smoothly, turn off the faucet.

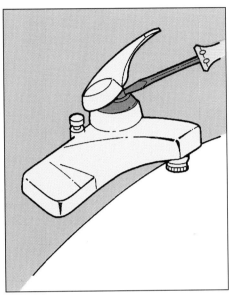

Figure 2. Begin repair by removing the setscrew, which may be a conventional straight-slot type, a Phillips-head screw or an Allen screw.

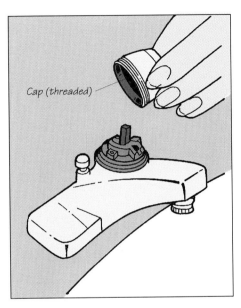

Figure 3. Remove the cap, which may or may not be threaded to the faucet body.

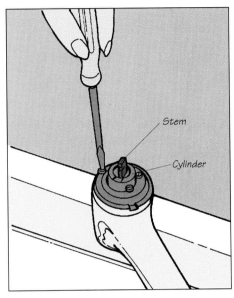

Figure 4. Undo the screws holding the cylinder in the faucet body and remove the cylinder. If the cylinder sticks, grab the stem with pliers and pull.

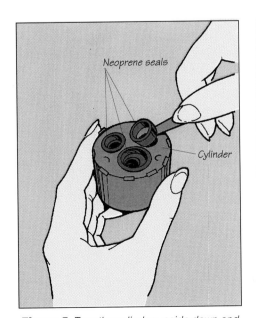

Figure 5. Turn the cylinder upside down and remove the seals.

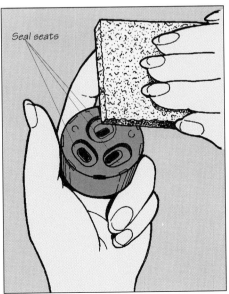

Figure 6. Clean the base of the cylinder and the seats in which seals fit. Be sure to flush the cylinder with water to get rid of deposits.

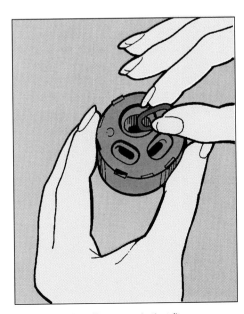

Figure 7. Install new seals that fit your particular make of faucet. Reinsert the cylinder, tighten screws and reassemble the other parts. Move handle to a partially open position and slowly turn on the water shutoff valves.

REPAIRING FAUCETS
BALL-TYPE ONE-HANDLE

Tools & Materials:
- ❏ conventional or Phillips screwdriver
- ❏ Allen wrench
- ❏ adjustable pliers
- ❏ electrical tape
- ❏ flashlight
- ❏ tension-ring spanner wrench
- ❏ seal and spring repair kit
- ❏ ball replacement kit
- ❏ tension ring, cam, & gasket repair kit

Remember: *Turn off the water shutoff valves or the main valve (see Figure 1, page 8) before beginning work.*

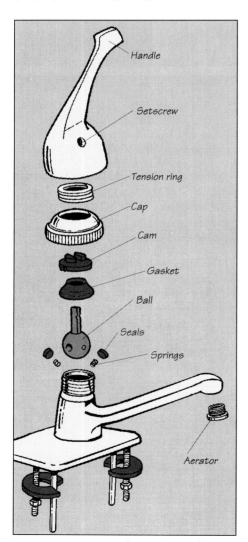

Figure 1. *A common variation of the ball-type one-handle faucet has a tension ring which, if loose, will allow water to drip from the spout.*

Of all faucets, this one is the most temperamental when it comes to repairs. The leak may seem to be fixed, only to reappear a few days later. You may have to exercise patience until the problem is finally resolved. Repair kits for this faucet are available containing individual parts or all parts (Figure 1), including the tension-ring spanner wrench.

Disassembly

Remove the handle, using a screwdriver or Allen wrench (Figure 2). You will spot the tension ring, which is a threaded part with notches. Many times a leak is caused by a loose tension ring. Fit a tension-ring spanner wrench into the notches of the ring and tighten it (Figure 3). Reinstall parts and turn on the water to see if the leak has been fixed. If not, turn off water and proceed to remove the handle, cover or cap, tension ring, cam, gasket, ball, seals and springs (Figures 4-8).

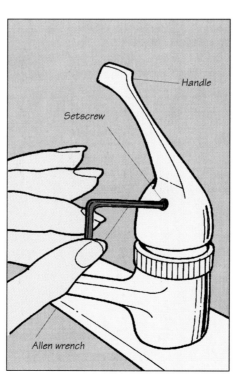

Figure 2. *To try to stop a leak without disassembling the faucet, first loosen the handle setscrew and remove the handle.*

Reassembly

Since it is usually not possible to determine which part is causing a leak, you can save yourself considerable time and effort by installing all new parts. Notice that seals and springs fit into water inlet ports with springs facing down into the part.

Obviously, new parts of the unit are installed in the reverse order that you removed old parts out of the faucet. But there is one thing to watch out for. The cam will probably have a tiny lug on it (Figure 9). The lug should fit securely into the notch in the faucet housing.

➡PLUMBER'S TIP:
If the ball you take out of the faucet is plastic and your water tends to scale, replace it with another plastic ball.

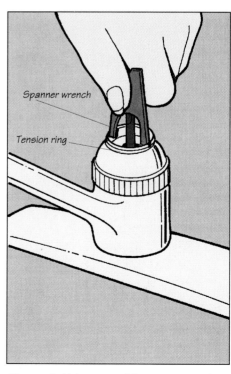

Figure 3. *Using a special spanner wrench, tighten the adjustable tension ring. Be sure to use a spanner wrench for your make of faucet.*

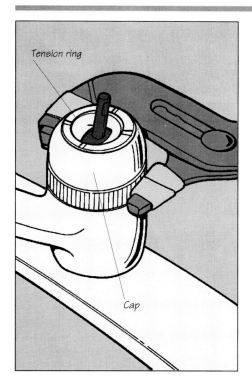

Figure 4. If tightening the tension ring does not get results, rebuild the faucet. After removing the handle, loosen and remove the cap and tension ring.

Figure 5. Place a rag around the base of the spout to absorb water that may splash and lift off the cam and washer. Then lift the spout off the faucet body.

Figure 6. Lift out the ball. Notice that the slot in the ball slides onto a pin in the faucet body. When you reinstall the ball, make sure the slot and pin fit together.

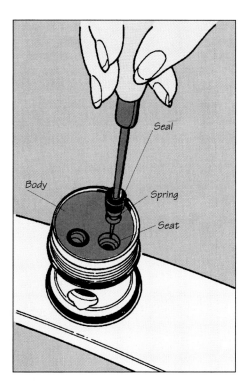

Figure 7. Remove the seals and springs in the faucet body and replace them with new parts contained in a rebuild kit for your make of faucet.

Figure. 8. If water has been leaking from around the base of the spout of a swivel faucet, also install new O-rings. Pry off the old ones. Roll the new ones into place.

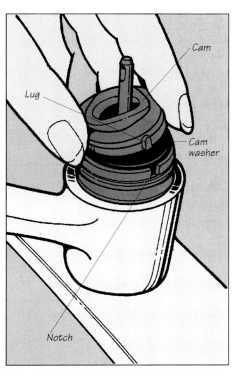

Figure 9. In reassembling the faucet, make sure that the lug of the cam fits securely into the notch of the faucet body.

REPAIRING FAUCETS
TIPPING-VALVE ONE-HANDLE

Tools & Materials:
❏ adjustable pliers
❏ electrical tape
❏ conventional screwdriver
❏ valve seat wrench
❏ valve seats
❏ tipping valves

Remember: *Turn off the water shutoff valves or the main valve (see Figure 1, page 8) before beginning work.*

➡PLUMBER'S TIP:
Occasionally, a particle in the water will be deposited on one of the seats and prevent a tipping valve from closing all the way (Figures 1 and 2). Before you disassemble the faucet, you may be able to flush the particle away by opening and closing the faucet a few times. Draw the faucet to one side and then quickly to the other.

Disassembly
1. Unscrew and remove the spout (Figure 3). If the spout nut is stuck, use adjustable pliers to loosen it, but wrap electrical tape around plier jaws so you don't scar the spout.

2. Lift off the cover (Figure 4).

3. Using a screwdriver, remove the slotted nuts over the tipping valves.

4. Remove the tipping valves (Figure 5).

Making the Repair
In all likelihood, the leak is caused by a damaged valve seat. Tipping valves seldom go bad.

1. Using a valve seat wrench, remove valve seats.

2. Get matching replacements from your local hardware or home center supply store and install the new seats.

3. Reinstall the tipping valves so the valve stems are facing down into the faucet.

4. Put the cover and spout back on, and turn on the water.

5. If the leak persists, one or both tipping valves are faulty. Disassemble the unit again, but this time replace the tipping valves.

6. If there is a leak from around the base of the spout, replace the O-ring before screwing the spout back onto the faucet (Figure 6).

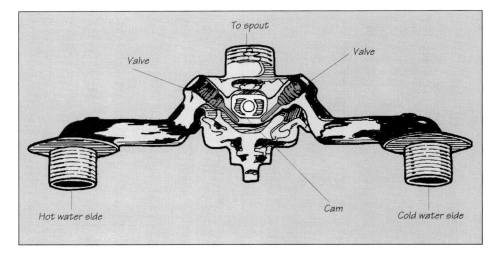

Figure 1. *The heart of a tipping-valve faucet is a cam that rotates when you turn the handle. In this position, the cam is not engaging the tipping valve, therefore, the faucet is turned off.*

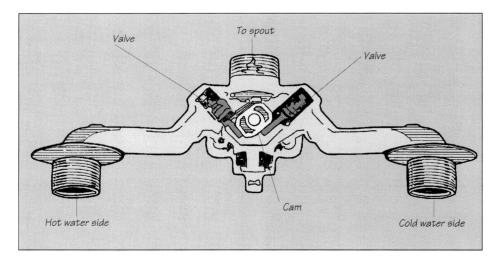

Figure 2. *Here, the cam is placing more pressure on the hot water tipping valve than on the cold water tipping valve, which means that the water coming from the spout is tepid.*

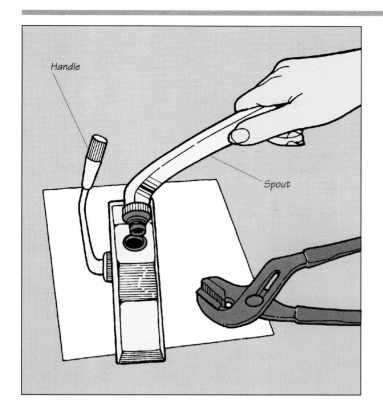

Figure 3. To begin repair, unscrew and remove the spout. Notice the unique position of the handle.

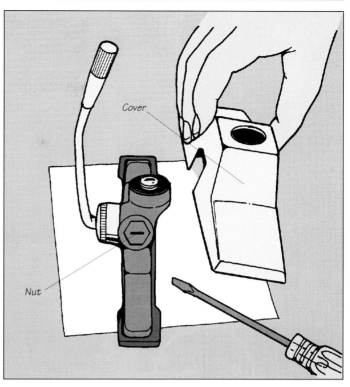

Figure 4. When the spout is off, the cover can be removed to reveal a slotted nut on each side of the faucet body.

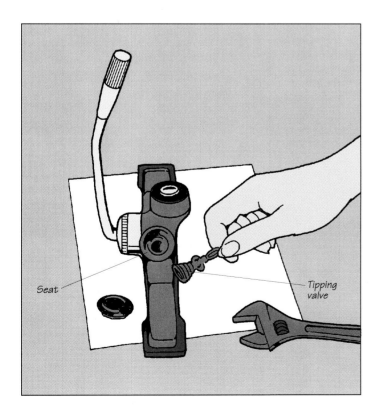

Figure 5. Remove the nut, which allows you to remove the tipping valve. You can now replace the seat and/or the tipping valve.

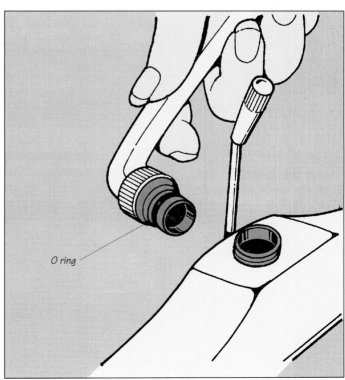

Figure 6. If there is a leak from around the base of the spout, replace the O-ring before screwing the spout back onto the faucet.

REPAIRING FAUCETS
CARTRIDGE-STYLE ONE-HANDLE

Tools & Materials:
- ❏ conventional or Phillips screwdriver
- ❏ Allen wrench
- ❏ utility knife
- ❏ pliers
- ❏ replacement cartridge
- ❏ O-rings
- ❏ petroleum jelly or heatproof grease

Remember: *Turn off the water shutoff valves or the main valve (see Figure 1, page 8) before beginning work.*

Disassembly

This type of one-handle faucet gets a "2-hammer" difficulty rating by virtue of the fact that the fastener holding the cartridge in the faucet may be difficult to spot and, therefore, to remove.

The problem involves a cartridge retaining clip, which is either on the outside of the faucet or on the inside under the handle (Figures 1 and 2).

Closely examine the outside of the faucet body below the handle for a ridge projecting out of the body. If you spot one, it's probably the retaining clip. Using a screwdriver and/or pliers, pry or pull out the clip (Figure 3). When this has been done, twist or lift the handle and cartridge out of the faucet (Figure 4). Separate the handle and cartridge.

If there is no opening in the faucet body, find the screw holding the handle (Figure 5). It might be under a cap that you have to pry off (Figure 6). Then again, it might be at the base of the handle, so you'll have to lift the handle to get at the screw (Figure 7).

Once the handle is off, you'll see the cartridge. At the base of the cartridge, there might be a retainer (Figure 8). Remove that to get at the cartridge retaining clip. Pry or pull the clip out and then remove the cartridge (Figure 9).

Repair

The repair is made by replacing the cartridge. A hardware, plumbing or home center supply store that sells your particular brand of faucet will be able to supply you with the new part.

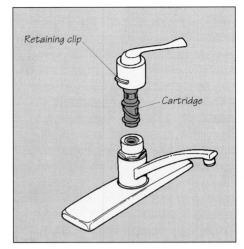

Figure 1. *This illustration shows where you may find an external retaining clip that has to be removed in order to free a cartridge. The handle is held to the cartridge by a screw, probably an Allen screw.*

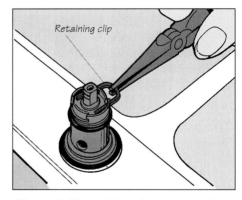

Figure 3. *The retaining clip can be easily removed with needle-nose pliers.*

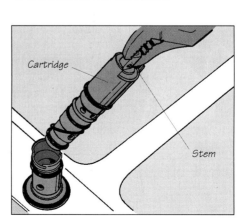

Figure 4. *Grasp the cartridge stem with pliers and pull the part from the faucet body. Replace the cartridge.*

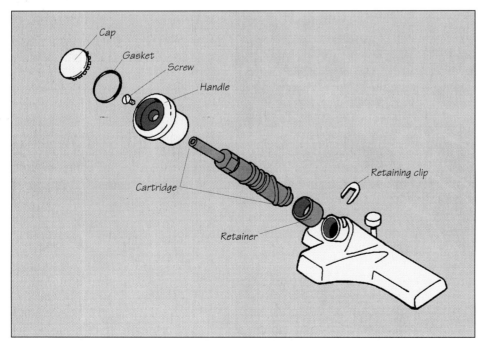

Figure 2. *Here are the parts that have to be removed to replace the cartridge. In order, they are a cap and gasket, screw, handle, retainer, retaining clip, and cartridge.*

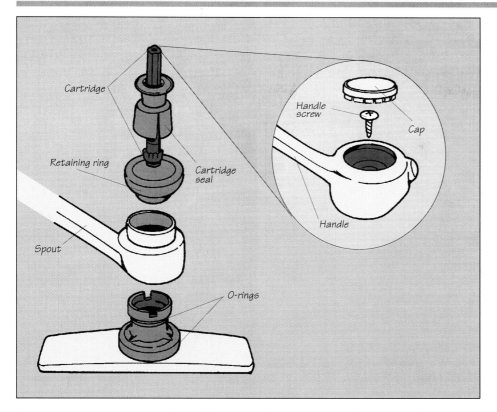

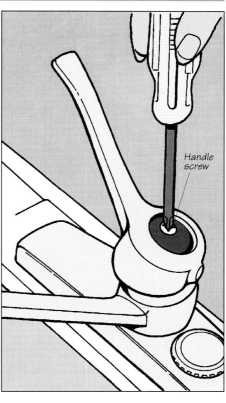

Figure 5. *This newer version of a cartridge faucet has the same premise as others in that you need to replace the cartridge to repair a leak.*

Figure 6. *To get at a faulty cartridge, pry off the cap over the handle screw and remove the screw.*

➥PLUMBER'S TIP:
After replacement of the cartridge, turn on the water and confirm that the hot and cold water is properly oriented (hot-left, cold-right). If not, remove the handle and rotate the cartridge 180 degrees. Improper orientation may result in burns.

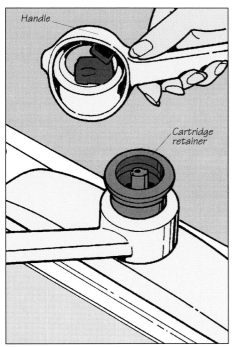

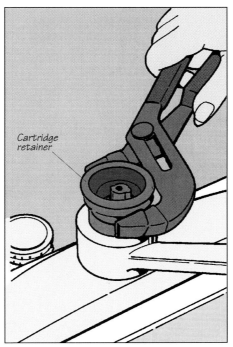

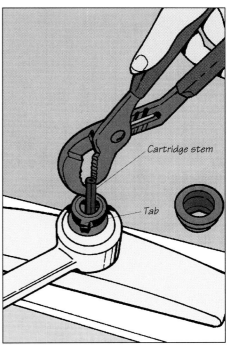

Figure 7. *Lift the handle up and tilt it back to remove it, uncovering the cartridge retainer.*

Figure 8. *To remove the retainer, grab it with adjustable pliers and turn counterclockwise. In addition, you may also find a retaining clip similar to the one shown in Figure 3.*

Figure 9. *Grasp the cartridge stem and pull the cartridge from the faucet body. The tab on cartridge faces toward front of faucet.*

REPAIRING FAUCETS
CARTRIDGE-STYLE TWO-HANDLE

Tools & Materials:
❏ conventional or Phillips screwdriver
❏ utility knife
❏ plastic-headed hammer
❏ adjustable wrench or adjustable pliers
❏ electrical tape
❏ can of compressed air
❏ replacement cartridge
❏ O-rings
❏ petroleum jelly or heatproof grease

Remember: *Turn off the water shutoff valves or the main valve (see Figure 1, page 8) before beginning work.*

Over the years, several types of two-handle faucet designs, commonly referred to as compression faucets, have been used. Figures 1, 2 and 3 below compare the three most common types.

Figure 3 is the cartridge-style two-handle faucet that this section describes.

It is the latest compression faucet design. In addition to having a ceramic stem cartridge, this style uses a rubber seal rather than a metal seat inside the body as the other two do. The ceramic stem cartridge raises off or closes down over the rubber seal to allow the water to flow or to turn off.

Disassembly
If handles of a cartridge-style faucet are rammed down, they become too tight. The result can be a leak from the spout. Loosen screws of handles and retighten them just enough to hold handles in place. If the leak continues, follow the instructions on page 16, "Repairing Washer-Style Two-Handle Faucets," to remove handles and cartridges.

Leak from a Spout
Deposits are the primary reason for spout leaks with this type of faucet. Aim the nozzle of a can of compressed air at the spokes at the base of the cartridge and give a short burst or two to blow away deposits that are keeping the movable disc from seating against the stationary disc. Flush with water. If a spout leak persists, however, the cartridge is damaged. Take the damaged cartridge to a home center supply or plumbing supply store so you can match it with a replacement cartridge since not all are alike.

Leak from Around a Handle
The cartridge-type two-handle faucet uses O-rings to prevent water from leaking around handles. If there is a leak, replace the O-rings. Spread a thin coat of petroleum jelly or heatproof grease on O-rings before placing them into the grooves.

Reassembly
Follow the instructions that apply as presented on page 16, "Repairing Washer-Style Two-Handle Faucets."

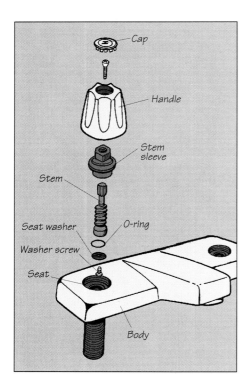

Figure 1. The washer faucet is the most popular of all compression faucets.

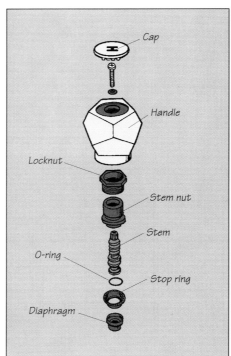

Figure 2. This version followed the development of the washer faucet and uses a neoprene cap (diaphragm) instead of a washer. When the faucet drips, the repair involves pulling off and replacing the diaphragm.

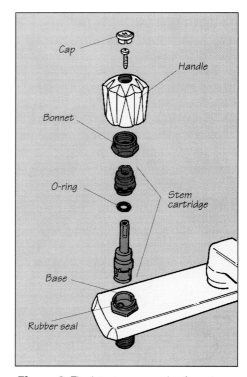

Figure 3. The latest compression faucet design is the cartridge-style two-handle faucet, which is described in this section.

REPAIRING FAUCETS
LEAK FROM THE BASE OF A SPOUT

Tools & Materials:
- ❑ adjustable pliers
- ❑ electrical tape
- ❑ knife or awl
- ❑ spout O-ring
- ❑ petroleum jelly or heatproof grease

Remember: *As a precaution to avoid accidental opening of faucets, turn off the water shutoff valves or the main valve (see Figure 1, page 8) before beginning work.*

Disassembly

If water leaks from around the base of a swivel spout of the type used in kitchen and utility room sinks, loosen the swivel nut holding the spout to the faucet (Figure 1). Use adjustable pliers, but wrap electrical tape around the jaws to keep from putting scars into the nut. Loosen the nut all the way and pull the spout free.

Making the Repair

You should find an O-ring around the threaded portion of the spout. Use the point of a knife or awl to slip the O-ring from place (Figure 2). Get a replacement of the same size. Spread a thin coat of petroleum jelly or heatproof grease over it and put it into position on the spout. A different style is illustrated in Figures 3, 4 and 5.

Reassembly

Screw the spout back onto the faucet by hand until you can't turn the swivel nut. Be careful that you don't cross thread the nut and its seat in the faucet. Using adjustable pliers, turn the swivel nut 1/8 turn more (Figure 6). Open the faucet. If there is a leak around the spout, tighten the swivel nut 1/8 turn at a time until it stops.

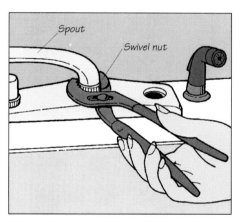

Figure 1. *To get at the spout O-ring, loosen the swivel nut.*

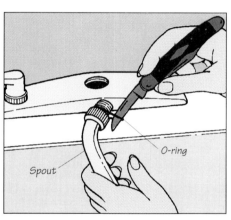

Figure 2. *Remove and discard the damaged O-ring, replacing it with one of the same size.*

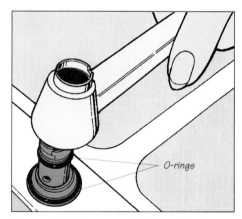

Figure 3. *This newer swivel spout design (shown here and in subsequent drawings) still requires replacement of O-rings when water leaks from around the base of the spout.*

Figure 4. *You can cut off the worn O-rings sealing a swivel faucet with a sharp knife. Before installing new O-rings, coat them with a heat-resistant lubricant.*

Figure 5. *Clean deposits from inside the spout cover and seat the spout securely on the faucet body.*

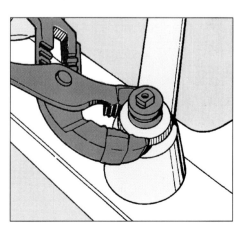

Figure 6. *The swivel spouts of all faucets are held to the assembly in some way. Here, with this cartridge faucet, it's by means of a retaining nut.*

REPAIRING FAUCETS
FROM THE BASEPLATE

Tools & Materials:
- ❏ adjustable wrench
- ❏ basin wrench
- ❏ utility knife
- ❏ plumber's putty
- ❏ putty knife

Remember: *Turn off the water shutoff valves (under the sink or faucet) or the main valve (see Figure 1, page 8) before beginning work.*

When water seeps out from around the baseplate of a faucet, the gasket or plumber's putty that was installed under the baseplate has deteriorated. A gasket is more likely to fail than putty. To make the repair, remove the faucet from the sink and restore the seal.

Remove the Faucet

1. Examine the water lines leading to the faucet to find fittings that connect the lines to the faucet. Using an adjustable or basin wrench, loosen these fittings and disconnect the lines from the faucet (Figures 1 and 2).

2. Slip the wrench onto one of the faucet mounting nuts holding the faucet to the sink. Turn the wrench counterclockwise to remove the nut. Then, remove the faucet mounting nut on the other side. Use a lubricant if the mounting nuts are stuck (Figure 3).

3. If working on a lavatory, disconnect the pop-up stopper (Figure 4). Release the lift rod holding the lever by unscrewing the clevis screw and disconnect the spring clip. Then, unscrew the retaining nut and turn the pivot rod, if necessary, and detach the rod from the stopper.

If working on a kitchen sink, you may have to release the hose feeding water to the spray unit (Figure 5).

4. With parts that have been attached to the faucet now released, lift the faucet and gasket (if there is a gasket) off the sink (Figure 6). Discard the gasket.

Seal the Baseplate

1. Use a putty knife to clean off particles of the old gasket or putty from the sink and the faucet baseplate (Figure 7). Both areas have to be clean.

2. Then install the new gasket (Figure 8) or spread a 1/8-inch bead of plumber's putty around the entire perimeter of the baseplate (Figure 9).

3. Reseat the faucet and press it down against the sink. A line of putty should ooze out beyond the baseplate (if you are using putty).

4. Reattach the faucet mounting nuts. Reattach lines, and lavatory pop-up stopper or sink spray unit hose. Then, use a utility knife to trim off excess putty (if you are using putty).

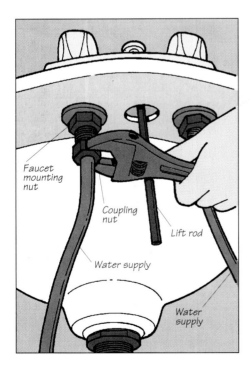

Figure 1. *Hot and cold water lines can be disconnected from the faucet with an adjustable wrench.*

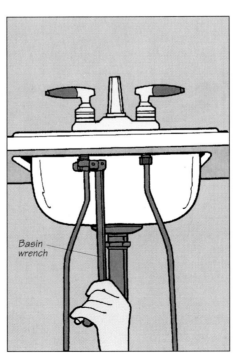

Figure 2. *If you have trouble reaching fasteners, use a basin wrench. It allows you to loosen and tighten fittings that are inaccessible with an adjustable wrench.*

Figure 3. *If faucet mounting nuts are stuck because of corrosion, spray them with a penetrating lubricant. Let the lubricant seep in for several minutes before attempting to free nuts.*

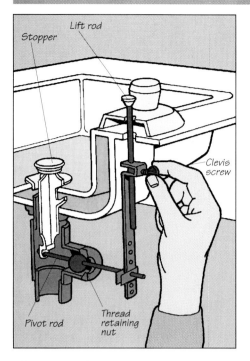

Figure 4. *To free the lift rod from the faucet of a lavatory, simply unscrew the clevis screw and pull the lift rod out. The text describes how to disassemble the entire unit for when you are replacing the lavatory.*

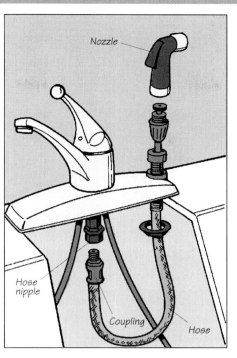

Figure 5. *With many sinks, you must free the spray hose at the faucet. This is done by unscrewing the coupling nut from the spray outlet shank of the faucet.*

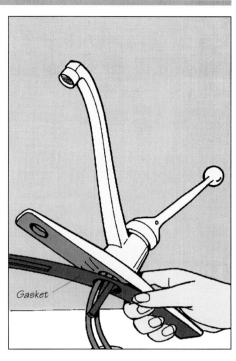

Figure 6. *Remove the faucet and gasket, if there is a gasket. Discard the gasket.*

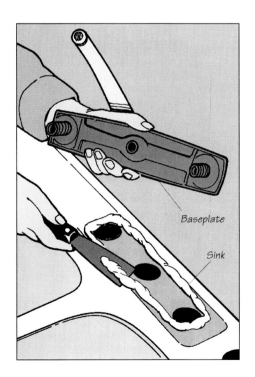

Figure 7. *If plumber's putty was used instead of a gasket to seal the baseplate of the faucet, scrape the old putty off the mounting surface of the sink and off the faucet. Both surfaces must be clean.*

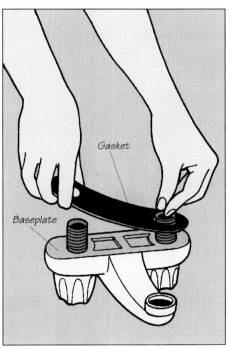

Figure 8. *Whether you use a gasket or plumber's putty is up to you. Some professional plumbers prefer putty because they contend that gaskets have a tendency to dry out and fail quicker than putty.*

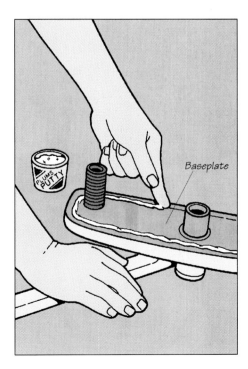

Figure 9. *Apply a 1/8-inch bead of plumber's putty around the perimeter of the baseplate. Reinstall the faucet.*

REPAIRING SPRAY ATTACHMENTS
CLEANING AN AERATOR

Tools & Materials:
❑ adjustable wrench
❑ screwdriver
❑ adjustable pliers
❑ conventional pliers
❑ electrical tape
❑ diverter valve
❑ toothbrush
❑ aerator

Repairing Spray Attachment

If little or no water comes out of the spray head of a sink's spray attachment, look under the sink to see that the hose that extends from the faucet to the spray unit is straight (Figure 1). If it's kinked, water can't get through to the spray head. You may have to disconnect the hose to straighten it (Figure 2).If the hose is straight, the reason for a restricted spray could be a dirty spray head nozzle (Figure 3).

1. Unscrew the nozzle from the head and wash it out or use a thin piece of wire to remove lime deposits (Figure 4). If it doesn't come clean, you can buy a replacement. To clean the other parts of the spray attachment, turn on the water and press the spray head handle before screwing the nozzle back into the spray head.

2. If none of these procedures are effective in restoring the spray, unscrew the faucet spout nut using adjustable pliers. Don't forget to wrap electrical tape around the spout nut to protect it. Remove the spout and lift or screw the diverter valve from the faucet (Figures 5 and 6).

3. Open the cold or hot water faucet slowly so water gushes from the vacated hole where the diverter valve sits. This will flush out residue that may be impeding the diverter valve.

4. Wash the diverter valve with a brush saturated with vinegar (Figure 7); then, reinstall it and the faucet spout. Try the spray. If the restriction persists, replace the diverter valve.

Cleaning an Aerator

An aerator is screwed into the nozzle of every sink and lavatory spout to lessen the force of the flow of water from the nozzle (Figure 8). If the flow ever seems sluggish, the aerator may be clogged.

Removing an aerator from a nozzle isn't a difficult task, but do it carefully to keep from damaging the part. If the aerator cannot be unscrewed by hand, wrap electrical tape around the jaws of pliers, engage the aerator with the pliers, and turn counterclockwise to loosen the aerator. Then, unscrew it by hand.

Flush deposits from the aerator screen. Use an old toothbrush to loosen stubborn residue (Figure 9). If cleaning doesn't improve the flow of water, replace the aerator. Screw it on hand-tight.

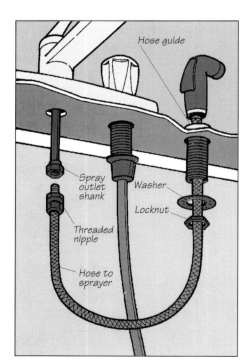

Figure 1. *If the spray attachment malfunctions, check that the hose is straight. It may need to be disconnected from the spray outlet shank of the faucet in order to straighten.*

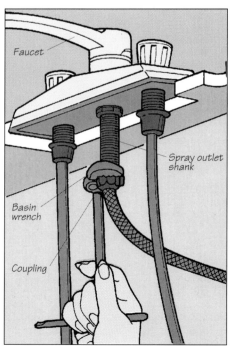

Figure 2. *If you can't get at the coupling of a spray hose, use a basin wrench. It gives you more flexibility than an adjustable or open-end wrench.*

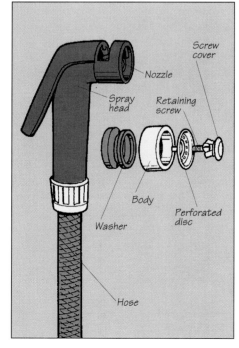

Figure 3. *Usually you can flush deposits from the assembly, but you may have to disassemble it entirely for cleaning.*

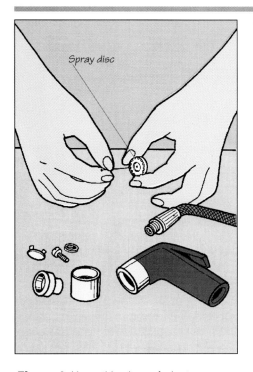

Figure 4. *Use a thin piece of wire to remove any lime deposits that may be clogging the spray disc.*

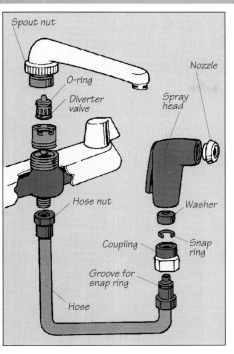

Figure 5. *The diverter valve of a spray attachment for a two-handle faucet lies beneath the spout. Remove the spout to service or replace the diverter valve.*

Figure 6. *Diverter valves for spray attachments that are coupled to one-handle faucets are usually positioned in the front or back of the faucet body. To reach the valve, you will probably have to disassemble the faucet.*

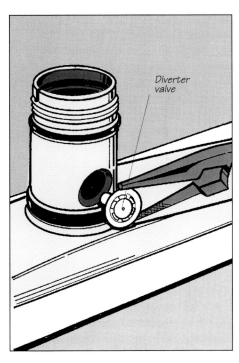

Figure 7. *After pulling the diverter valve out of the faucet body, clean it with a brush saturated with vinegar. If this fails to work, replace the diverter.*

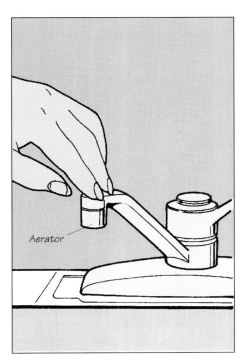

Figure 8. *There should be an aerator in the spout of every faucet in your house.*

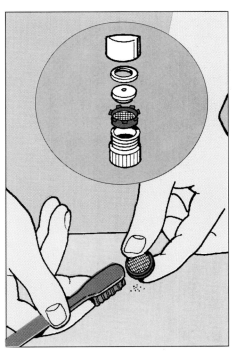

Figure 9. *An aerator is easily serviced. Simply take it apart and brush off any debris on the screen.*

FREEING CLOGGED SINK DRAINS
PLUNGING & SNAKING

Tools & Materials:
❑ For plunging: plumber's helper
  (type with flat-rimmed rubber cup)
❑ rags/paper towels/pipe cleaners
❑ C-clamp
❑ petroleum jelly
❑ For snaking: auger
❑ adjustable wrench
❑ adjustable pliers
❑ Teflon sealing tape

Next to leaking faucets, clogged sink and lavatory drains are probably going to be your biggest plumbing headache. It's usually not the fault of the system, but of those using the system. Traps and waste pipes are intended to handle liquid, not solids. Hair, bits of soap, scraps of food, and grease flowing into the system can cause a clog. So can debris put into a sink by a do-it-yourselfer who washes off paint brushes and putty knives.

Traps and waste pipes of kitchen sinks outfitted with food waste disposers can handle ground-up slush. They will not clog as long as slush is washed away with an ample flow of water.

The steps for clearing a clogged sink or lavatory drain should proceed from the easiest to the more difficult to perform. Begin with plunging. If that doesn't work, use an auger (snake).

Chemical drain cleaners are not recommended. Mechanical procedures are usually more effective. However, if you are going to use a chemical drain cleaner, despite the recommendation not to do so, follow the directions on the container carefully, and wear goggles, heavy rubber gloves and protective clothing.

Note: If you are working on a lavatory drain that's clogged, the first thing to do is to release the pop-up stopper and withdraw the stopper from the drain hole (see pages 28 and 29). You might be surprised at the amount of soap scum and hair that's built up on the stem of the stopper. It could be causing slow drainage. Cleaning off this accumulation with paper towels and pipe cleaners may clear the clog. If not, proceed with plunging.

Plunging a Clog

Here's the correct way to use a plumber's helper or plunger:

1. Using rags, block all openings that are part of the sink or lavatory setup. This includes overflow holes and the drain hole of the other sink if the clogged sink is part of a double sink setup (Figure 1).

2. The drain hose of a dishwasher should be closed by placing blocks of wood on its top and bottom surfaces and pressing them together with a C-clamp (Figure 2).

3. Spread a thin layer of petroleum jelly on the rim of the plumber's helper to affect a more perfect seal between the rubber cup and the sink or lavatory (Figure 3).

4. With two to three inches of water in the basin, place the rubber cup over the drain hole (Figure 4). Use steady, rhythmic, and forceful downward strokes to clear the clog. Try ten strokes at a time; then, test the flow of water down the drain. If the drain is clear, let the hot water run for about five minutes to wash away residue left by the clog.

5. Don't forget to remove rags from

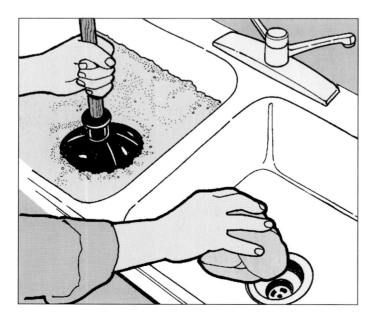

Figure 1. *For a plumber's helper (plunger) to exert maximum effect on a clog, all openings to the sink, including the drain holes of a double sink, should be blocked with rags.*

Figure 2. *To close the drain hose of a dishwasher, place two blocks of wood on the hose and press them together with a C-clamp.*

openings that you closed off, and the C-clamp and wood blocks from the drain hose of a dishwasher.

If plunging doesn't have an effect on the clog after five attempts, it's time for the more drastic measure of snaking.

Snaking a Clog

There are several ways to approach this operation.

1. Try clearing the clog by inserting the auger through the drain hole in the sink (Figure 5).

2. If this doesn't work and the trap has a cleanout plug, remove the plug (Figure 6) and try clearing the clog by inserting the auger through the hole into the waste pipe (Figure 7). When you reinstall the cleanout plug, wrap a layer of Teflon sealing tape around the threads to prevent a leak.

3. If there is no cleanout plug, use adjustable pliers or a wrench to undo the fasteners holding the trap (Figure 8). Place a pail under the trap to catch whatever flows out as the trap comes down (Figure 9).

4. Clean out the trap by running a cloth through it. Whatever it is that's causing the clog could be sitting in the trap.

5. Insert an auger into the waste pipe to make sure the pipe is clear (Figure 10). Reinstall the trap and let hot water flow down the drain for about five minutes.

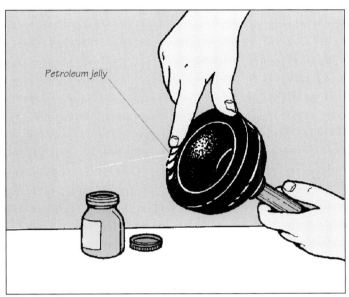

Figure 3. *A layer of petroleum jelly on the rim of the plumber's helper will create a solid seal between the tool and sink.*

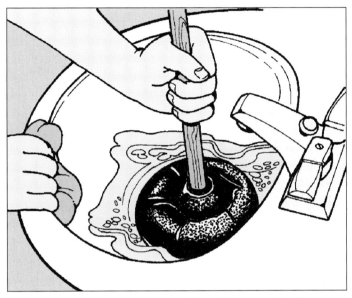

Figure 4. *Use steady, rhythmic, and forceful downward strokes to clear the clog.*

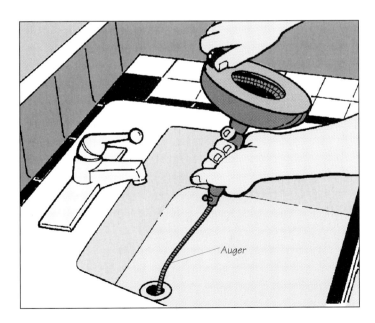

Figure 5. *You might be able to clear the drain by snaking through the drain hole, so try this first.*

Figure 6. *If the trap has a cleanout plug, loosen and remove it.*

➡ PLUMBER'S TIP:
If a sink or lavatory is outfitted with plastic waste pipes, be careful in using an auger. Excessive force may poke a hole through the plastic. If you encounter stiff resistance, withdraw the auger and start again. That resistance is probably being caused by the auger hitting against the plastic pipe. Material that causes clogs is usually soft, and an auger should go right through it without trouble.

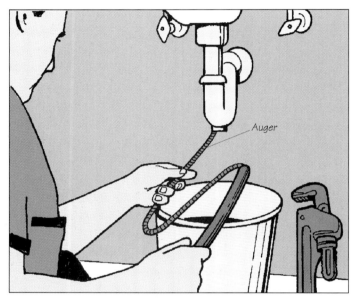

Figure 7. *Work the auger into the hole in the trap and try to clear the clog in this way.*

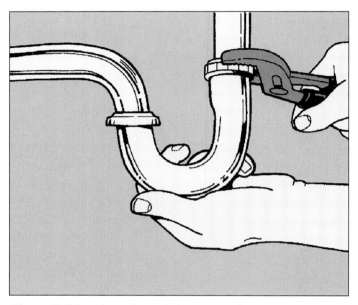

Figure 8. *If there is no cleanout plug, remove the trap.*

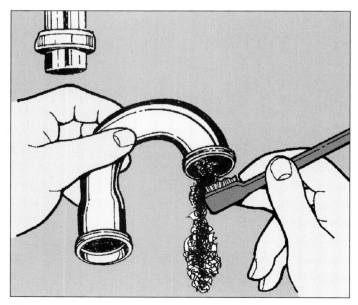

Figure 9. *The clogging matter may be located right in the trap, so clean that out.*

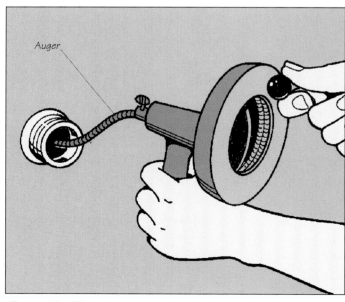

Figure 10. *With the trap removed, work the auger into the waste pipe.*

FREEING CLOGGED DRAINS
WHEN ALL ELSE FAILS

Tools & Materials:
- ❏ power auger
- ❏ penetrating oil
- ❏ newspapers
- ❏ gloves

*This job might be better performed by a professional serviceman.

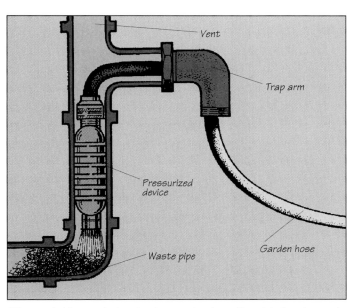

Figure 1. *It's rare that a clog in a waste pipe will resist plunging and augering. If it does, you might want to try a device that exerts tremendous water pressure against the clog before calling a professional. You can buy or rent one from a plumbing supply dealer.*

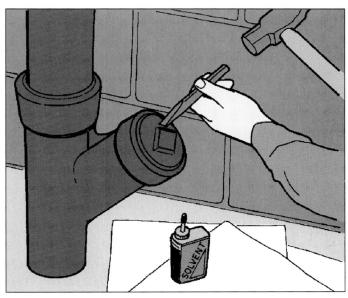

Figure 2. *The most serious clog occurs when matter, such as tree roots, invades the lateral leading to the sewer. A professional will probably be needed to deal with this. He will first open the cleanout plug to allow access to the main drain and lateral.*

Figure 3. *The cutting end of the power auger will be fed into the network through the cleanout.*

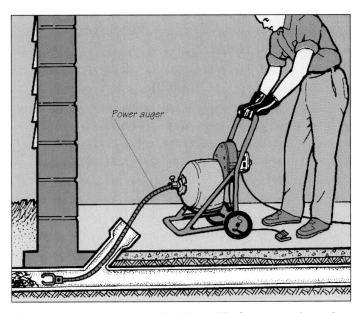

Figure 4. *A clog cannot usually withstand the force exerted upon it by the power auger.*

LEAKY WATER SUPPLY LINES
REPAIRING CONNECTING NUT & REPLACING SUPPLY LINE

Hot and cold water supply lines (risers) extending to a faucet from hot and cold water pipes may in time begin to leak (Figure 1). If you can turn off water from the pipe to the leaking supply line by shutting a valve between the two (Figure 2), which is possible in the vast majority of homes, the repair is simple to make.

However, if there are no water shutoff valves, the leaking supply line has to be cut off with a saw or pipe cutter, in which case you might as well install a shutoff valve (see pages 60-62).

Stopping a Leak

If the leak is from the nut connecting the supply line to the stub of the shutoff valve on the water pipe (Figure 3), close the shutoff valve.

1. Using an adjustable wrench, undo the nut that attaches the line to the stub. Slide the nut up onto the line and carefully pull the line out of its seat in the stub until the ferrule (usually brass) on the line is completely exposed.

2. The ferrule provides a seal between the water pipe and supply line. If the ferrule is damaged, the seal is broken and water will leak from around the nut.

3. Wrap a layer of Teflon tape around the ferrule. Reinsert the end of the line into the stub so the ferrule is secure. Slide the nut down and turn it by hand until it's tight. Then, using the adjustable wrench, turn the nut one-half turn.

4. Open the shutoff valve, turn on the water, and check to see if the leak has stopped. If not, turn the nut a little at a time with the wrench until it has ceased.

Replacing a Leaking Supply Line

If a water supply line spouts a leak, you'll have to replace the line. The job is easy using a replacement made of braided stainless steel instead of copper or plastic. Braided stainless steel is flexible and easier to manipulate (Figure 4).

1. Close the water shutoff valve. Undo the nuts holding the supply line to the stub and to the tailpiece of the faucet. Use an adjustable wrench if you can. The tailpiece nut is sometimes not easy to reach with an adjustable wrench. In this case, a basin wrench will allow you to loosen the nut (Figure 5).

2. When the nuts are off, draw the

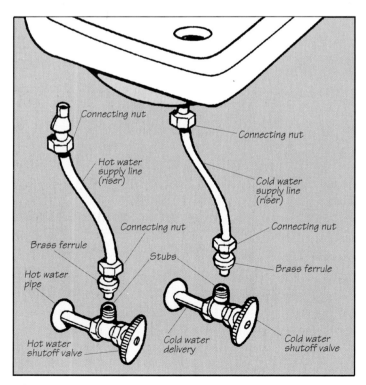

Figure 1. *Shown are the particular parts you have to deal with when repairing a leaking hot or cold water supply line.*

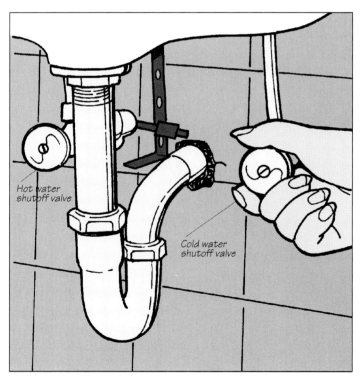

Figure 2. *If a hot or cold water supply line in your home begins to leak, turn off the fixture's shutoff valve. Hopefully, you will find that the contractor who built your house equipped every faucet with a shutoff valve.*

ends of the line from position, remove the line, and throw it away.

3. As a precaution, wrap a layer of Teflon tape around the male threads of the faucet tailpiece and the male threads of the shutoff valve stub. If you prefer, use pipe joint compound instead. Cover the threads with a thin coating.

4. Place the ends of the braided stainless-steel water supply line onto their respective seats, secure the nuts by hand (Figure 6), and then tighten them one-half turn with the wrench.

5. Turn on the water and check for leaks. If there is a leak, attach the wrench pliers to the nut and turn it a little at a time until the leak stops.

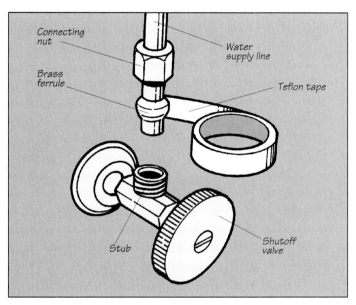

Figure 3. *A leak from around the nut that connects a metal supply line to the stub of the valve can often be sealed using Teflon tape.*

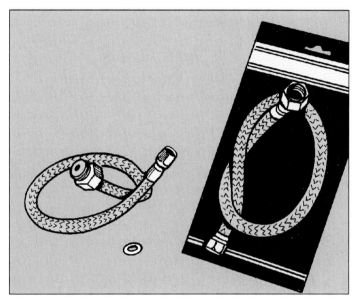

Figure 4. *Flexible braided stainless-steel water supply lines cost more than copper or plastic, but they are easier to handle and install.*

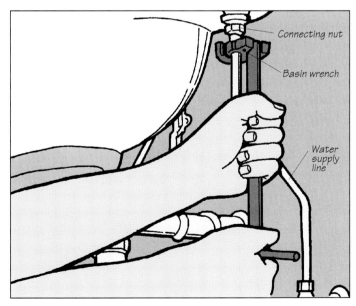

Figure 5. *When there isn't enough clearance to get at upper connecting nuts with an adjustable wrench, use a basin wrench, which has a head that swivels to allow you to maneuver the wrench onto nuts located in confined areas.*

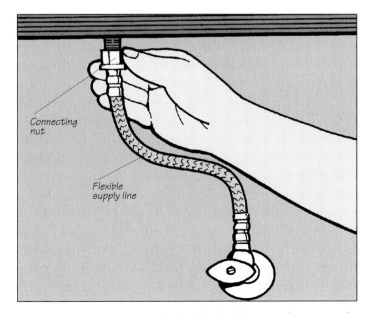

Figure 6. *Place the ends of the braided stainless-steel water supply line onto their respective seats. The compression-type connecting nuts may be tightened by hand and then with a wrench.*

PREVENTING LEAKING WATER PIPES

Tools & Materials:
❏ insulation
❏ electrical tape or duct tape

Note: In this book, we use the term copper pipe to refer to both copper pipe and copper tubing.

Although the subject of preventing water pipes from damage is addressed here under the major heading "All About Sinks," it is obviously applicable to pipes that deliver water to all other plumbing fixtures and plumbing appliances in a home.

Pipes that deliver water to sinks, lavatories, toilets, water heaters, washing machines, and other plumbing fixtures and appliances are most commonly made of copper, galvanized steel, or plastic.

Copper pipe is the most popular.

Figure 1. *A popular type of material used for protecting water pipes from the cold is foam tubing that comes spliced as shown here or in lengths that have to be split.*

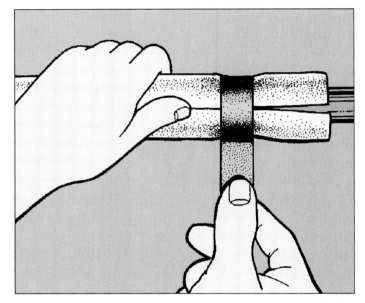

Figure 2. *After wrapping the foam around the pipe, seal the slit with electrical tape or duct tape.*

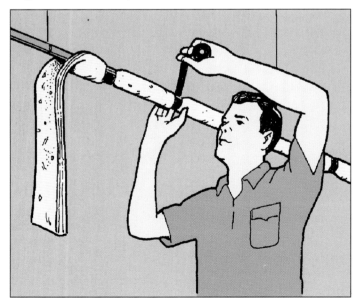

Figure 3. *If you have any fiberglass insulation left over from the attic, you can use that instead of foam to protect pipes.*

Figure 4. *Another kind of water pipe protector is UL-listed electric heat tape which is wrapped around the pipe and plugged into an electric outlet.*

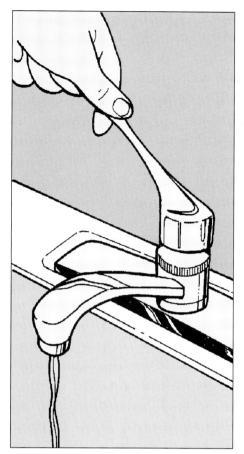

Figure 5. *An expensive way to keep pipes from freezing is to open the faucet so that a slow but steady stream of water flows.*

Where municipal plumbing codes permit, chlorinated polyvinyl chloride (CPVC) plastic pipe has attained wide acceptance in newer homes. Galvanized steel water pipe is found in homes built in the 1940s and prior years.

If copper pipe is leaking, the damaged piece has to be cut out and a new length of copper pipe soldered into place. A leaking galvanized steel pipe can often be repaired with an epoxy compound, clamps, or both. If plastic pipe is leaking, the section is easily replaced with a new piece of plastic pipe.

Before discussing how to repair leaking copper, galvanized steel, and plastic water pipes, there is a related topic that should be addressed: how to prevent pipe from developing a leak. Taking precautions is a lot easier to do than making a repair.

Prevention: Better Than a Cure

Age doesn't usually affect copper and plastic pipe. On the other hand, galvanized steel pipe may start to leak as it gets older. Leaks generally develop at a seam or around a fitting (see pages 46-50).

The one condition that affects all three kinds of pipe, causing them to split and leak, is exposure to freezing temperature. Water turns to ice, and the expanding ice splits the pipe.

Prevention involves insulating all water pipes in your home that could be exposed to freezing. If the pipe is accessible, wrap it with insulation. There are several varieties available (Figures 1-3). Foam wrapped with tape, though, is suitable in most instances. Another solution is electric heat tape (Figure 4).

Where exposed pipe is close to a foundation sill above a cinder block or concrete basement wall or crawl space, packing batts of insulation into the crevices of the sill and wrapping it around pipe will usually afford enough protection (Figure 6).

Where a section of pipe travels within a wall that's exposed to cold air, the only way to provide it with protection is to have insulation blown into the wall cavity (Figure 7). The expense incurred will be more than offset by preventing the trouble and expense that you'll experience if water in the pipe freezes, causing the pipe to split and leak. The wall will then have to be torn down to make the repair.

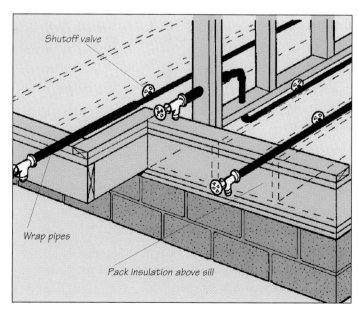

Figure 6. *Pipes that come close to or pass through exterior walls are particularly susceptible to freezing at that point. Packing fiberglass insulation above the sill is a wise precaution to take.*

Figure 7. *If the walls of a house are not insulated, pipes running up the wall to fixtures and appliances may freeze and split. Consider having these walls packed with foam insulation that's blown inside the walls with special equipment.*

REPAIRING LEAKS
COPPER PIPE & TUBING

Tools & Materials:
- ❏ tubing cutter
- ❏ hacksaw
- ❏ miter box
- ❏ reamer
- ❏ emery cloth
- ❏ propane torch
- ❏ solder and flux
- ❏ copper pipe or tubing
- ❏ copper-to-copper fittings

Remember: *Turn off the water shutoff valve or the main valve (see Figure 1, page 8) before beginning work.*

Although the subject of permanently repairing leaking copper pipe or tubing is addressed here under the major heading "All About Sinks," it is obviously applicable to copper pipes and tubing that deliver water to all other plumbing fixtures and plumbing appliances in a home.

Before beginning, certain terms need to be clarified. One is the term "permanently repairing," which is used in the paragraph above. There are various methods you can use to stop copper pipe or tubing from leaking, such as a special clamp that fits over the split. But all methods are temporary measures (see "Some Temporary Measures," below), except the permanent one of cutting out the damaged piece and replacing it as described in this section.

The other terms that need clarification are "copper pipe" and "copper tubing." Although they are frequently used interchangeably, in this section the term "copper pipe" will apply to the rigid (hard-tempered) material that comes in straight lengths of 10 and 20 feet. The term "copper tubing" will apply to the flexible (soft-tempered) material that comes in coils of 10 and 20 feet.

Copper pipe and tubing are available in three grades: K, L, and M. K is the heaviest; M is the thinnest and L falls between the two. M-grade copper pipe is used for water delivery in most homes. However, there are municipal plumbing codes that require the use of L-or K-grade copper pipe or copper tubing.

Each grade comes in various diameters, but the sizes usually required in home water delivery systems are 3/8, 1/2, 3/4 or 1 inch. The size of a copper

SOME TEMPORARY MEASURES

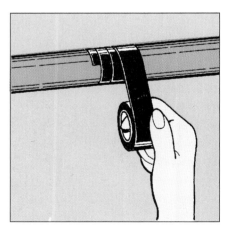

Figure A. *If there's a pinhole in a pipe, you may be able to stop the leak temporarily by draining the pipe, drying it thoroughly, and wrapping layers of electrical tape around it.*

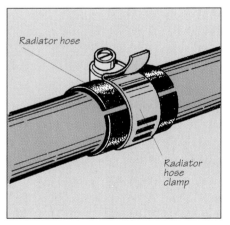

Figure B. *Another way to stop a copper pipe from leaking at least temporarily is with an auto radiator hose clamp and a piece of radiator hose that you've sliced open. Place the hose around the pipe so the opened end is opposite the leak, open the clamp and put it around the hose. Then tighten the clamp.*

Figure C. *Still another temporary measure is the use of a pipe sleeve that is specifically made to stop a leak. This part can be obtained from a plumbing supply dealer or your local home center store.*

pipe or tubing is given as a nominal measurement. If you are going to use copper pipe and fittings that are going to be soldered, order material using the inner diameter. If you are going to use tubing and compression fittings, then order material using the outer diameter.

The easiest way to find out the grade, diameter and hardness of the copper pipe or tubing you have in your house, and thus the kind you should buy to replace a piece that's leaking, is to cut off the damaged piece and take it to the plumbing supply, hardware or home center supply store. Store personnel can help you select the copper fitting you will need.

The fitting is the coupling, joint or tee, which is used to connect pipe or tubing together. A coupling has two ends. A tee has three ends like the letter T. A joint (or elbow) is a curved connector that's used to attach two pieces of pipe or tubing where an angle of 45 or 90 degrees is necessary.

Preparing Pipe or Tubing for Soldering

1. Close the main shutoff valve near the water meter or turn off the submersible pump. Flush toilets and open all faucets, including those on the outside of the house. Keep faucets open until the repair is completed and the water is turned on again.

2. Measure out at least six inches beyond each side of the split in the pipe or tubing. Lock the cutter onto the pipe or tubing at one measured spot and turn the tool one complete revolution (Figure 1). Tighten the cutter's handle and turn the tool again. Continue this way until the cut is completed.

3. Repeat the procedure where you measured on the other side of the damage. Work deliberately to make sure the ends of the pipe are cut squarely.

4. You now have to cut a length of replacement pipe or tubing that is the same size as the piece you removed. It's important to make sure that the end is square, so use the tubing cutter or hacksaw and miter box (Figure 2).

5. After cutting out the damaged pipe or tubing and the replacement, use a reamer to remove burrs from the ends of each piece of pipe or tubing—four ends in all (Figure 3).

6. The final step in preparation for soldering is to use emery cloth to polish the ends of all pieces and also the insides of the connectors (Figures 4 and 5). This will remove oxidation, which can affect the integrity of the soldered joints. Apply a thin coating of noncorrosive flux to the cleaned ends and to the fittings.

Soldering

The National Standard Plumbing Code requires that solder and flux contain not more than 0.2 percent lead. Solder containing 50-percent lead and 50-percent tin (so-called solid-core 50:50 solder) was the standard for many years. The concern over the effect of lead on health, however, has resulted in an alteration of the formula. Your municipality may, in fact, have outlawed solder containing any lead. The alternative may be silver phosphorous solder.

The soldering method described here is the traditional one of fluxing and soldering as separate steps. (Soldering is also referred to as sweating.) Fluxing is necessary to prevent the formation of oxidation as heat is applied to the pipe.

CAUTION: Flux is an irritant. Wear eye protection and avoid rubbing your eyes. Wash hands thoroughly after working with flux and solder.

Some solder products already contain flux so you may not have to apply flux to the ends of the pipe or tubing as a separate step. Therefore, when you buy solder, read the instructions carefully or ask store personnel for help.

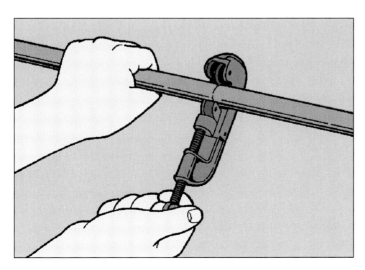

Figure 1. Use a cutter to cut out the damaged section of copper pipe or tubing. Remove at least 6 inches, allowing at least 1 inch between the ends of the rupture and where you make the cut.

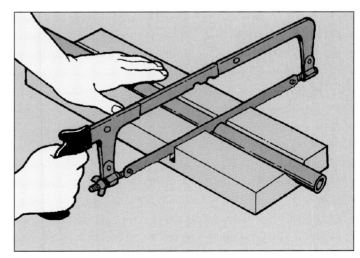

Figure 2. If a tubing cutter is not available, use a miter box and hacksaw when cutting a replacement piece of copper pipe or tubing to insure that the ends will be square.

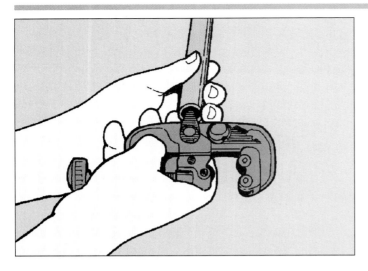

Figure 3. *Remove burrs from the inside of copper pipe or tubing with a reamer, which may be a part of the cutter you've purchased.*

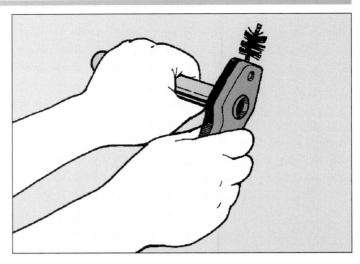

Figure 4. *Clean the ends of all parts that will go together. This multipurpose tool features an abrasive for doing this as well as a wire brush.*

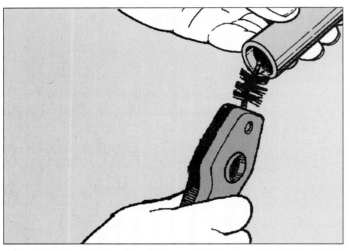

Figure 5. *The insides of the fitting and all pipes must be clean. Use a wire brush.*

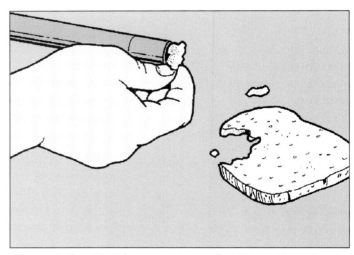

Figure 6. *If a trickle of water persists, stuff white bread into the pipe or tubing to absorb trapped water.*

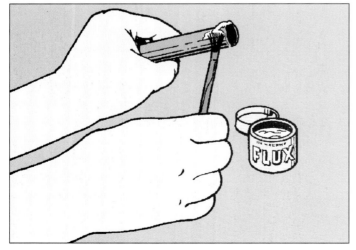

Figure 7. *Apply a light coating of flux to the ends of the pipe or tubing. Flux inhibits oxidation as the pipe or tubing is being heated. Oxidation can prevent solder from taking hold, which will result in a leak.*

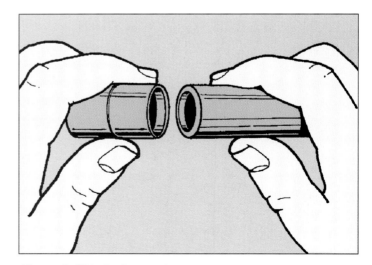

Figure 8. *Slide the fitting as far as possible onto one end of the cut pipe. Then, slip the other end of the cut pipe into the fitting. Maneuver the fitting around until half of it is on one pipe and the other half is on the other pipe.*

1. Pull down the ends of the pipe or tubing between which the replacement pipe will be connected to allow trapped water to drip out. If any droplets of water remain trapped, they will turn to steam as you apply heat and cause pinholes in the solder joint through which water will leak.

➡PLUMBER'S TIP:
Roll some fresh white bread into a loose ball and push it into the pipe or tubing (Figure 6). Do not pack it tightly. Bread will absorb trapped droplets of water and prevent them from affecting the solder. When water is turned back on, the rush of water through the pipe or tubing will flush out the bread. Remove aerators from faucets so they don't block the passage of the bread.

2. If the solder you are using does not contain flux, now is the time to apply it. Using a small brush apply a light coating of flux to the ends of the existing pipe or tubing, to the ends of the replacement piece, and to the insides of the fittings (Figure 7).

3. Slide the fittings onto the existing pipe or tubing, position the replacement piece in the opening, and move the fittings into place to couple the existing pipe or tubing to the replacement piece (Figure 8).

4. Using the propane torch, heat the area around one of the joints as you hold the tip of the solder in the joint (Figure 9).

CAUTION: Wear heavy work gloves in case your hand comes into contact with the pipe or tubing, which is going to get red hot. If you are soldering near a joist, wallboard, or some other material that is flammable, tack a cookie sheet over its surface (Figure10). Always keep a fire extinguisher close by—just in case.

Do not apply the flame to the solder. As the pipe or tubing gets hot, the solder will run freely all the way around and into the joint. After the solder hardens, wipe the joint with a cold wet cloth to cool the pipe or tubing (Figure 11). Solder each joint this same way.

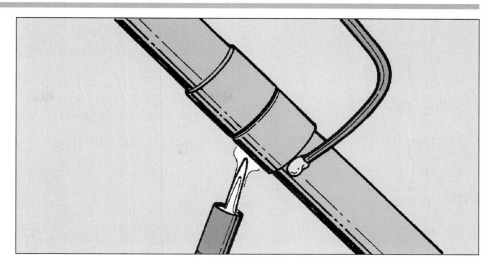

Figure 9. *Heat the pipe for about five seconds. Then, move the torch to the fitting as you hold the solder at the joint. The solder will melt and run into the joint to seal it.*

Figure 10. *Don't take chances starting a fire. If you're soldering close to joists, tack a cookie sheet in place to serve as a barrier between the wood and flame.*

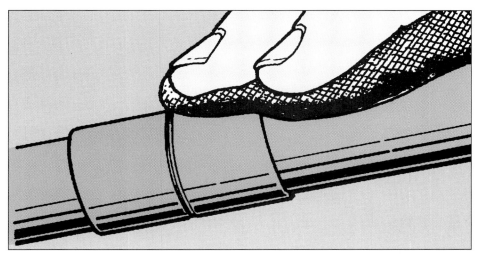

Figure 11. *Cool the pipe with a wet rag. Then, test the joint. If it leaks, try more solder, but in the end you may have to break the joint and try again.*

REPAIRING LEAKING WATER PIPES
CPVC PIPE

Tools & Materials:
- ❏ cutter
- ❏ backsaw
- ❏ miter box
- ❏ utility knife
- ❏ CPVC pipe
- ❏ CPVC fittings
- ❏ CPVC primer
- ❏ CPVC solvent
- ❏ cement
- ❏ eye protection

Remember: *Turn off the water shutoff valve or the main valve (see Figure 1, page 8) before beginning work.*

Although the subject of repairing a leaking CPVC water pipe is addressed here under the major heading "All About Sinks," it is obviously applicable to CPVC pipes that deliver water to all other plumbing fixtures and plumbing appliances in a home.

CPVC (chlorinated polyvinyl chloride) pipe is rigid. A replacement piece is joined to an existing pipe that has sprung a leak by cutting out the damaged section and installing the new piece of pipe using a process called solvent welding. Solvent cement is spread onto the ends of the pieces, which are joined together with CPVC fittings.

CPVC pipe is available in 1/2- and 3/4inch diameters and in 10-foot, and longer, lengths. It is rated to perform at temperatures up to 180 degrees F under 100 pounds per square inch of pressure. Thus, CPVC meets the requirements necessary for pipe to carry hot water to plumbing fixtures and plumbing appliances.

CPVC pipe isn't the only kind of plastic pipe used for water delivery. Where municipal plumbing codes allow, polybutylene (PB) is also used. This material, which is flexible enough to be rolled up like a garden hose, is available in coils of 25, 100, and 500 feet.

If PB pipe is used in your home and it starts to leak, a replacement piece of PB can be transplanted. However, you can't use the solvent welding procedure. PB pipes have to be connected together with compression fittings. Ask personnel at a plumbing supply or home center store to explain this to you.

Getting Ready

1. Flush toilets and open all faucets, including those on the outside of the house. Keep faucets open until the repair is completed and the water is turned on again.

2. Measure out at least two inches beyond each side of leak. Lock a tubing cutter onto the pipe at one measured spot and turn the tool one complete revolution (Figure 1). Tighten the cutter's handle and turn again. Continue this way until the cut is completed.

3. Repeat the procedure where you measured on the other side of the damage. Make sure the ends of the pipe are cut squarely.

4. When the damaged section has been removed, measure the space between the two ends of the pipe. Cut a replacement piece of CPVC pipe to this size using a tubing cutter or backsaw and a miter box so the ends will be cut straight and smooth (Figure 2).

5. After cutting the replacement, use a utility knife to shave burrs off the ends of all pieces (Figure 3). Then, bevel the edges to provide a secure weld.

Slip fittings on the ends of each pipe to make sure they slide freely (Figure 4).

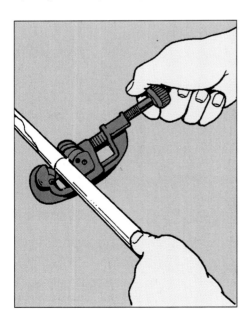

Figure 1. *Using a plastic-tubing cutter, remove that section of the existing CPVC pipe that is split. Work carefully so ends are cut straight.*

Figure 2. *Using a backsaw and miter box, cut a replacement to a size that will fill the space between the ends of the existing pipe.*

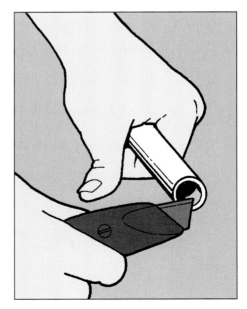

Figure 3. *Use a sharp utility knife to remove burrs and to bevel slightly the edges of the pipes to be joined.*

The Installation

1. The purpose of CPVC primer is to clean the parts that are going to be joined. Therefore, spread primer inside the fittings as well as around the ends of the pipes (Figure 5). While the primer is still wet, spread CPVC solvent cement on all these parts (Figure 6).

2. Slide the fittings onto the replacement piece of pipe. Hold the replacement piece between the existing pipe and bring fittings into place to make the replacement piece part of the water pipe.

3. Twist each fitting back and forth several times, then hold the parts tightly together for about 20 seconds before releasing. This action will evenly spread the solvent around the entire joint to ensure a tight fit (Figure 7). Work quickly, but carefully, to get pieces locked together before the solvent hardens. The solvent cement will form a continuous bead all around the joints if the job is done properly (Figures 8 and 9).

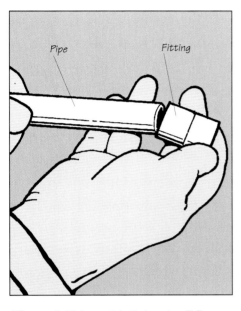

Figure 4. Make certain that parts will fit together before applying primer and solvent cement.

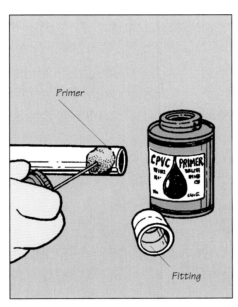

Figure 5. Coat the ends of each pipe and the insides of fittings with CPVC primer. Use a liberal amount.

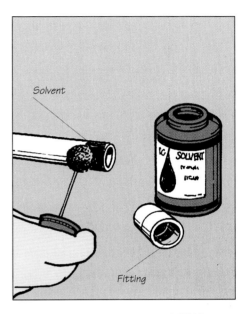

Figure 6. Apply a heavy coat of CPVC solvent cement to the ends of each pipe and to the insides of the fittings. Make sure the surfaces are completely covered.

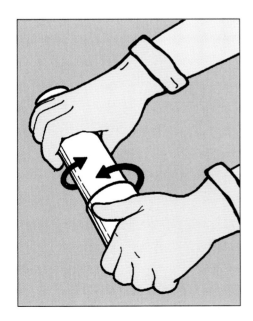

Figure 7. In putting the various components together, twist the parts as shown to make sure the solvent cement spreads to all spots.

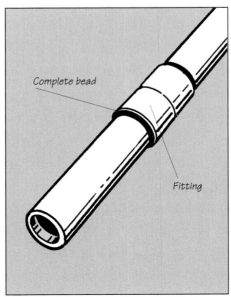

Figure 8. If the job is done properly, solvent cement will form a continuous bead at joints.

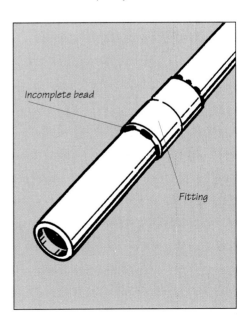

Figure 9. If a bead such as this forms, do the job again. Water can leak through gaps in solvent cement.

REPAIRING LEAKS
GALVANIZED STEEL PIPE

or

Tools & Materials:
- ❏ epoxy plumbing repair compound
- ❏ pipe clamp
- ❏ pipe wrenches
- ❏ hacksaw or reciprocating saw
- ❏ sandpaper
- ❏ penetrating oil
- ❏ propane torch
- ❏ galvanized steel pipe nipples
- ❏ three-part union fittings
- ❏ pipe joint compound

depends on repair needed

Remember: *Turn off the water shutoff valve or the main valve (see Figure 1, page 8) before beginning work.*

Although the subject of repairing a leaking galvanized steel water pipe is addressed here under the major heading "All About Sinks," it is obviously applicable to galvanized steel pipes that deliver water to all other plumbing fixtures and plumbing appliances in a home.

Leaks from galvanized steel water pipes occur either at a threaded fitting or in the pipe's surface (Figure 1).

CAUTION: Wear eye protection.

The order of repair presented here proceeds from easy to difficult:
1. If the leak is at a threaded fitting, flush toilets and open all faucets, including those on the outside of the house. Keep faucets open until the repair is completed and the water is turned on again.

When water has stopped dripping from the threaded fitting, clean the circumference of the fitting using a piece of sandpaper. Work on the area until all corrosion has been eliminated and the fitting virtually gleams.

Now, mix together the two-part epoxy contained in the repair kit (Figure 2). Read the package directions, but usually a repair patch is made by kneading together equal quantities of the two materials in the kit. Form the compound into a rope and wrap it around the fitting, pressing it firmly into place (Figure 3). Give the material time to take hold. About an hour should do it.

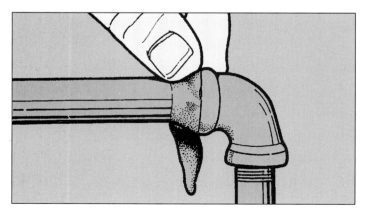

Figure 1. *Galvanized steel (also called "iron" or just "galvanized") water pipes can start to leak at threads (black arrow) or in the body of the pipe (white arrows).*

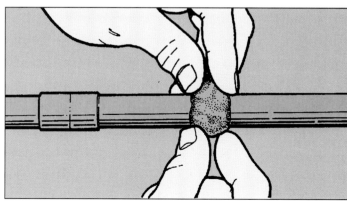

Figure 2. *A small leak around a threaded fitting or in the pipe's surface of a galvanized steel water delivery system may be stopped with a repair kit of epoxy.*

Figure 3. *Clean the area. Then, wrap the compound around the threaded parts, working it into the joint where pipe and fitting meet.*

Figure 4. *To try to stop a leak in the midsection of a galvanized steel pipe, drain the system, prepare the epoxy patch and press it over the damaged area.*

2. If the leak is in the body of the pipe, the two-part repair patch described above plus a pipe clamp may stop it. After turning off the water, draining pipes, and cleaning the damaged area with sandpaper, press the epoxy patch over the leak (Figure 4). Then, wrap a pipe clamp (Figure 5) around the damage and tighten the clamp bolts (Figure 6).

3. If the procedures described above fail, the pipe has to be replaced and the repair gets difficult. But it can be simplified by removing the entire run between the fittings instead of trying to piece in a section.

After turning off the water and draining the pipes, follow these steps:

a. Measure and record the length of the pipe from the flange of one fitting to the flange of the other. Assuming the pipe diameter is 1/2 or 3/4 inch, as is probably the case, add 1 inch to the measurement to allow for the 1/2 inch that the pipe extends into each fitting (Figure 7). If the pipe is 1 inch in diameter or larger, add 1 1/4 inches to the measurement to allow for an extension into each fitting of 5/8 inch. Take this measurement with you when you go to buy a replacement. The replacement parts you get in the form of nipples and a three-part union fitting must equal the measurement.

b. Use a reciprocating saw or hacksaw to cut the damaged pipe about 12 inches from one of the fittings (Figure 8).

c. Grasp the fitting with one pipe wrench; grasp the short length of pipe with another pipe wrench. Position the wrenches so their jaws face each other (Figure 9). Hold the fitting tightly with one wrench and unscrew the pipe by turning the other wrench counterclockwise. If the fitting is shot, unscrew that too and buy a new one.

➡ PLUMBER'S TIP:

If the threads of the pipe and fitting are so badly corroded that you can't budge them (Figure 10), apply penetrating oil. Give oil time to work and loosen things up before you try to separate the pipe and fitting. If oil doesn't work, heat the threaded area with a propane torch for about 30 seconds. It should do the trick. But watch out for flammable material in the surrounding area. Tape a cookie sheet over the material to avoid trouble.

d. Cut the rest of the pipe off, but leave about 12 inches attached to the other fitting. Then, remove that piece from the fitting in the same way.

e. Replacing the section of pipe now becomes a matter of screwing together galvanized steel nipples and three-part union connectors (Figure 11) to equal the length of the old pipe. It's impossible to insert a full length of pipe from one fitting to the other. In order to do this, you would have to disassemble the entire network from its terminus back to where you are working.

Let's start by assuming that you have to replace one or both of the fittings (Figure 12). After applying pipe joint compound (Figure 13) to the threads of the adjacent pipes to which those fittings are screwed, install the new fittings. Tighten them with the pipe wrenches, leaving them off-center about 1/8 inch to make it easier to get the other components into position.

Note: Be sure to apply pipe joint compound to male and female threads.

Screw a galvanized steel nipple to one of the fittings (Figure 14). Tighten the nipple. A nipple is a length of pipe 12 inches or less in length that is threaded externally on both ends.

Separate the three parts of a union connector and place the large ring nut onto the nipple (Figure 15). Then, screw the hubbed part of the three-part union nut onto the nipple. Apply pipe joint compound to the face of the hub.

Working at the other fitting, screw a nipple into that (Figure 16). Assuming that you're going to be using just two nipples and one three-part union nut, screw the third part of the union nut to this nipple. Note that this part of the union nut is externally threaded so the ring nut can be screwed to it (Figure 17).

Turn both fittings so everything lines up and the lip of the hubbed part of the union nut fits into the externally threaded part of the union nut. Slide the ring nut into place and tighten it securely to lock together the union nut and the nipples (Figure 18).

Following this procedure, you can screw together as many galvanized steel nipples and three-part union nuts as it takes to cover the space left vacant between fittings.

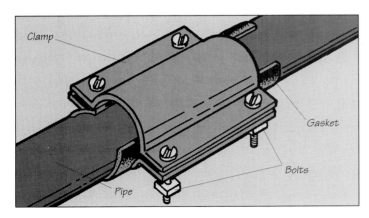

Figure 5. *Shown are the parts of a pipe clamp and how they are to be assembled around a leaky galvanized steel pipe.*

Figure 6. *Place the pipe clamp over the damage so the gasket of the clamp presses against the epoxy covering the leak. Tighten the clamp.*

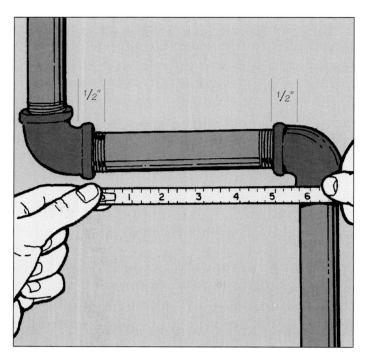

Figure 7. When figuring the length of a new piece of galvanized steel pipe, be sure to allow 1 inch extra for the 1/2 inch that the pipe must extend into each fitting.

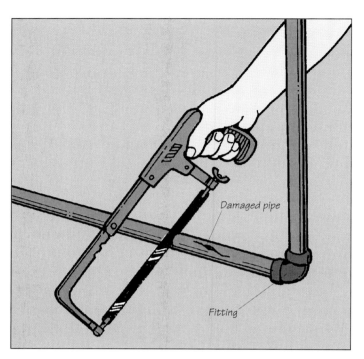

Figure 8. Cut the pipe about 12 inches from one of the fittings.

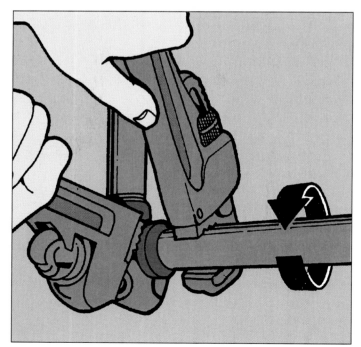

Figure 9. Unscrew the cut pipe from the fitting. Note the position of the wrenches.

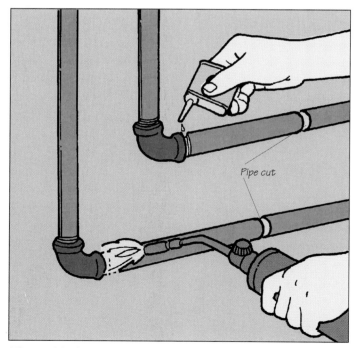

Figure 10. If you can't get the pipe to budge, apply penetrating oil to threads. Give it time to work before trying again. If penetrating oil doesn't work, try heat.

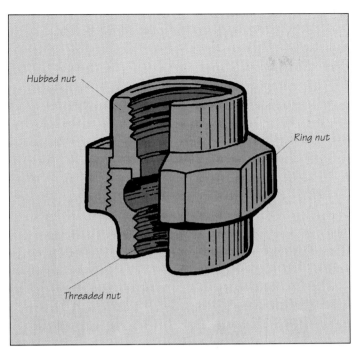

Figure 11. *The two steel nipples (pieces of pipe) that replace the leaking length of pipe are joined together by a three-part union nut. The hubbed nut is screwed onto one nipple; the threaded nut is screwed onto the other nipple; and the two are joined together by the ring nut. Figures 12-18 illustrate the procedure to follow.*

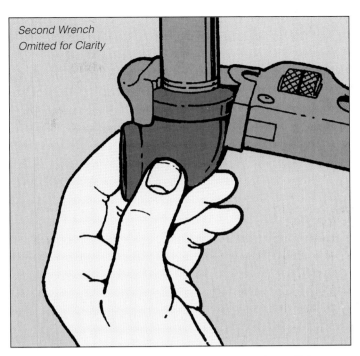

Figure 12. *If old fittings are shot, replace them with new fittings.*

Figure 13. *Be sure to seal all male threads with pipe joint compound.*

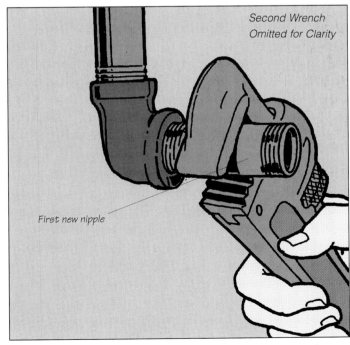

Figure 14. *Screw a nipple into one of the fittings. Turn as much as possible with your pipe wrench.*

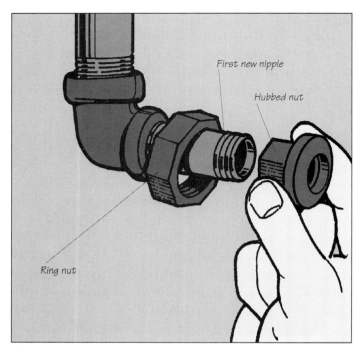

Figure 15. *Slide the ring nut of the three-part union nut onto the nipple. Then, screw the hubbed nut onto the nipple and tighten it with two pipe wrenches. Apply pipe joint compound to the face of the union.*

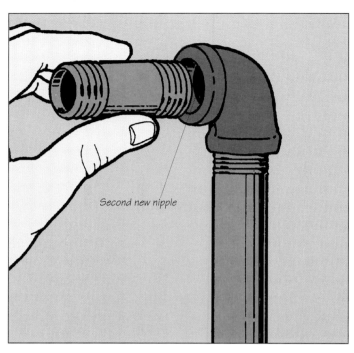

Figure 16. *Screw another nipple into the fitting opposite the one you've been working at.*

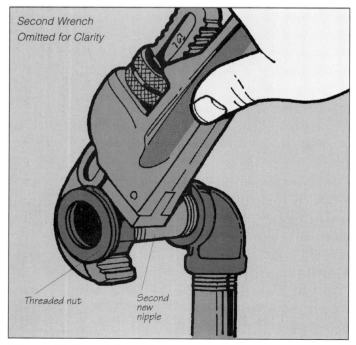

Figure 17. *Screw the threaded nut of the three-part union nut onto this second nipple and tighten with a pipe wrench.*

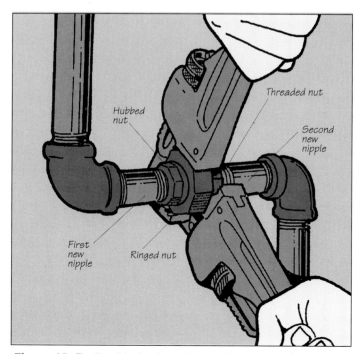

Figure 18. *Finally, slide the ring nut toward the second nipple, screw to threaded nut and tighten using two pipe wrenches—one to hold the threaded nut and one to turn the ring nut securely.*

REPAIRING A LEAKING TRAP

Tools & Materials:
❏ garden hose plastic stretchable tape
❏ adjustable pliers or pipe wrench
❏ pail
❏ plastic or metal trap
❏ rags
❏ pipe joint compound (for metal)
❏ Teflon compound (for plastic)

Sink and lavatory traps come in various designs such as the swivel P or J bend, may be metal or plastic, and with or without a cleanout plug (Figure 1). Another version is a fixed P trap that is connected directly to the drain pipe rather than to an elbow.

Temporary Repair

If the metal trap of a sink corrodes and begins to leak, try a temporary repair using plastic, waterproof, stretchable tape—the type used for repairing garden hoses. Wrap several layers of tape around the trap (Figure 2). It should stop the leak for a few days. Keep a bucket under the trap—just in case.

Permanent Repair

You can replace a corroded metal trap with another or one made of plastic. An advantage of plastic is that it will resist corrosion. Here's how to proceed.

Place a pail under the trap. By hand, try to unscrew the locknuts holding the trap to the tailpiece and extension. If you can't budge them, use adjustable pliers or a pipe wrench to free them (Figure 3). Then, unscrew the locknuts and remove the old corroded trap (Figure 4).

Stuff a rag into the drain pipe extension to prevent sewer gas from entering the room. Take the trap with you to ensure that you buy a replacement of the same shape and dimensions. Lavatory traps are normally 1¼ inches in diameter, while sink traps are 1½ inches in diameter.

Install the new trap. You need to tighten locknuts by hand only (Figure 5). Then, run the water. If there's seepage, tighten locknuts just a bit with adjustable pliers or a pipe wrench. If the leak persists, remove the trap, apply paste-type Teflon compound to the threads of a plastic trap or conventional pipe joint compound on the threads of a metal trap.

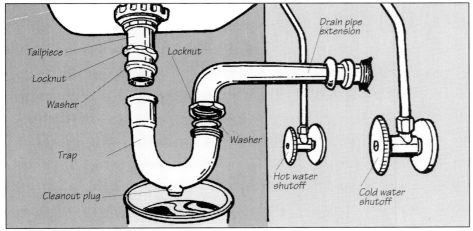

Figure 1. *Shown are the various parts a trap arrangement. The trap may or may not have a cleanout plug.*

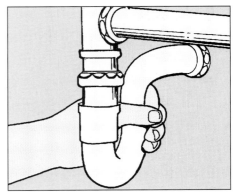

Figure 2. *Wrapping a few layers of water-proof plastic tape around the corroded, section of a trap may stop the leak temporarily.*

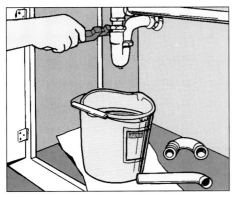

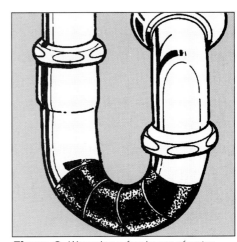

Figures 3-5 *This sequence shows the steps to take when replacing a trap (from left): (3) loosen locknuts; (4) remove and discard the old trap; (5) install new trap, tightening locknuts.*

INSTALLING A DIFFERENT FAUCET

Tools & Materials:
- ❏ ruler
- ❏ adjustable wrench
- ❏ basin wrench
- ❏ braided stainless-steel or vinyl-mesh supply lines (risers)
- ❏ penetrating oil
- ❏ putty knife
- ❏ mineral spirits
- ❏ plumber's putty or silicone caulking
- ❏ pipe joint compound

Remember: Turn off the water shutoff valve or the main valve (see Figure 1, page 8) before beginning work.

Is one of the faucets in your home so worn out that you can't stop it from leaking? Or are you just tired of the same old look? Well, you've turned to the right section of this book.

Don't let the difficulty scale assigned to this project scare you. If you can easily reach the nuts holding the faucet to the sink and those fittings are easy to loosen (Figure 1), it may be an easier job than the rating suggests.

On the other hand, you may have to work in an area that provides 1/2 inch or less clearance between faucet fittings and a wall. Then, the rating could seem overly generous.

Replacing one type of faucet is done the same way as replacing another type. Thus, the following instructions apply whether you are replacing a two-handle faucet with a two-handle faucet, a one-handle faucet with a one-handle faucet, a one-handle faucet with a two-handle faucet, or a two-handle faucet with a one-handle faucet.

Getting Started
Working beneath the sink, measure the distance between the faucet tailpieces or remove the old faucet and measure the distance between the mounting holes in the sink (Figure 2).

With most, the distance is either 4 or 8 inches from the center of one mounting hole (or shank) to the center of the other.

But sometimes you can run across an odd-ball size of 6 inches. The measurement between the shanks of the new faucet must be identical to the measurement of the old faucet.

Removing the Old Faucet
1. With the water shutoff valves closed, open the faucet to let water drain. Then, set up a flashlight so it's aimed at the work area.

CAUTION: Don't use a light that has to be plugged into an outlet. Water and high voltage, if they mix, can cause serious injury or death. Since there's a chance of gettting wet, use a flashlight.

2. Examine the setup. You will be facing one of two possibilities. First, the hot water supply line (riser) may connect to the left-side tailpiece of the faucet and the cold water riser may connect to the right-side tailpiece of the faucet (Figure 3).

Note: "Left" means your left as you face the faucet. "Right" means your right as you face the faucet.

The second possibility is that the tailpiece have nothing to do with supplying water to the faucet—that they're used only to hold the nuts securing the faucet to the sink. In this case, hot and cold water risers converge in the center of the faucet (Figure 4) and connect to copper tubes that are part of the faucet.

In the kitchen faucet illustrated in Figure 4, the center tailpiece serves two functions: one is to provide a way to help secure the faucet to the sink, and the other is to provide the medium through which water is delivered to the sprayer.

Types of faucets can be interchanged as long as the distance between the end

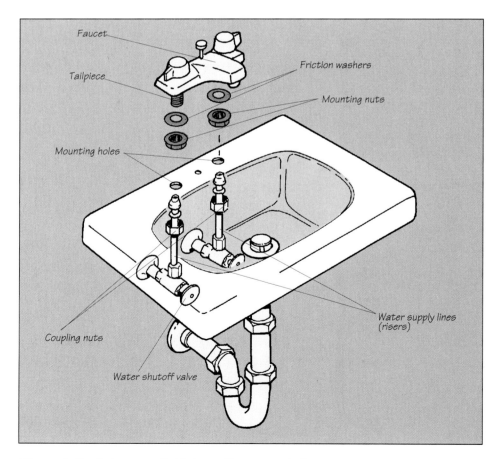

Figure 1. Familiarize yourself with these different parts before proceeding.

bolts equals the distance between the tailpieces (Figures 5 and 6).

3. Disconnect the nuts holding the risers to the tailpieces or to the copper tubes. Use an adjustable wrench, if you can get it on the nuts. If space is tight, use a basin wrench. If possible, use two wrenches—one to hold the riser and one to turn the nut (to avoid the possiblility of twisting the riser).

Consider replacing old risers with new braided stainless-steel (see page 36-37) or vinyl-mesh supply lines (Figure 6).

There are two reasons for doing this. First, if the old risers have been in use for a long time, there's a chance that once they're disconnected from the faucet they won't reseat themselves properly and will leak.

Second, braided stainless steel and vinyl mesh are flexible while chrome copper isn't. If you have to disconnect risers in the future, the job will be easier.

4. Reach up and attach the wrench to the faucet mounting nut on one tailpiece. Turn counterclockwise to loosen and turn the nut and washer off the tailpiece. Do the same on the other side of the faucet. If a nut is frozen in place, spray the area with penetrating oil. Let oil soak into threads for several minutes before trying again.

If you're replacing the faucet of a kitchen sink disconnect the spray hose. Undo the nut holding the hose to the faucet. Use a bucket to catch water.

5. When all the hardware has been freed, pull the old faucet off the sink. If necessary, slip a putty knife under the baseplate and pry off. Then, use the putty knife to scrape crumbled gasket material or putty off the surface of the sink. Using a cloth moistened with water, wash the mounting surface (it must be clean, Figure 7).

Installing the New Faucet

1. If the new faucet comes with a gasket, place it between the baseplate of the faucet and the mounting surface (Figure 8). If there is no gasket, spread a 1/8 to 1/4 inch of plumber's putty or silicone caulking around the faucet baseplate (Figure 9), insert the faucet tailpieces into the mounting holes, and press down on the faucet so putty or caulking eases out beyond the baseplate to make an even border.

Note: Plumber's putty causes marble to stain. Use silicone caulking when working with marble.

2. Working beneath the sink again, secure and tighten by hand the new mounting nuts and washers that come with the faucet (Figure 10). Using an adjustable wrench or basin wrench, turn each nut until it's secure (Figure 11). Do not overtighten nuts.

3. Attach the risers to the faucet and to the shutoff valves (Figures 12 and 13).

4. If the faucet comes equipped with copper supply tubes, spread them apart carefully so you can get them hooked up (Figure 14). Do not overtighten compression fittings. You may distort pipes or strip threads. If applicable, attach the sprayer hose to the center tailpiece (Figure 15).

5. Turn on the water and check connections. If there's a leak, turn the connection a little at a time until the leak stops.

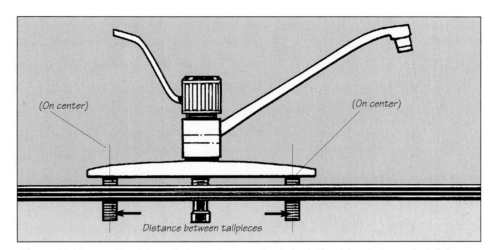

Figure 2. *Measure the distance between the mounting holes in the sink or between the tailpieces; from the center of one to the center of the other. Your new faucet must have the same measurement.*

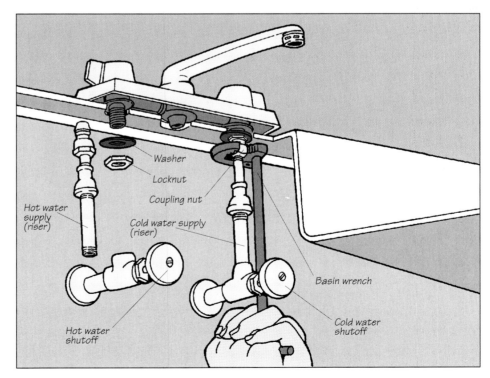

Figure 3. *This type of faucet connects the hot water supply line to the tailpiece of the hot water faucet (left side) and the cold water supply line to the tailpiece of the cold water faucet (right side). If space is tight, use a basin wrench to turn coupling nuts.*

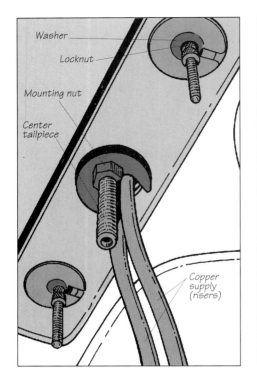

Figure 4. *Another type of faucet has hot and cold water risers converging in the center of the faucet. To remove this faucet, you have to remove hardware in three locations: at each end and at the center tailpiece.*

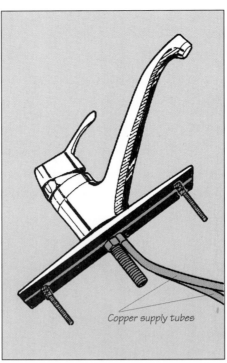

Figure 5. *The two faucet arrangements shown in Figures 3 and 4 are interchangeable. Also, the type in Figure 3 can be replaced with the type shown here if measurements match.*

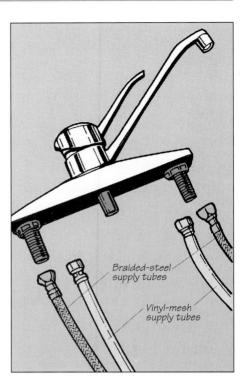

Figure 6. *You can replace the faucet in Figure 4 with this type if measurements match. Also shown are examples of braided-steel and vinyl-mesh flexible supply tubes.*

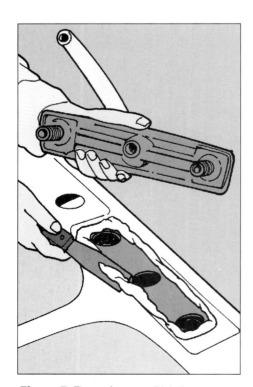

Figure 7. *The surface on which the new faucet is to be placed must be clean.*

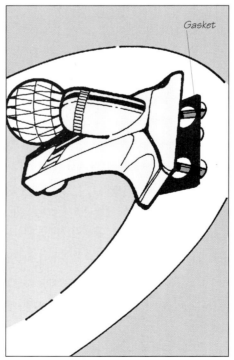

Figure 8. *You must use either a gasket or a sealant around the base of the faucet to provide a seat for the faucet and to prevent water from running down into the cabinet below.*

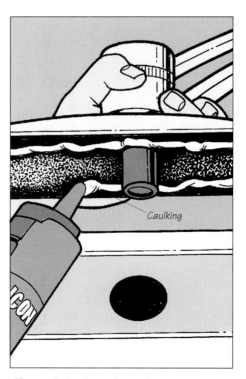

Figure 9. *In place of a gasket, use plumber's putty or silicone caulking to seal the base of the faucet. Do not use plumber's putty on a marble sink or lavatory.*

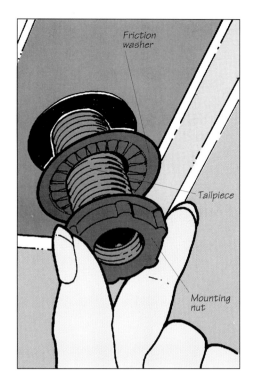

Figure 10. Modern faucets come equipped with plastic mounting nuts that are easily screwed to tailpieces of faucets. The friction washer goes on first, followed by the mounting nut.

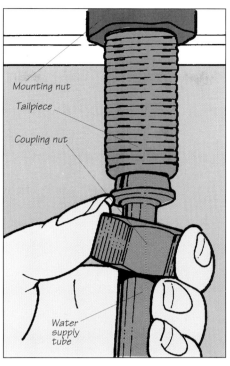

Figure 11. After the mounting nuts have been secured (Figure 10), connect the water supply tube to the tailpiece and secure it with the coupling nut. After tightening connections with your wrench, turn on the water and check for leaks.

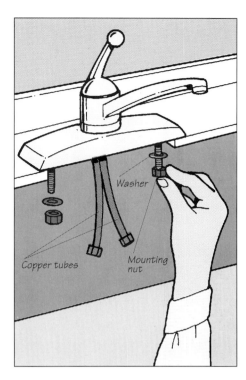

Figure 12. If the new faucet has copper tubes already attached (see Figure 5), set the faucet into the sink and secure it with washers and mounting nuts.

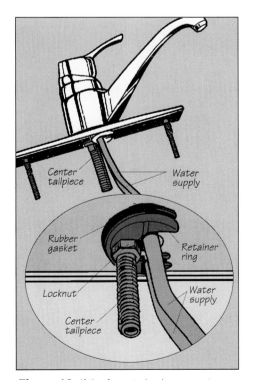

Figure 13. If the faucet also has a center tailpiece for a sprayer, secure this shank with locknut. This illustration shows the arrangement for the securing hardware.

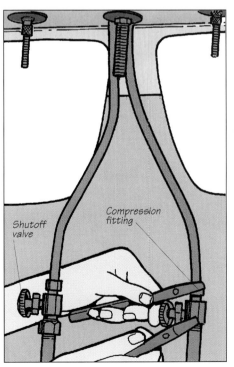

Figure 14. Spread the flexible copper tubes lines and connect them to water shutoff valves with compression fittings.

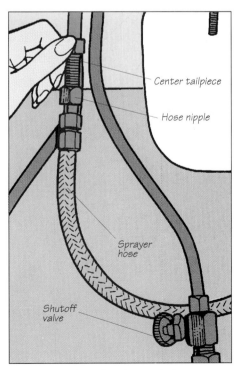

Figure 15. If applicable, attach the sprayer hose to the center tailpiece.

REPAIRING A SINK

Tools & Materials:

❏ porcelain repair compound
❏ high-gloss, alkyd-base paint
❏ medium-grit emery cloth
❏ rubbing alcohol
❏ single-edged razor blade
❏ dowel stick or tongue depressor
❏ fingernail polish remover
❏ 1/2-inch-wide masking tape
❏ silicone caulking
❏ caulking gun
❏ putty knife

Chipping is one problem homeowners face with a sink or lavatory that has a porcelain enamel finish. If the chip is on a side that stays dry most of the time, a repair is possible. However, the repair won't last long if the damage is in the basin.

A second problem involves the joint between a sink and countertop . If the joint wasn't caulked properly to begin with or if the caulk has dried out and cracked, water that splashes can leak into the cabinet.

Repairing Porcelain Enamel

Note: The following repair can also be made to the porcelain enamel surface of a bathtub or toilet:

1. Buy porcelain repair compound at your local home center or hardware store. You also need a can of alkyd-base paint that matches the sink color.

2. Using a piece of medium-grit emery cloth, sand the chipped area (Figure 1). Remove all soap scum and rust, but confine sanding to the damage. Sanding porcelain beyond the damaged spot will cause scratches.

3. Clean the spot using a cloth that you've dampened with rubbing alcohol. Wait for the alcohol to completely dry before applying the repair material.

4. Mix the repair compound with high-gloss alkyd-base paint. Be careful to add a little at a time until it matches the color of the sink as closely as possible. If the color is too dark, mix a new batch with less paint (Figure 2).

➡ PLUMBER'S TIP:

To avoid contaminating the repair compound, mix the compound and paint on a clean piece of glass or a ceramic tile using a wooden dowel stick or tongue depressor.

5. Scoop a little of the compound onto a single-edged razor blade and apply it to the damaged area (Figure 3). Scrape off excess until the compound lies flush with the surface of the surrounding area.

6. After the patch dries, dip a cotton swab in fingernail polish remover and remove excess repair compound to blend the edges into the porcelain (Figure 4).

Sealing Joint Between Sink and Cabinet

1. Brush out crumbled pieces of old caulk in the joint. Then, clean the joint with an alcohol-dampened cloth. Allow it to dry.

2. Apply a strip of 1/2-inch-wide masking tape on and around the sink to

Figure 1. Sand the damaged spot with medium-grit emery cloth until no chipped porcelain remains and the surface is smooth.

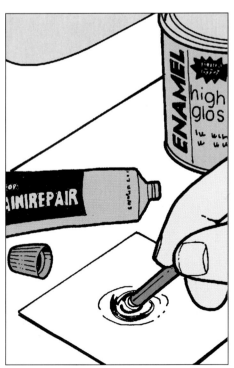

Figure 2. Mix a couple of drops of paint at a time with the repair compound until it matches the color of the porcelain.

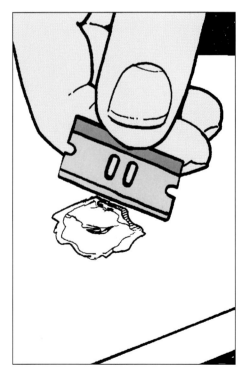

Figure 3. Build up the spot by starting in the hole. Then, keep adding repair compound until it overlaps the edges of the damage slightly.

protect the fixture (Figure 5). The edge of the masking tape should lie just above the joint formed by the rim of the sink and the cabinet.

3. Snip off the end of a tube of silicone caulking to provide the narrowest bead of caulk possible. Place the tube into a caulking gun and slowly move the tip of the tube around the rim of the sink so caulking fills the joint (Figure 6).

When that's been done, dip your finger into water and run that around the caulking to smooth the bead. If caulking has also gotten onto the cabinet, wash it off while it's still wet.

4. Leave the repair alone to allow caulking to cure for several hours. Then, carefully pull off the masking tape.

If necessary, use a single-edged razor blade to remove caulking that's gotten on the sink (Figure 7) and a putty knife to remove any excess on the countertop (Figure 8).

Figure 4. *After the repair compound dries, use a cotton swab saturated with nail polish remover to smooth the edges and blend the compound into the surrounding porcelain.*

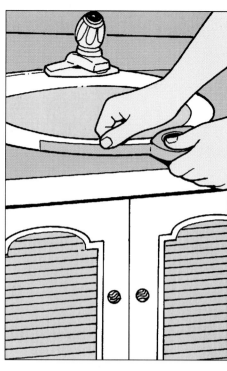

Figure 5. *To keep silicone caulking off porcelain, spread masking tape around the sink.*

Figure 6. *Apply an even bead of caulking compound to the joint.*

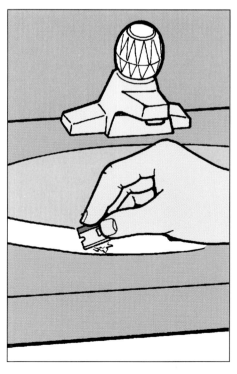

Figure 7. *If any caulking has gotten on the sink, remove it with a razor blade.*

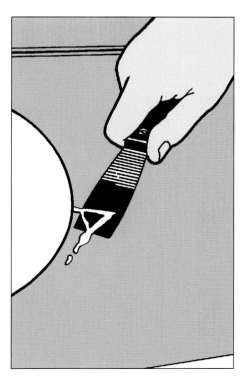

Figure 8. *Using a putty knife, remove excess compound that has gotten on the countertop, but don't disturb the bead around the sink.*

INSTALLING A LARGER LAVATORY

Tools & Materials:

❏ pail
❏ sponge
❏ adjustable wrench
❏ basin wrench
❏ adjustable pliers
❏ pipe wrench
❏ drywall utility knife or pizza cutter
❏ hammer
❏ putty knife
❏ wood chisel
❏ saber saw
❏ ruler
❏ plumber's putty
❏ silicone caulking
❏ caulking gun
❏ braided stainless-steel lines (risers)

Remember: Turn off the water shutoff valve or the main valve (see Figure 1, page 8) before beginning work.

The project described here replaces the lavatory in a bathroom vanity with a larger unit and assumes you're going to reuse the faucet. The same techniques can be used to replace a kitchen sink.

Remove the Present Lavatory

1. With the water turned off, open the faucet to let water drain. Position a pail to catch water that will leak from the cold and hot water supply lines (risers) when they're disconnected.

2. Disconnect the risers from the faucet tailpieces or copper tubes and the shutoff valves (see page 52, "Installing a Different Faucet," for details). Reach up with a basin wrench to loosen and remove the nuts screwed on the faucet tailpieces so the faucet is freed from the lavatory. Use a sponge to sop up any water that missed the pail and has fallen to the floor of the cabinet.

3. Detach the drain from the sink. Place the pail under the trap. Undo the trap locknuts and remove the trap. Then, use adjustable pliers or a pipe wrench to loosen the nut holding the drain tailpiece to the drain flange if a tailpiece is used.

4. Free the stopper (Figure 1). With the setup shown here, this is done by releasing the clevis strap holding the lift rod to the pivot rod and freeing the pivot rod. If you're going to reuse the stopper,

you will also have to unscrew the retaining nut to remove the pivot rod.

5. Remove the lavatory. It's probably secured to the vanity with caulking compound so you'll have to break the seal. Depending upon what type of caulking was used, this can be easy or difficult. If silicone caulking was used, you can break the seal by slipping a sharp instrument under the rim of the lavatory and scouring the caulk around the perimeter. Use a sharp drywall utility knife or pizza cutter.

6. If the lavatory won't come free, an industrial-type of caulking was probably used. You'll have to chip the caulking away. Use a hammer and a putty knife. If the putty knife doesn't work, try a wood chisel having a cutting edge that measures about 1/4 inch. This is a tough job, so be patient. When the lavatory disengages from the vanity, lift the lavatory out.

Although sinks are usually installed using only caulking compound, angle braces and screws also may have been used. Examine the inside of the vanity to be sure this isn't the case. If it is, unscrew the braces.

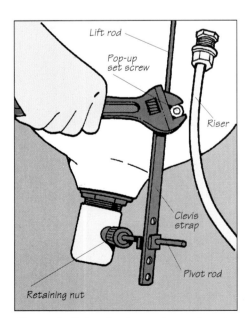

Figure 1. To free the stopper, loosen the set screw holding the lift rod to the clevis strap and release the pivot rod from the clevis strap. Then, undo the retaining nut to free the pivot rod.

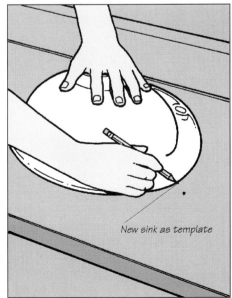

New sink as template

Figure 2. After centering the larger lavatory over the hole, trace its perimeter onto the countertop. Then, scribe a circle 3/8- to 1/2-inch inside the template and erase first line.

Sink opening

Figure 3. Use a saber saw to enlarge the opening, so the new lavatory will fit. Be sure to follow the inside line.

Enlarge the Opening

Center the new larger lavatory, bottom side up, over the opening in the vanity (Figure 2). Then, circumscribe the perimeter of the sink onto the vanity.

Measure the rim of the new lavatory and deduct 3/8 to 1/2 inch from it. Then, measure inward from the outline on the vanity to this measurement and circumscribe another perimeter. Erase the first perimeter line. Using a saber saw, cut along this second perimeter line to cut out the opening for the new lavatory (Figure 3).

Install Faucet and Drain

1. Before you install the lavatory, attach all hardware (Figure 4). Clean the baseplate of the faucet, making certain that no particles of old caulking compound remain. Spread silicone caulking around the baseplate and insert the faucet into the lavatory. Then, attach the locknuts and washers to the faucet tailpieces and secure the faucet to the lavatory (Figure 5).

2. Coat the base of the lavatory drain flange with silicone caulking and insert that into the drain hole. Now, screw the drain piece to the drain flange using the gasket and coupling nut. Spread pipe joint compound on the threads before attaching the two. You should also connect the parts of the pop-up stopper.

3. Spread a bead of silicone caulking around the perimeter of the vanity and set the lavatory in place (Figures 6 and 7). Press down so an even bead of silicone caulking forms from around the joint where the lavatory and vanity meet.

4. To complete the task, hook up the faucet to the water shutoff valves and the drain. Connecting the faucet will probably involve installing new risers. Make things easy on yourself by buying braided

stainless-steel lines or vinyl mesh rather than chrome copper, which has to be shaped (see page 52, "Installing a Different Faucet," for details).

5. As for the drain (Figure 8), after determining the extent of the space you have to fill and the drain parts you have available, take the information to a home center or plumbing supply store. Personnel there can provide you with the parts you'll need.

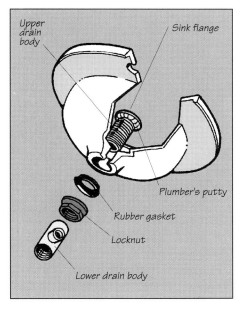
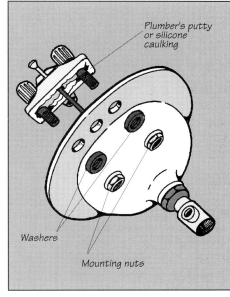

Figures 4 and 5. Install the faucet and drain piece to the lavatory before you set the lavatory in the vanity. Use plumber's putty where noted.

Figure 6. Spread waterproof silicone caulk around the perimeter of the vanity. Aim for an even bead that is 1/4 to 1/2 inch wide.

Figure 7. Install the new lavatory and press it down. Smooth the bead of caulking; then, leave things alone until caulking cures.

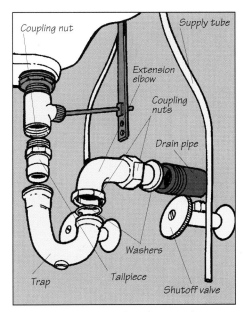

Figure 8. This illustration shows various drain system components you may need for a new lavatory.

INSTALLING WATER SHUTOFF VALVES

Tools & Materials:
- ❏ tube cutter or hacksaw
- ❏ receptacle
- ❏ sponge
- ❏ adjustable wrench or basin wrench
- ❏ tube bender
- ❏ chrome copper supply lines (risers)
- ❏ shutoff valves
- ❏ two compression fittings each consisting of a compression ring and a compression nut
- ❏ coupling nut
- ❏ joint compound or Teflon tape

Remember: *Turn off the main water valve near the water meter (see Figure 1, page 8) before beginning work.*

It hasn't always been a requirement to have shutoff valves on water supply lines (risers) going to sink and lavatory faucets (Figure 1). If the sinks in your house fit this category, consider installing shutoff valves. If you have to make repairs or if there's an emergency, you can use valves to turn off water at the particular faucet instead of running to the basement and shutting off the home's main water valve or the submersible pump.

There's more than one way to make this improvement, and a visit to a plumbing supply or home center store will reveal several different types of valve kits. You may prefer one of them rather than the type described here, which assumes the installation of copper risers and employs the traditional method that uses metal components for installing the shutoff valves (Figure 2).

Getting Ready

1. Decide where you want shutoff valves. The best spot is beneath the sink or lavatory. If space is tight, however, you can install valves in the basement close to where the water supply pipes to the faucets project through the floor. Although you'll still have to run to the basement to turn off water to the faucet, at least you won't have to turn it off throughout the house.

2. Open the faucet you're working on. Also open a faucet in the basement to drain off as much water as possible. Leave faucets open until the procedure has been completed and the water has been turned back on.

3. Place a receptacle under one of the lines to catch water.

4. Using a tube cutter or hacksaw, cut the line (Figure 3). If the water pipe comes through the floor and runs straight to the faucet, make the cut at a point that allows the best location for the valve.

If the water pipe comes through the wall and then angles toward the faucet, the ideal place to make the cut is in the pipe coming through the wall (horizontal segment), behind the 90-degree elbow. Allow enough room for the valve and an escutcheon.

The cut must be straight so take your time. Use a sponge to sop up water that drips onto the floor.

5. Using an adjustable wrench or basin wrench, disconnect the coupling nut holding the cut line to the faucet tailpiece and take it to the plumbing supply store to get the correct size shutoff valves. Explain what you're going to do, where valves are going to be placed (under the sink or in the basement), and whether water pipes run straight or at an angle.

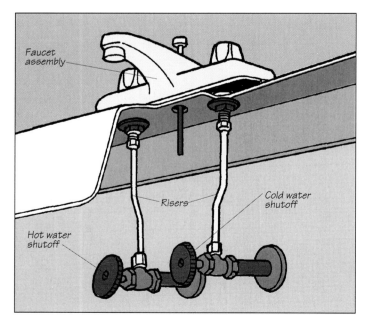

Figure 1. *Water shutoff valves on a sink or lavatory are a convenience.*

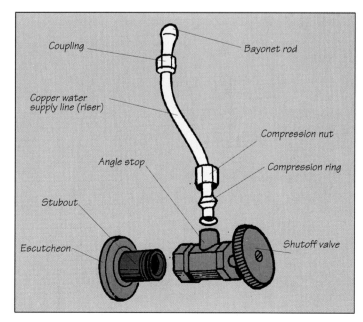

Figure 2. *Although there are different ways to install a shutoff valve, the traditional and widely accepted method described here makes use of these parts. Note that the valve is threaded to the stubout when galvanized steel is involved.*

Installing the Shutoff Valve

1. Slip a compression nut on the new copper riser about 1 inch from the end.

2. Slip a compression ring on the riser and slide it back to where the nut is positioned (Figure 4).

3. Apply a coating of pipe joint compound to the compression ring.

4. Wrap Teflon tape or apply a coating of pipe joint compound around the threads of the shutoff valve. Hold the valve on the pipe as you bring the compression ring and compression nut against the base of the valve (Figure 5). Tighten the compression nut by hand.

5. With that done, use double-wrenching to turn the compression nut 1/2 to 3/4 turn with an adjustable wrench. Double-wrenching means that you use one wrench to hold the valve steady as you turn the compression nut with another wrench. This prevents pipe distortion.

6. Prepare the new copper supply line (riser) for installation. Notice that one end is the bayonet end (Figure 6). This end fits into the faucet tailpiece to provide a seal. Hold this end in the tailpiece and judge the amount that the line will have to be bent so it will line up with the valve. Place the line into a tube bender and carefully bend it to this shape (Figure 7).

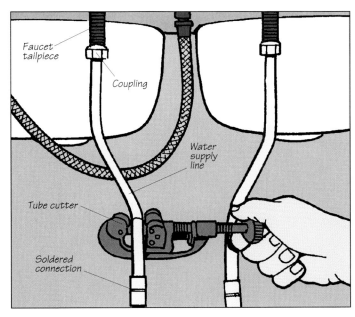

Figure 3. The first step in installing water shutoff valves is to turn off the water and drain the water supply line. The next step is to cut the line.

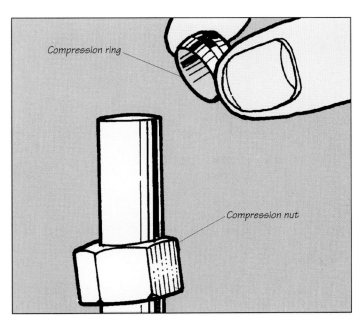

Figure 4. The compression fitting consists of a compression ring and a compression nut. When the nut is tightened to the water shutoff valve, it secures the ring and makes a leakproof connection.

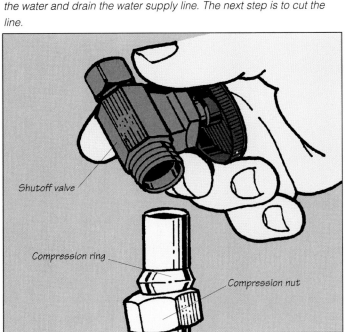

Figure 5. This illustration shows the relation of the compression nut and compression ring to the shutoff valve.

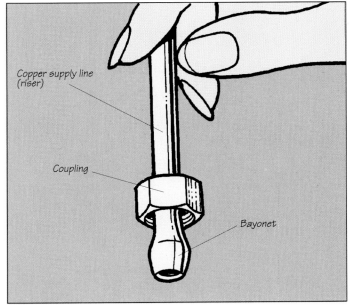

Figure 6. The copper supply line you buy should have a bayonet end. This end fits into the faucet shank and is attached to the shank with a coupling nut.

Note: *If you are leery about your ability to shape copper line, buy braided flexible stainless-steel or vinyl-mesh line (see page 36-37) to use for the riser.*

7. Holding the riser so the bayonet end is in the faucet tailpiece, mark the line at the valve for length (Figure 8).

8. Cut to the proper length.

9. The remainder of the procedure involves hooking up the copper supply line. Apply joint compound or Teflon tape to the threads of the tailpiece. Slip a coupling nut onto the riser, slide it up to the bayonet end, and screw this end of the riser to the faucet tailpiece.

10. Slide a compression nut and compression ring onto the other end of the riser, insert the end into the shutoff valve, apply pipe joint compound to the compression ring and threads of the valve, and secure this end to the valve.

Note: You will probably have to flex the riser a bit to get the end into the valve. Do this carefully.

11. Use double-wrenching to tighten the nuts (Figure 9). Turn on the water and check for leaks around the nuts. If there is a leak at one of the compression nuts or at the coupling nut, tighten the nut a little at a time until the leak stops (Figure 10).

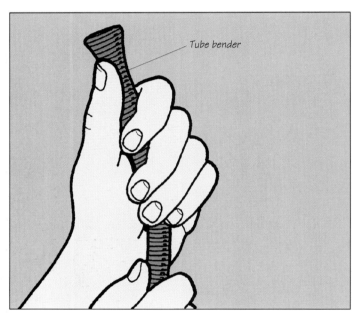

Figure 7. *Using a tube bender, bend the chrome copper supply pipe to shape so it can be connected to the faucet tailpiece and new shutoff valve.*

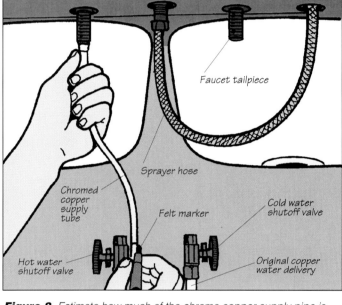

Figure 8. *Estimate how much of the chrome copper supply pipe is excess. Then, cut it off.*

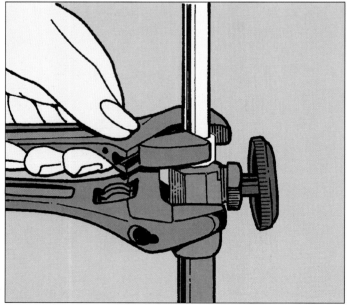

Figure 9. *Using two wrenches—one to hold the valve and the other to turn the compression nut—tighten the nut securely. Do not overtighten.*

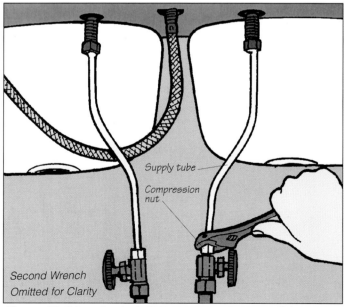

Figure 10. *If there is a leak, tighten compression nuts a little at a time until the leak stops.*

ANATOMY OF A TOILET

Most residential toilets consist of a bowl and a tank with bowls resting on the floor. Others are mounted on the wall so the bowl is off the floor and the tank sits on top of the bowl. A toilet can have a separate tank and bowl, or they can be manufactured as one piece.

When you flush a toilet, gravity forces water to rush from the tank into the bowl. This surging water creates a siphon within the trap that pulls the contents out of the bowl into the drain.

The mechanisms inside the tank, which are used to control the flow of water, are involved either with the replenishment of water into the tank from the home's water supply system or the discharge of water from the tank into the bowl.

Water-Intake System

The water-intake system, which replenishes water in the tank, consists of a water-supply riser connected to a water-intake valve and a float. The water supply line is attached to a water shutoff valve.

Another term for the water-intake valve is "ballcock." Various ballcock designs are in use. One of the oldest types (Figure 1) is a brass or plastic assembly with a plunger that governs the flow of water into the tank. The plunger is controlled by the float, which is a hollow ball.

A more recent design has the float as part of the ballcock (Figure 2). Another does away with the float altogether (Figure 3) and incorporates a pressure-sensitive component that senses when the water level has dropped below the preset level so it can release the water-intake port, which opens.

There are only two things that can be done with this type of ballcock: (1) You can lower or raise the water level in the tank by turning the adjustment screw counterclockwise or clockwise, respectively and (2) if the ballcock fails to control the intake of water as it should, you have to replace the entire assembly.

Water-Outlet System

The water-outlet system inside a toilet tank consists of a flush valve (rubber ball or flapper) that sits over a wide opening we call the flush-valve seat.

Another important part is the overflow tube, which allows water to flow out of the tank into the bowl should the ballcock fail to shut.

The Bowl

As water flows out of the tank, it spirals into the bowl through several small holes around the rim of the bowl and through a larger opening called the siphon jet hole. Its velocity pushes the bowl contents up through a discharge channel (or trap) into the drain (Figure 1). Water that sits in the bowl blocks sewer gases entering the bathroom.

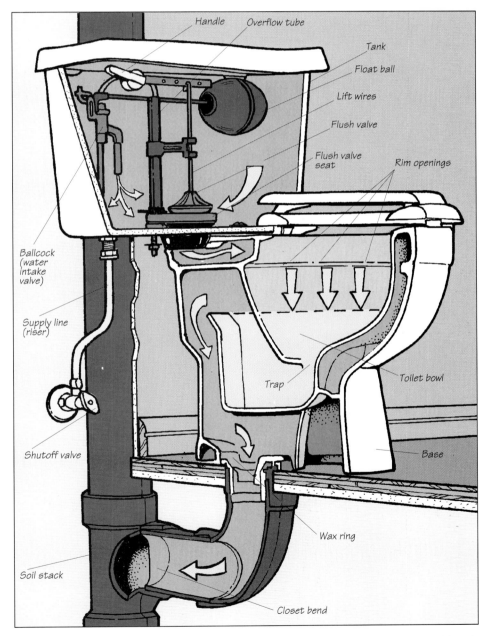

Figure 1. Gravity-operated flush toilets are basically the same from one unit to another although there are variations in the design of some components.

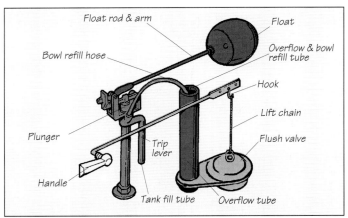

Figure 2. *When a plunger-valve ballcock toilet is flushed, the ball and float arm drop, opening the brass water-intake port.*

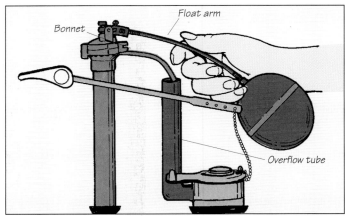

Figure 3. *When a diaphragm ballcock toilet is flushed, the ball and float arm drop, opening the rubber diaphragm water-intake port in the plastic bonnet.*

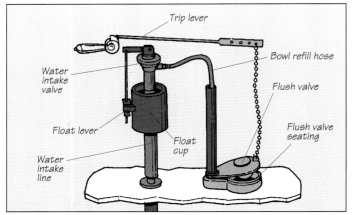

Figure 4. *When the float cup ballcock toilet is flushed, the float slides down the ballcock, drawing a diaphragm off the water-intake port.*

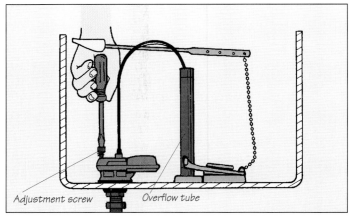

Figure 5. *When a pressure-sensitive ballcock senses the water level has dropped below the preset level, it opens the water-intake port.*

HIGH-PRESSURE, FLUSH-VALVE SYSTEM

The low-flush pressure-tank toilet features a smaller tank (the pressure tank) within the tank. A pressure regulating valve compresses ambient air pressure in the small tank to 35 pounds per square inch. When the push-button is pressed to flush the toilet, the pressurized air pushes 1.6 gallons of water into the bowl at an extraordinary rate that is equal to 70 gallons per minute. The force creates a vortex effect that allows water to flush away whatever is in the bowl and creates a scouring effect by the swirling water against the sides to clean the bowl. Using just 1.6 gallons of water allows this toilet to meet every code that defines the characteristics of a low-flush toilet.

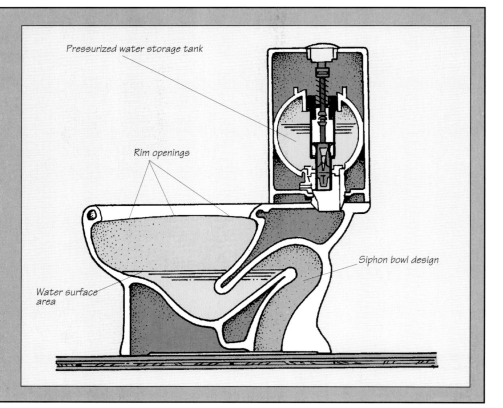

TOILET TROUBLESHOOTING

The following chart summarizes causes of and solutions for problems with toilets.

Problem	Cause	Solution
Water trickles into bowl	• Dirt on flush-valve seat • Damaged flush-valve seat • Flush valve drifts • Defective flush valve	• Clean flush valve seat (page 66) • Replace flush valve (page 66) • Adjust position of flush valve (page 66) • Replace flush valve seat or toilet (page 66)
Toilet momentarily flushes itself(phantom flush)	• Damaged flush valve	• Replace flush-valve (page 66)
Water flows continuously into bowl	• Handle assembly hanging up • Float set too high • Damaged float	• Service handle assembly (page 67) • Adjust float (page 67) • Replace float (page 67)
Water trickles continuously into tank; hissing noise in tank	• Misadjusted or damaged float • Damaged or waterlogged ballcock	• Adjust or replace float (page 67) • Replace seals (page 68) or replace ballcock (page 69)
Tank doesn't completely empty	• Loose flush-valve chain or bent lift wire • Water flow into bowl is sluggish because of clogged flush and siphon jet holes	• Adjust flush-valve chain (page 70); straighten or replace lift wire (page 67) • Clean out flush and siphon jet holes (page 70)
Bowl overflows	• Clogged trap	• Clear clogging material (page 71)
Tank "sweats"	• Warm air condenses on cool sides of tank	• Insulate tank (page 73)
Tank leaks	• Fasteners holding tank to bowl have loosened or seals have deteriorated • Tank cracked	• Tighten fasteners (page 73) or replace seals (page 73) • Replace tank or toilet (page 75)
Bowl leaks	• Seal has deteriorated	• Install a new seal (page 75)

REPLACING A TOILET SEAT

Tools & Materials:
❑ pliers
❑ new toilet seat
❑ screwdriver

To replace a cracked toilet seat, or one that has seen better days, follow these steps:

1. Lower the seat and cover.

2. If they're present, pry open the lids covering the bolts that hold the seat to the bowl (Figure 1).

3. Reach underneath and grasp the nut on one side of the bowl. Then, loosen and remove this fastener. Do the same thing on the other side. Lift the old seat off the bowl (Figure 2).

4. Wash and dry the rim of the bowl before installing the new seat. Turn the fasteners fingertight and then give them one-half turn with a wrench. Do not overtighten; they could crack.

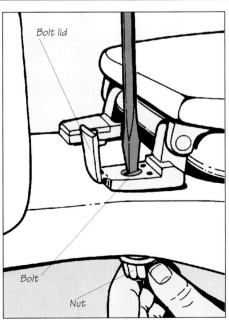

Figure 1. *Lift the lid, hold the bolt, and unscrew the nut.*

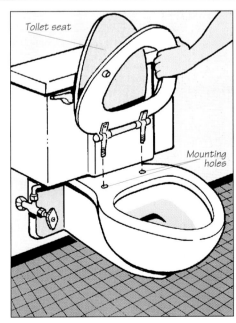

Figure 2. *Remove the old seat and install the new one.*

WATER TRICKLES INTO BOWL
OR PHANTOM FLUSHES

Tools & Materials:
- ❑ sponge
- ❑ rags or paper towels
- ❑ fine steel wool or vinyl-cleaning pad
- ❑ replacement flush valve
  (rubber ball or flapper)

Remember: *Turn off the water shutoff valve or the main valve (see Figure 1, page 8) before beginning work.*

This section describes how to repair the following conditions:

1. Water trickling into the bowl most often is the result of a deteriorated flush valve (rubber ball or flapper). Sometimes, it is caused by a dirty flush valve seat, which is preventing the ball or flapper from seating securely. The problem could also be caused by a misaligned ball.

2. The toilet seems to flush itself momentarily. This brief rush of water into the bowl, called a phantom flush, is caused by a flush valve.

Servicing Flush Valve Seat

With the water shutoff valve closed, flush the toilet. Use a large sponge to sop up water remaining in the tank. Wipe the flush valve seat with rags or paper towels to clean off sediment. For stubborn deposits, use fine steel wool if rim is brass or a pad made for cleaning vinyl-coated cooking utensils if plastic (Figure 1).

Replacing Rubber Ball or Flapper Flush Valve

If your toilet is equipped with a rubber ball flush valve, lift the ball off the flush valve seat and unscrew it from the lift wire (Figure 2). Screw on the replacement. Be careful not to bend the lift wire or the alignment between the ball and seat will be thrown out of kilter.

If your toilet has a flapper flush valve, unhook its chain from the handle lever. Take note of which hole in the handle lever the chain is hooked. If the flapper is attached to lugs on the side of the overflow tube, unhook it from those lugs (Figure 3). If it fits over the overflow tube instead, slide it off the tube. Install the new flapper valve the same way (Figure 4).

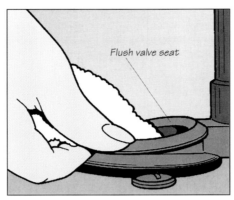

Figure 1. *The first step in stopping a trickle into the bowl from the tank is to clean the flush valve seat.*

Figure 3. *Unhook the old flapper from the lugs on the overflow pipe, as illustrated, or slide it off the overflow pipe.*

Repositioning Rubber Ball

Unscrew the lift wire from a rubber ball flush valve. If the wire is bent, straighten or replace it. Seat the rubber ball squarely in the flush valve seat. Loosen the lift wire guide screw and turn it until the lift wire is squarely over the rubber ball. Tighten the lift wire guide and screw the lift wire onto the rubber ball (Figure 5). Be careful not to bend the lift wire. Fill the tank to see if the adjustment has stopped the trickle.

Replace Flush Valve Seat

If the flush valve seat is badly worn, it may need to be replaced. Remove the tank if it's a two-piece toilet and replace the part. If this is a one-piece toilet, you'll probably have to install a new toilet.

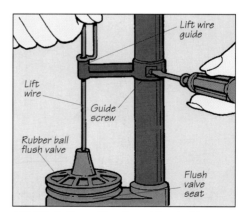

Figure 2. *Replace a defective rubber ball by unscrewing it from the lift wire. Secure the new ball to the lift wire.*

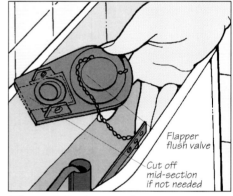

Figure 4. *Replacement flappers are designed to fit over the overflow pipe or to hook onto lugs that are part of the overflow pipe. If lugs are present, use scissors to cut off the mid-section as shown here.*

Figure 5. *Reposition the rubber ball to make sure it is falling squarely into the flush valve seat.*

WATER FLOWS CONTINUOUSLY INTO BOWL

Tools & Materials:
- ❏ adjustable wrench
- ❏ wire brush
- ❏ vinegar
- ❏ needle-nose pliers
- ❏ lift wire
- ❏ float

Remember: *Turn off the water shutoff valve or the main valve (see Figure 1, page 8) before beginning work.*

When water won't stop running into the bowl, try jiggling the handle to dislodge the stuck flush valve (rubber ball or flapper) handle assembly. If this doesn't work, the fault lies with a misadjusted or damaged float.

Handle Assembly Repairs
If jiggling the handle stops the flow of water, the handle assembly is probably sticking because of lime deposits on the mechanism.

With the water shutoff valve closed, flush the toilet. Using an adjustable wrench, loosen the nut holding the handle to the inner wall of the tank. Clean lime deposits off the threads of the handle mechanism with a wire brush saturated with vinegar. Flush with water. Then, tighten the nut securely. If this doesn't work, the next step is to check on the lift wire or chain.

If the handle assembly lifts a rubber ball flush valve, it has a lift wire (Figure 1). If the lower lift wire is bent, unscrew the rubber ball, slide the lower wire from the upper wire to the lower wire and straighten or replace the wire.

If the handle assembly uses a chain to draw a flapper flush valve off the flush valve seat, the chain probably has too much slack (Figure 2). Unhook the chain from the hole in the handle lever and switch it to another hole to reduce the slack. There should be about 1/2 inch of slack to the chain. If the chain is too long, use needle-nose pliers to remove links, which will reduce the length.

Servicing the Float
If jiggling the handle doesn't stop the flow of water into the bowl, the float is lying too low in the water and is keeping the water-inlet valve from closing (Figure 3). The float is not adjusted properly or it's too heavy. A heavy float can result when the hollow float ball develops a hole that allows water to get inside it. In either event, the result can be a float that doesn't rise to a level that is sufficient to allow the water-inlet valve to close.

Water will rise above the top of the overflow tube and pour into the bowl through that tube. If you remove the tank lid, you'll be able to see this. Do the following:

1. Turn the float onto the threaded float arm. Flush the toilet. Does the water again rise over the top of the overflow and bowl-refill tube?

2. If the answer is "yes," and with the water shutoff valve closed, flush the toilet. Unscrew the float and replace it with a new one.

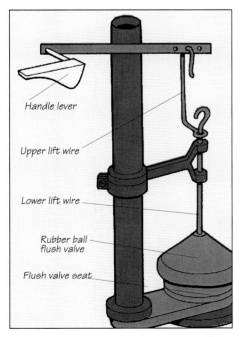

Figure 1. *The lift wire must not be bent if a rubber ball flush valve is to fall squarely into the flush valve seat.*

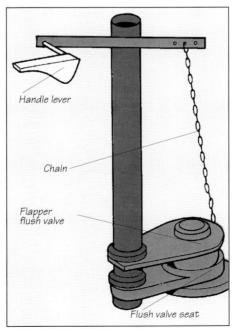

Figure 2. *Slack in the chain to a flapper flush valve should be about 1/2 inch. If greater, move the chain to another hole to reduce the slack.*

Figure 3. *Lift the float. If the flow of water stops, tighten or replace the float.*

WATER TRICKLES CONTINUOUSLY INTO TANK
HISSING NOISE IN TANK

Tools & Materials:
- ❏ float
- ❏ pliers
- ❏ screwdriver
- ❏ ballcock plunger or plunger seal replacement kit
- ❏ ballcock (anti-siphon)
- ❏ nylon pad
- ❏ sponge
- ❏ adjustable wrench
- ❏ adjustable pliers or pipe wrench
- ❏ joint compound (for metal)
- ❏ Teflon compound paste (for plastic)

*depends on repair needed

Remember: *Turn off the water shutoff valve or the main valve (see Fig. 1, page 8) before beginning work.*

When there's a constant trickle of water into a toilet tank or a hissing sound comes from the tank, the reason is a misadjusted or damaged float or defective water-inlet valve (ballcock).

Servicing the Float
For information on this procedure, see page 67.

Servicing the Ballcock
To install new seals in a brass ballcock, proceed in this way:

1. With the water shutoff valve closed, flush the toilet.

2. Remove the wing nut or screw holding the float rod to the ballcock and remove the float rod and float.

3. Pry the plunger out of the ballcock.

4. Take the plunger to a plumbing supply or home center store to determine if replacement seals (Figure 1) or a new plunger is available. If so, buy one or the other and reassemble the unit.

With a traditional-style plastic ballcock, remove the screws holding the top of the ballcock and lift it off. If parts are corroded or cracked, replace the ballcock. If parts look okay, replace the seals on the plunger and the diaphragm if these parts are available (Figure 2).

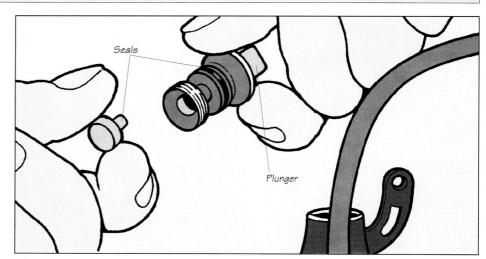

Figure 1. *Traditional brass ballcock assemblies have two seals.*

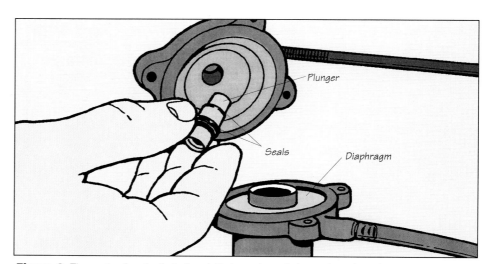

Figure 2. *The parts of a plastic ballcock that may have to be replaced are the seals and diaphragm.*

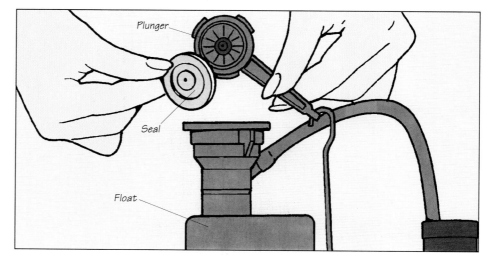

Figure 3. *The seal inside the plunger of an assembly that has the float as part of the ballcock is the component that has to be replaced.*

With a ballcock that uses a round plastic float that encircles the ballcock, lift off the ballcock cap, press down on the plunger, and turn it to lift it off. If parts look sound, remove the seal from inside the plunger and replace it (Figure 3).

In all cases, when you reassemble the ballcock, use a nylon pad to clean sediment from the water-intake port before installing the plunger.

Replacing a Ballcock

Purchase an anti-siphon ballcock to comply with the National Standard Plumbing Code. Follow these steps to replace a ballcock (Figure 4):

1. With the water shutoff valve closed, flush the toilet, and use a sponge to sop excess water from the tank.

2. Unscrew the float and float rod from the ballcock.

3. Using an adjustable wrench, unscrew the water supply line.

4. Using adjustable pliers or a pipe wrench, loosen and remove the locknut and washer holding the ballcock to the underside of the tank.

5. Lift the old ballcock out of the tank. Before you install a new metal ballcock in the hole in the base of the tank, spread pipe joint compound around the threads that fit through the hole. If the new ballcock is plastic, use Teflon paste compound around the threads. Install the new ballcock.

CAUTION: Do not overtighten connections. When you turn on the water, check for leaks. If there is a leak, tighten that connection a little at a time until the leak stops.

6. You may have to adjust the float when you attach the float and rod to the ballcock. Water should lie about 3/4 of an inch below the top of the overflow tube. Carefully bend the middle of the float rod down a little to lower the float (Figure 5) or bend the rod up to raise the float. Check the result. Proceed in this way until the water rises to the proper level vis-a-vis the overflow tube.

7. See that the refill hose is attached to the ballcock and that 1/4 inch or so is down the throat of the overflow tube (Figure 6).

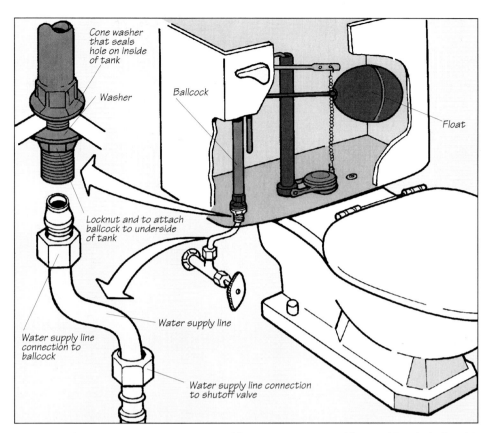

Figure 4. Shown is the usual arrangement of fasteners that are used for attaching the ballcock to the toilet tank.

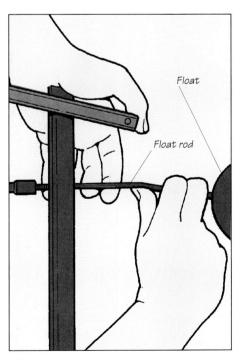

Figure 5. If the float level has to be adjusted, gently bend the float rod.

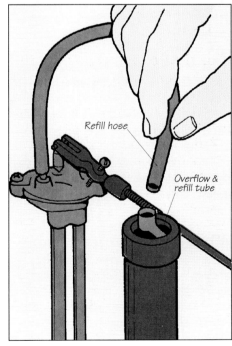

Figure 6. Attach the refill hose so that 1/4 inch is down the throat of the overflow tube.

TOILET DOESN'T FLUSH PROPERLY

Tools & Materials:
- ❏ pliers
- ❏ flapper flush valve and chain
- ❏ wire coat hanger
- ❏ pocket mirror
- ❏ anti-lime compound
- ❏ funnel

Two types of flushing problems are described in this section: (1) the tank doesn't empty completely unless you hold the handle down and (2) the tank empties completely, but the flow of water into the bowl is sluggish and doesn't allow complete discharge.

Tank Doesn't Empty Completely

The cause of this problem is often confined to toilets with chain-lifted flapper flush valves. The chain probably has too much slack, restricting the height of the flapper as you activate the handle. The pressure of water on the flapper flush valve causes it to reseat itself before the normal amount of water in the tank can empty unless you keep the flapper off the valve seat by holding on to the handle.

The thin metal hook that attaches the end of the chain to the trip lever may have stretched a bit. Unhook the chain from its present hole in the trip lever and bend it or attach it to a hole that's closer to the handle (Figure 1).

If this doesn't resolve the problem, the flapper flush valve may have deteriorated, so replace the valve and the chain (Figure 2).

Sluggish Flow Into Bowl

If you must flush the toilet more than once to empty the bowl, it's often due to partially blocked flush holes around the rim of the bowl and/or a partially blocked siphon jet hole. By holding a pocket mirror under the rim of the bowl (Figure 3), check to see if lime deposits are clogging the flush holes. Here's how to clean the holes:

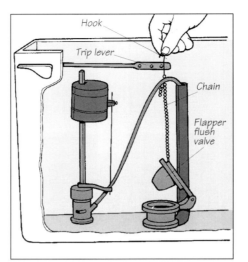

Figure 1. *If you must keep pressure on the handle of a chain-type mechanism in order for the tank to empty completely, try moving the hook of the chain to a hole in the trip lever that is closer to the handle.*

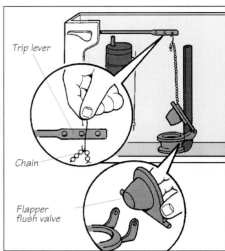

Figure 2. *If moving the chain to another hole doesn't help empty the tank completely, you may have to replace the flapper and chain.*

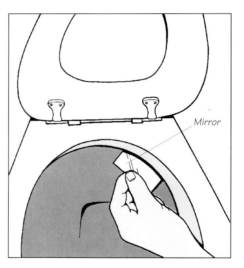

Figure 3. *You can usually see lime deposits that clog bowl flush holes by holding a mirror under the rim.*

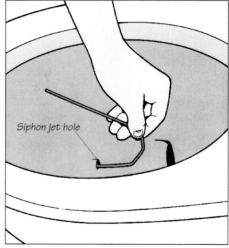

Figure 4. *A coat hanger makes an effective tool to loosen the deposits clogging the siphon jet hole.*

1. Straighten a wire coat hanger and carefully poke the end of it into each flush hole. Move the hanger back and forth a couple of times to clear deposits, but be careful that the hanger doesn't slip and damage the porcelain.

2. Insert the hanger into the siphon jet hole and scrape deposits from that (Figure 4).

3. Buy anti-lime compound from a hardware or home center store and mix it according to directions. Bail water from the bowl to below the siphon jet hole.

4. Remove the tank lid, insert a funnel into the overflow tube, and pour the solution down that tube.

5. After one hour, flush the toilet several times.

BOWL CLOGS

Tools & Materials:
❑ cup or tin can
❑ pocket mirror
❑ flashlight
❑ wire coat hanger
❑ plumber's helper
❑ closet auger

*depends on repair needed

If the water in a bowl rises to the rim or overflows,it is likely that something is clogging the channel (trap), preventing the water and contents from entering the drain. Usually, the restriction is easily cleared.

Try the Easy Way

1. Use an old cup or a tin can to bail water from the bowl.

2. Place a small mirror at an angle in the drain hole and shine a flashlight into the mirror so the beam reflects into the channel for better visibility (Figure 1).

3. If you can spot the obstruction, try to fish it out using a wire coat hanger that has been straightened out, and has a hook at one end.

Plumber's helper

If the clog can't be relieved the easy way, use a plumber's helper. The type of plumber's helper you want for a toilet is one that has a bulb (flange) on the end of the cup (Figure 2). You can clear most toilet bowl stoppages with this tool.

Insert the bulb into the drain, press down, and vigorously pump the handle of the plumber's helper several times. Then flush the toilet to test results.

CAUTION: Keep your hand on the water shutoff valve in case water begins to rise to the point of overflowing.

Repeat the procedure four or five times before giving up and turning to a closet auger.

Closet Auger

The closet auger is designed to flex around the turns in the channel that form the trap while still being stiff enough to force its way through practically any obstruction. It is a fairly expensive tool so you may want to rent one instead of purchasing.

To use a closet auger, place the working end of the auger into the bowl. Turn the handle to snake the end through the channel (Figure 3). When you hit the obstruction, turn and push harder. Repeat the snaking action several times. Follow by flushing the toilet with the above caution in mind.

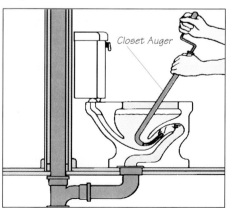

Figure 1. *By using a small mirror and flashlight, you may be able to see an obstruction in the top of the trap. If so, try fishing it out with a wire coat hanger.*

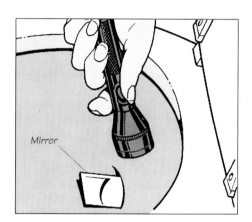

Figure 3. *A closet auger is flexible enough to make the turns in the trap. Insert the auger and turn the handle.*

Testing Results

To test the results, throw 20 to 30 feet of toilet paper into the bowl and flush. Keep your hand on the water shutoff valve just in case. If the paper swirls vigorously down the drain, you've succeeded. If not, more plunging or auger action is needed.

Drastic Action

If the obstruction in the trap is so solidly stuck that even a closet auger won't clear it out, detach the bowl from the floor, turn it upside down, and clear the obstruction from the bottom side of the bowl (Figure 4). How to remove a bowl is described on page 74.

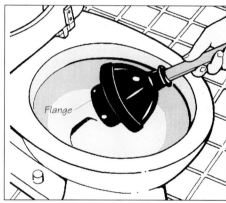

Figure 2. *A plumber's helper with a bulb or flange on the end of the cup provides greater force to clear an obstruction than one without.*

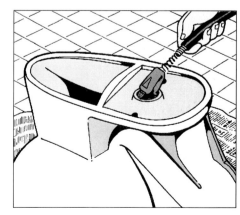

Figure 4. *In the event that you still can't clear an obstruction after using the plunger and closet auger, you'll have to remove the bowl (see page 74) and tackle the problem from below.*

Repairing a Minor Leak
and Preventing Condensation

Tools & Materials:
- ❏ adjustable wrench
- ❏ Teflon tape
- ❏ pipe joint compound,
- ❏ braided stainless-steel water supply line
- ❏ sponge
- ❏ ballcock gasket
- ❏ screwdriver
- ❏ tank-to-bowl fasteners
- ❏ toilet tank insulation kit

Remember: *Turn off the water shutoff valve or the main valve (see Figure 1, page 8) before beginning work.*

A two-piece floor-mounted unit can leak water from seven spots. A one-piece floor-mounted unit can leak from five spots. A one-piece wall-mounted toilet can leak from three spots.

Minor leaks, defined as the following, are discussed in this section:
- ♦ A leak from the water-supply line. This applies to all designs.
- ♦ A leak from around a deteriorated water-inlet pipe gasket. This applies to all designs.
- ♦ A leak from around the bolts that hold the tank of a two-piece toilet to the bowl.

Stopping a Leak From Water-Supply Line
If there's a drip of water from around one of the nuts that attaches the water-supply line to the water shutoff valve and ballcock, tighten the nut using an adjustable wrench. If the leak persists, with the water shutoff valve closed, loosen the nut, and wrap Teflon tape or spread pipe joint compound around the compression ring and/or around the female threads. Tighten the nut.

If the water-supply line has sprung a leak, replace it (Figure 1). The job is done the same way as replacing a faucet water-supply line (page 36). Braided stainless-steel water-supply line instead of chrome brass is easier to work with.

Stopping a Leak From Water-Inlet Pipe Gasket
1. With the water shutoff valve closed, flush the toilet, and remove the tank lid. Using a sponge, sop up the water remaining in the bottom of the tank.

2. Loosen and unscrew the nuts holding the water-supply line. Remove the water-supply line.

3. Hold or have a helper hold the ballcock. Working beneath the tank, loosen the nut holding the ballcock to the tank. Then, remove the nut and gasket. Take these to a plumbing parts supply store or home center store and get replacements.

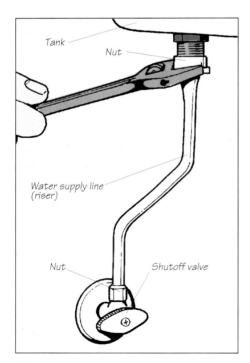

Figure 1. *To replace the water-supply line, undo the nuts on the top and bottom. Replace with a line of braided stainless steel or a chrome brass line, which will have to be curved with a tube bender.*

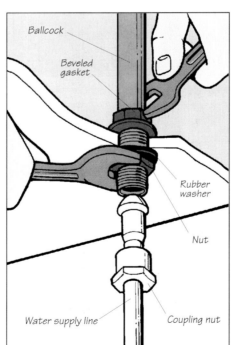

Figure 2. *Remove the ballcock by loosening the nut while a helper holds the ballcock. Replace the gasket and the nut and its rubber washer.*

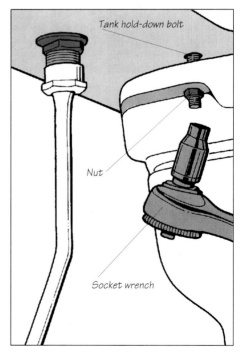

Figure 3. *If there's a leak from around a tank mounting bolt, securing the nut may draw the washer more firmly against the hole, causing the leak to stop. Do not over-tighten the nut.*

4. Install the new ballcock nut and gasket (Figure 2). Tighten the nut with your fingers. Then holding the ballcock, tighten the nut snugly without overtightening. Overtightening the nut can crack the tank.

5. Apply Teflon tape (on plastic parts) or spread pipe joint compound (on metal parts) around the compression rings and/or female threads of the water-supply line and tighten (but do not overtighten) the nuts.

6. Turn on the water and check for leaks around each connection. If there is a drip from any connection, tighten that connection a little at a time until the drip stops.

Stopping a Leak From Tank Mounting Bolts

To stop a leak from around a bolt that holds the tank to the bowl (there are two of these bolts), follow these steps:

1. From beneath the tank, snug up the nut a bit to see if you can get the drip to stop, but do not ram it against the bowl (Figure 3). You can crack the bowl or tank.

2. If the drip persists, with the water shutoff valve closed, flush the toilet, and sop up water that remains in the bottom of the tank.

3. Have an assistant hold the nut steady with a wrench from under the tank as you unscrew the hold-down bolt inside the tank (Figure 4). Remove the bolt, nut and washer. Buy replacements that are identical.

4. Install the new fasteners (Figure 5), but be sure you don't tighten the fasteners excessively. You can crack the tank or bowl.

Preventing Condensation

Condensation on the sides of a tank occurs when air in the room is warm and when the humidity is high. The warm air against the cool sides of the tank condenses.

Although technically not a leak, don't take the moisture that drips off the tank onto the floor lightly. If it isn't wiped up, it can seep beneath the floor covering and cause subflooring to rot.

Constantly having to clean up this water is a nuisance. Therefore, take the following steps to eliminate condensation:

1. With the water shutoff valve closed, flush the toilet, remove the lid and sop up water remaining in the bottom of the tank.

2. Using rags, thoroughly dry the sides and bottom of the tank.

3. Turn on the air conditioner or open the window and allow the toilet to remain dormant with the tank lid off for 24 hours.

4. Buy a toilet tank insulation kit from a home center store. Liners in the kit are foam rubber or Styrofoam. Cut the liners to size and apply the adhesive, which is included in the kit, as directed. Install the liners (Figure 6).

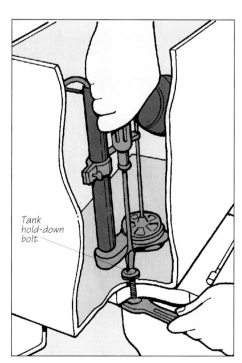

Figure 4. *To replace a tank hold-down bolt and nut that allow water to drip, hold the nut and undo the bolt.*

Tank hold-down bolt

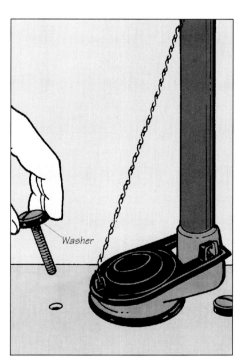

Figure 5. *The washer under the head of the hold-down bolt is the part that permits water to drip. In time, it may deteriorate, causing the trouble.*

Washer

Insulation liner

Figure 6. *The easiest way to stop tank condensation is with a liner kit.*

REPAIRING A MAJOR LEAK

Tools & Materials:
- ❏ adjustable wrench
- ❏ screwdriver
- ❏ adjustable pliers
- ❏ penetrating oil or anti-corrosion compound
- ❏ overflow tube or washers
- ❏ spud wrench
- ❏ hacksaw
- ❏ putty knife
- ❏ bowl mounting bolts and nuts
- ❏ alcohol or mineral spirits
- ❏ bowl seal
- ❏ plumber's putty
- ❏ Teflon paste

Remember: *Turn off the water shutoff valve or the main valve (see Figure 1, page 8) before beginning work.*

The information in this section covers floor-mounted toilets and can be used to repair a leak around the base of the bowl, to replace a worn flush valve because you can't stop a leak (page 66), or to install a new toilet because the tank or bowl of the present unit is cracked or you simply wish a different look.

Prepare to Demount

1. With the water shutoff valve closed, flush the toilet, sop up water remaining in the bottom of the tank, and disconnect the water-supply line.

2. If this is a two-piece toilet, unscrew the nuts from the bolts that hold the bowl and tank together (page 66). Use a penetrating oil or anti-corrosion compound to free the nuts if they are stuck tight.

3. Lift the tank off the bowl and lay it aside. Be careful not to crack the tank, if it will be used again.

Replacing Flush Valve Seat

If you are replacing a flush valve seat, because the leak can't be stopped by using the procedure described on page 66, here's what to do:

1. Turn the tank upside down. Take off the large washer on the threads of the opening. Then, use a spud wrench to loosen and remove the spud nut holding the overflow and tube to the tank (Figure 1). The design of most toilets is such that the flush valve seat is part of this tube.

2. Set the tank right side up and remove the overflow and flush valve seat assembly tube. If the tube is damaged or badly corroded, replace it. If just the washer is shot, slide it off the threads of the tube. Get a new overflow tube or new washer from a plumbing supply or home center store.

3. Place a new washer on the threads of the overflow tube and flush valve seat

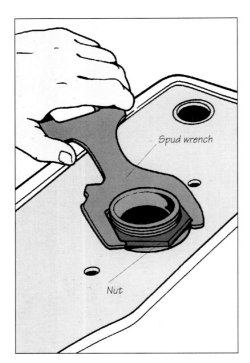

Figure 1. *Use a spud wrench to remove the nut that holds the overflow tube to the tank.*

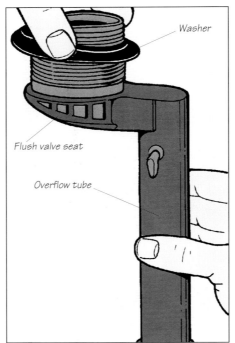

Figure 2. *Replace the entire overflow tube, if necessary, or just the washer.*

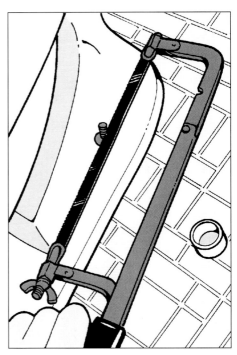

Figure 3. *If nuts holding the bowl to the floor won't come loose, cut off hardware.*

assembly (Figure 2) and insert the threaded end of the tube into the opening of the tank. Secure that end with the spud nut.

4. Install a new washer and place the tank back on the bowl if this is the only repair you are making.

Demounting the Bowl

If there is a leak between the bowl and floor, or if you're replacing the toilet, do the following:

1. Remove the caps over the bowl mounting bolts. If necessary, pry them off.

2. Loosen and remove the nuts holding the bowl to the mounting bolts and, thus, to the floor. If nuts and bolts are corroded in place, use penetrating oil or anti-corrosion compound. If this doesn't work, cut hardware off with a hacksaw (Figure 3).

3. Rock the bowl back and forth to break it free from the old seal. Then, lift the bowl off the floor and place it aside.

4. Stuff a rag into the closet drain opening to prevent sewer gases from permeating into the bathroom.

5. Use a putty knife to remove the old seal from the flange of the closet drain and to remove old putty that may be stuck to the floor. If bolts are corroded or had to be cut, slide them off the flange.

6. If the bowl is going to be reinstalled, use the putty knife to scrape residue left by the old seal and putty off the bottom of the bowl (Figure 4). Then, saturate a cloth with alcohol or mineral spirits and wash the bottom of the bowl.

Note: The floor and bowl must be clean to accept a new seal.

Installing Seal and Mounting Toilet

After buying a new seal, new mounting bolts and nuts if the old ones aren't reusable, and a new toilet if you're replacing the old one, here's what to do:

1. Slide new mounting bolts into position on the closet flange. Notice that the flange has a wide opening on each end of the slots to let you insert the wide ends of the bolts.

2. Center the new seal over the opening in the flange and press the seal into place (Figure 5).

3. Lift the bowl, right side up, position it over the closet flange, and bring it down to the floor so the mounting bolts protrude through the bolt holes in the bowl flange (Figure 6). Press the bowl down onto the seal.

4. Attach cap support washers and nuts. Tighten nuts by hand. Then, use a wrench to secure the nuts, but do not overtighten them. You may crack the bowl. Install caps.

5. If this is a two-piece toilet, install the tank and connect the water-supply line. Use plumber's putty or Teflon paste on threads to prevent a leak. Teflon paste must be used on plastic parts. Turn on the water and check for leaks.

6. Apply a bead of plumber's putty or silicone caulking compound around the perimeter of the bowl flange.

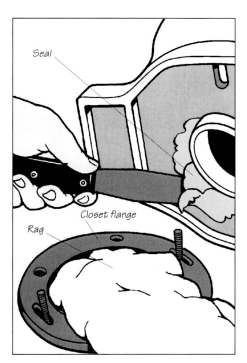

Figure 4. If the bowl is going to be reused, make sure that the bottom of it and the floor are clean.

Figure 5. Center the new seal over the drain hole in the bowl. If the seal has a flange, as shown here, it should be positioned so that it will fall into the closet drain when you install the toilet.

Figure 6. Place the toilet onto the closet flange and secure hardware.

REPLACING A WALL-MOUNT TOILET

Tools & Materials:
- ❏ sponge
- ❏ adjustable wrench
- ❏ putty knife
- ❏ adjustable pliers
- ❏ support unit
- ❏ closet drain
- ❏ seal
- ❏ pipe joint compound

Remember: *Turn off the water shutoff valve or the main valve (see Figure 1, page 8) before beginning work.*

If a wall-mounted toilet has to be replaced, the following steps will help guide you in doing this job yourself.

Preparatory Steps

1. With the water shutoff valve closed, flush the toilet and remove the tank lid. Use a sponge to sop up and get rid of any water that remains in the tank.

2. Loosen the nut holding the water-supply line. Remove the water-supply line.

3. Prop the toilet to keep it from falling to the floor when you detach wall-mounting bolts.

➡**PLUMBER'S TIP:**
Make a support from pieces of 4 x 4 or 2 x 4 lumber. Or, if you have an old wooden stool lying around that you have no further use for, measure the distance between the floor and bottom of the toilet bowl and cut the legs of the stool so the bowl rests on top of the stool when you slide the stool under the bowl.

4. With the toilet supported, use a putty knife to pry off the caps covering the bolts that mount the toilet to the wall. There are four bolts to locate (Figure 1). Remove the nuts and washers from mounting bolts. Then, with assistance from another person, move the toilet away from the wall.

Installing the New Toilet

1. Scrape the old seal from the flange of the closet drain. You should have purchased a seal when you purchased the new toilet (Figure 2). Clean the flange and install the seal, pressing it into place.

2. Again with assistance, raise the new toilet to the wall and place it on mounting bolts.

3. Place washers on bolts and screw on the nuts fingertight. Then, tighten the nuts with a wrench.

4. Install the water-supply line, tank lid, and new toilet seat. Turn on the water and check for leaks.

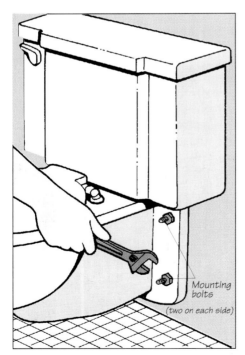

Figure 1. *Hardware must hold a wall-mounted toilet firmly to prevent pressure that's placed on it from allowing separation between the toilet and closet drain.*

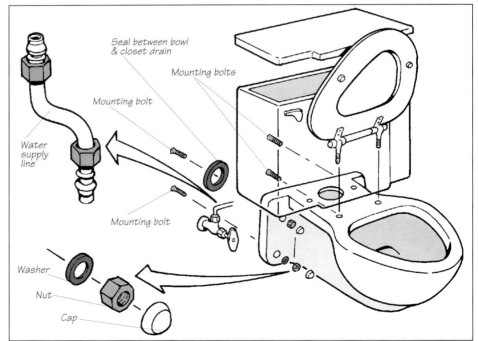

Figure 2. *The fittings that have to be taken off to remove a wall-mounted toilet, naturally, have to be reinstalled when installing a new wall-mounted toilet.*

ANATOMY OF A BATHTUB AND SHOWER

Bathtubs come in several materials, sizes and styles. They come with showers (Figure 1), which are also available separate from bathtubs in their own stalls. But that's not all there is to bathtub/shower combinations and shower stalls. They are precisely engineered units.

Makeup of a Bathtub

The waste outlet should be 1½ inches in diameter. The stopper can be a lever-operated pop-up type that when closed seals the waste outlet, a lever-operated metal plunger that when closed seals the waste pipe, or a rubber or metal plug that is inserted into the waste outlet by hand.

Bathtubs have overflows just as most lavatories have overflows. The purpose is to give excess water in the tub an outlet to the waste pipe. The overflow is a hole at least 1½ inches in diameter that is usually on the faucet side of the tub. It's covered by a plate. If the tub is equipped with a lever-controlled pop-up or plunger stopper, the lever controlling the stopper projects from this plate (Figure 2).

To adjust a pop-up stopper, turn the "turnbuckle-type" fitting with pliers and reseat in overflow and drain pipe. Adjust rod until stopper fits perfectly. The joints between the tub and the adjoining wall and floor are worthy of mention to remind you of a necessary maintenance task. The National Standard Plumbing Code says, "Openings or gaps between the fixture and the wall or floor are considered unsanitary as this open space may tend to collect dirt or harbor vermin. Cement or some other form of sealant may be used to seal these openings."

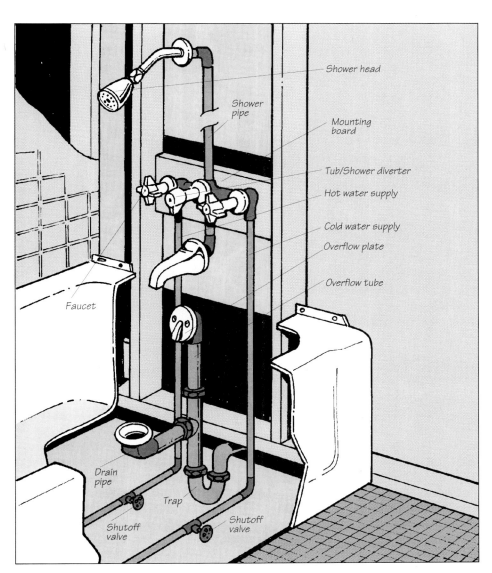

Shower head

Shower pipe

Mounting board

Tub/Shower diverter

Hot water supply

Cold water supply

Overflow plate

Overflow tube

Faucet

Drain pipe

Trap

Shutoff valve

Shutoff valve

Figure 1. *A typical bathtub arrangement may have water shutoff valves on pipes in the basement that lead to faucets. If there aren't any, water can be turned off by means of the house's main water valve (page 8).*

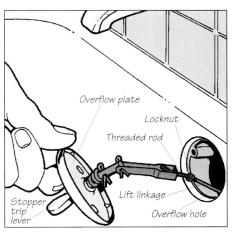

Overflow plate

Locknut

Threaded rod

Stopper trip lever

Lift linkage

Overflow hole

Figure 2. *To adjust a pop-up stopper, turn the "turnbuckle-type" fitting with pliers and reseat in overflow hole and drain pipe. Adjust rod until stopper fits perfectly.*

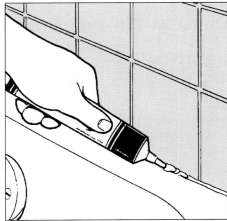

Figure 3. *If the joint between a bathtub and wall or bathtub and floor has to be renewed, prepare the surface and use a long-lasting, quality sealing compound.*

Thus, if old sealant between the wall and bathtub or floor and bathtub ever falls apart on you, it should be renewed by removing the crumbled material and applying new sealant (Figure 3). Silicone sealants available in hardware and home center stores are designed for this purpose and will maintain their effectiveness for an indefinite period.

Makeup of a Shower Stall

Where a shower is by itself in a stall, the National Standard Plumbing Code requires that the floor of the compartment be sloped 1/4 inch per foot toward the waste outlet. Furthermore, the waste outlet should be 2 inches in diameter and equipped with a strainer to stop hair and keep it from getting into the waste pipe and trap.

You should be able to remove the strainer for cleaning. Therefore, it can either be fastened to the floor with screws or be snapped into the outlet opening so it can be turned or pried free from the drain hole.

There's another detail about shower stall construction to note. The area beneath the floor—which is usually ceramic tile or fiberglass—should be made of a watertight, durable material. This sub-area is called the pan.

The pan should cover the entire base under the floor and extend up on all sides of the stall to a point that is above the stall threshold. Furthermore, the pan should be secured to the waste outlet in such a way as to make a watertight joint between the two.

The most durable pans are concrete and lead. If damage occurs and water leaks through a pan or around the joint formed by the pan and waste outlet, the floor has to be ripped up to repair or replace the pan.

Bathtub and Shower Hardware

Although they may look different, the faucets that serve bathtub/ shower combinations and shower stalls are in most instances internally the same as those used in sinks and lavatories. Bathtub/shower and shower-stall faucets that have two handles—one for hot water and one for cold water—are compression or cartridge faucets. If there's one handle, the faucet is of a disc, cartridge, or ball design (Figure 4).

Bathtub/shower combinations have a piece of hardware to keep water from going to the tub's spout and divert it to the shower head. This is called a diverter. It may be a handle between hot and cold water handles, making three handles in all. When the diverter handle is turned clockwise, water flows from the spout. When it's turned counterclockwise, water flows out the shower head. The handle type diverter is equipped with the same kind of mechanism as hot and cold water faucets; that is, it's either a compression or cartridge style. You

repair it the same as if you were repairing a two-handle compression or cartridge faucet (page 80-81).

The other type of diverter used by a bathtub/shower combination is a knob and stem assembly projecting from the top of the spout (Figure 5). When you pull up on the assembly, water is diverted from the spout to the shower head. This is called a lift-gate diverter. The pressure of the water flowing against the valve keeps the valve raised in place. When the water is turned off, the pressure recedes and the valve drops down. If a lift-gate diverter fails, the spout has to be replaced (page 85-86).

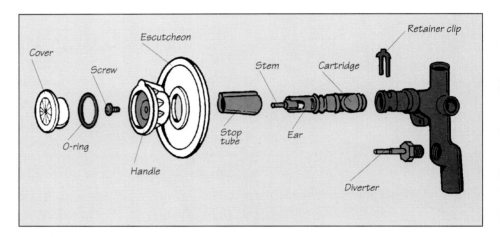

Figure 4. *Bathtub and shower stall faucets are often of the one-handle, pull-push design. Rotating the handle to the left or right increases the flow of hot or cold water, respectively. This faucet is a one-handle cartridge design.*

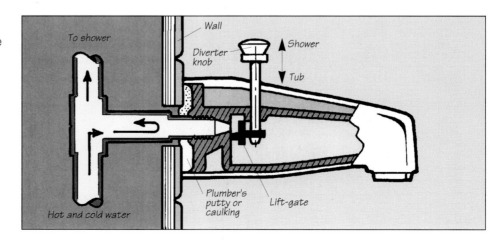

Figure 5. *When the knob of an in-the-spout diverter is pulled up, the lift-gate blocks the flow of water through the spout and diverts it to the shower head.*

BATHTUB & SHOWER TROUBLESHOOTING GUIDE

The following chart summarizes causes of and solutions for problems that occur with bathtubs and showers.

Problem	Cause	Solution
• Water drips from bathtub spout or shower head in a stall shower	• Faucet open • Worn or damaged faucet	• Close • Repair or replace (page 80)
• Water drips from shower head in a bathtub	• Damaged diverter	• Repair or replace (page 85)
• Spray from shower head is uneven; shower head doesn't stay in position	• Clogged shower head; worn shower head O-ring	• Clean shower head; replace O-ring (page 87)
• Water leaks out of bathtub	• Ineffective stopper	• Repair or replace (page 88)
• Sluggish flow of water from bathtub or stall shower into waste pipe	• Clogged stopper or waste pipe	• Clean (page 89)
• Leaking pipe; leaking shower-stall pan		• Repair (page 79)

HANDLING HIDDEN LEAKS

Protective shield

Figure 1. *If it's been determined there is a pipe leak in the wall, try to reach the pipe from the other side to avoid having to rip tile off the bathroom wall. After shutting off the water and draining the system, make repairs using one of the procedures outlined in Chapter 3 on repairing pipes.*

The most serious problem you can have with a bathtub is a leaking water pipe in the wall. The most serious problems you face with a shower stall are a leaking water pipe in the wall and a crack in the pan beneath the floor. These are not common failures, but if one occurs, a major renovation is necessary.

If a shower pan cracks and water drips to the floor below, the floor of the shower stall has to be torn up to repair or replace the pan. Then, a new floor has to be installed.

An in-the-wall pipe leak is repaired as a leak from the pipe of a sink or lavatory (see "All About Sinks," page 36-46). The most difficult part of the job, however, is getting to the pipe. If there is a closet or another room backing the bathroom wall (Figure 1), try to reach the pipe from that side so you don't have to rip tile off the bathroom wall to get at the pipe.

➡PLUMBER'S TIP:
If you aren't sure whether there's a leak from an in-the-wall water pipe and your house has a water meter, read the meter. Don't run water anywhere in the house for six hours. Then, read the meter again. If the second reading is higher than the first, there's a leak.

REPAIRING TWO-HANDLE FAUCETS & AN ON-THE-WALL DIVERTER

Tools & Materials:
❏ screwdriver or putty knife
❏ adhesive or electrical tape
❏ adjustable pliers
❏ adjustable wrench or
   ratchet wrench and socket
❏ faucet stem washer
❏ screw or
   faucet stem diaphragm cartridge
❏ wire brush
❏ heat-resistant lubricant
❏ valve-seat dressing tool
❏ ear syringe
❏ can of compressed air
   (from a photography supply store)

Remember: *Turn off the water shutoff valve or the main valve (see Figure 1, page 8) before beginning work.*

Two-handle faucets that control the flow of hot and cold water from bathtubs and shower heads are of similar design to two-handle faucets that serve sinks and lavatories. They can be compression-style faucets using washers or diaphragms on the ends of stems, or cartridge-style faucets having two interacting discs.

The major difference between sink/lavatory and bathtub/shower stall faucets is that the components of two-handle bathtub/shower stall faucets are larger than those of sink/lavatory faucets.

When there's a leak from the spout or shower head of a bathtub/shower stall equipped with two-handle faucets, the faulty component is a stem washer or stem diaphragm of a compression-style faucet or the discs of a cartridge-style faucet. You may not know which one you're dealing with until you've disassembled the faucet (Figures 1 and 2).

If there's a handle on the wall between the hot and cold water handles, it controls the diverter that switches the flow of water from the spout to the shower head and vice versa. When this diverter fails, water will come out of the spout and shower head at the same time or there will be a trickle of water from the shower head when the full flow should be from the spout.

The mechanism of the diverter is of the same style as the mechanism of the hot and cold water faucets, that is, compression or cartridge. Repair is done the same way as repairing the hot or cold water faucet—by replacing the stem washer or diaphragm, or servicing the cartridge.

Disassembly and Repair

1. With the water turned off, open the faucet to let water drain.

2. If there's a cap in the center of the handle, pry it off by inserting the tip of a screwdriver or putty knife into the ridge between the cap and handle.

3. Remove the screw; then, the handle. If the handle sticks, tap it lightly with the handle of the screwdriver and wiggle it back and forth until it comes off.

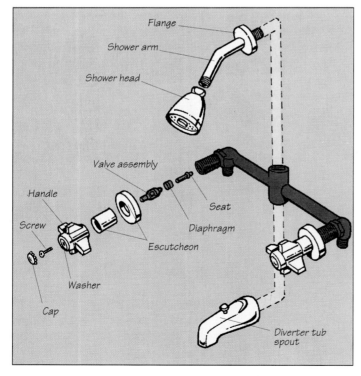

Figure 1. *When you disassemble a two-handle faucet on a bathtub or shower stall, it may be a compression faucet with a replaceable washer or diaphragm. Some, like the one shown here, also have replaceable seats.*

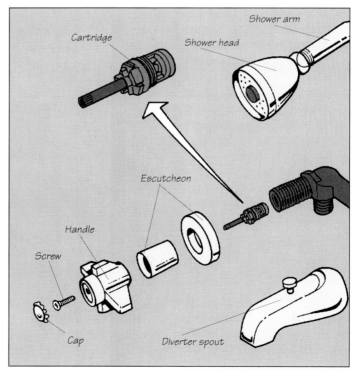

Figure 2. *A faucet of a two-handle design may be of a cartridge design. Cleaning usually doesn't help and the cartridge must be replaced.*

4. There's probably a decorative plate, called an escutcheon, over the hole in the wall in which the stem or cartridge sits. If you can't remove this plate by hand, wrap adhesive or electrical tape around the jaws of adjustable pliers, grasp the plate with the pliers, and turn it until it comes off.

5. There may or may not be a part called a spacer under the escutcheon. If there is, take it off.

6. You are now ready to remove the stem or cartridge (Figure 3). Most likely, there will be a six-sided brass nut that needs to be removed. If you can grab it with an adjustable wrench or adjustable pliers, turn it counterclockwise and remove it. If not, use a ratchet wrench and socket to remove it (Figures 4 and 5). Then, unscrew or pull the stem or cartridge from place.

7. If this is a compression faucet, undo the brass screw holding the washer to the stem (Figure 6) and remove the washer. Take the stem and seat to a plumbing supply or home center store, and buy a new washer of the same size and a new brass screw.

If a compression faucet doesn't have a stem washer, it has a cap called a diaphragm on the bottom of the stem. Pull it off and buy a new one that is identical.

If the faucet is a cartridge design, open the serrated spokes of the disks and use compressed air to blow dirt from between the spokes. Reassemble the faucet to determine if this action resolves the problem. If it doesn't, replace the cartridge.

8. If this is a compression faucet, service the washer seat before reassembling the faucet. Hold a valve-seat dressing tool against the seat. Using moderate pressure, turn the tool through two revolutions. Then, fill an ear syringe with water and flush out deposits. This action will eliminate burrs or other defects on the seat that could damage the new washer.

9. Use a wire brush to clean deposits from metal parts.

10. Reassemble the faucet.

Note: For specific details concerning the repair of compression and cartridge style two-handle faucets, refer to page 26.

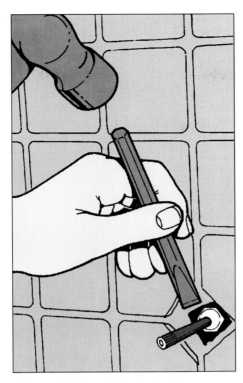

Figure 3. *After undoing the handle, spacer and escutcheon, the faucet bonnet nut is revealed. If the nut is deep in the wall and is blocked by mortar, put on eye protection, and chip away the mortar.*

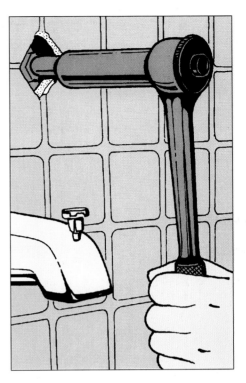

Figure 4. *Use a socket and ratchet to remove the bonnet nut and stem.*

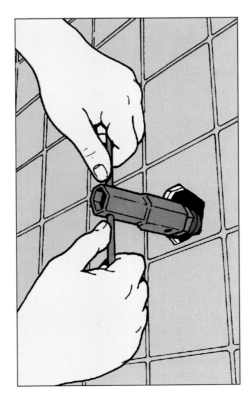

Figure 5. *A tool similar to this one is available from a plumbing or home center store for removing the stem or cartridge.*

Figure 6. *If the faucet has a washer or diaphragm, replace it as you would on a sink or lavatory faucet (see page 16).*

REPAIRING ONE-HANDLE FAUCETS

Tools & Materials:
- ❏ screwdriver
- ❏ adjustable wrench
- ❏ adjustable pliers
- ❏ replacement parts
  (depends on faucet design)

Remember: *Turn off the water shutoff valve or the main valve (see Figure 1, page 8) before beginning work.*

A one-handle faucet controls the flow of both hot and cold water to a bathtub spout or shower stall head. As with a one-handle faucet of sinks and lavatories, a one-handle faucet of a bathtub or shower stall is a cartridge, disc, or ball design.

Disassembly

1. Remove a cap over the handle screw, if necessary, and remove the screw and handle (Figure 1).

2. The escutcheon might be held by a screw, too. If so, unscrew to remove the escutcheon.

3. You may see slotted nuts on each side of the faucet control. These are the hot water and cold water shutoff valves (Figure 2). Insert a screwdriver into the slot and turn clockwise to shutoff the flow

of water on each side.

If these shutoff valves are not present, turn off the water at shutoff valves on the pipes going to the faucet, at the main water valve near the water meter, or by switching off the submersible pump.

4. There may be a length of tube called a stop tube over the faucet stem. If there is, pull it off.

Removing a Cartridge-Style Water Control

1. Determine if there's a threaded retaining ring in place over a cartridge faucet. If so, grasp the ring and turn it counterclockwise to remove it (Figure 3).

2. Grab the end of the cartridge and pull it out of the wall (Figures 4 and 5).

3. If there is no retaining ring or the cartridge won't come free, examine the

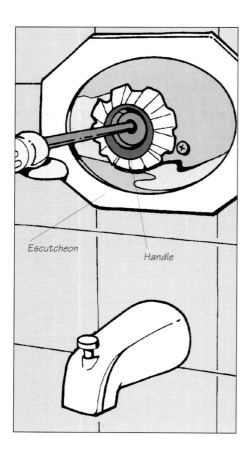

Escutcheon

Handle

Shutoff valve

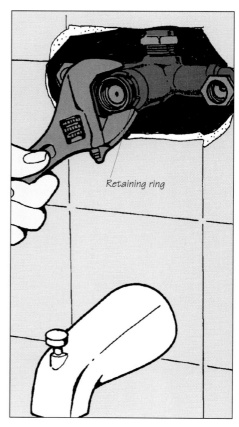

Retaining ring

Figure 1. *Remove the handle, then the escutcheon. Notice that a screw (arrow) holds this escutcheon in place.*

Figure 2. *Turn off the water by closing the built-in shutoff valves, if they are present. If not, turn off the home's main water valve or submersible pump.*

Figure 3. *If there's a threaded retaining ring in place over a cartridge faucet, grasp the ring with an adjustable wrench or adjustable pliers and turn it counterclockwise.*

housing that holds the cartridge. You will probably see a clip (Figure 6). Pry this clip from its seat. Then, pull the cartridge free.

4. Bring the cartridge to a plumbing supply or home center store to determine if there are replacement seals, but don't be surprised if personnel advise you to replace the cartridge. Replacing the part may be a lot easier than trying to replace the seals.

Handling Other Noncompression Designs

1. Once handle and escutcheon are removed, a disc-style one-handle bathtub or shower stall faucet is taken out of the wall by removing the screws holding the disc (Figure 7).

2. To repair the leaky faucet, replace the seals in the base of the disc. These seals are usually available in a kit.

3. As for a ball-type noncompression faucet (Figure 8), the same advice offered in the section on dealing with a ball-type faucet of a sink or lavatory (page 20) applies to bathtub and shower-stall faucets.

4. The ball-type noncompression faucet of a tub or shower stall is disassembled in the same way as a ball-type noncompression faucet of a sink or lavatory once the handle and escutcheon are removed. Replace all parts.

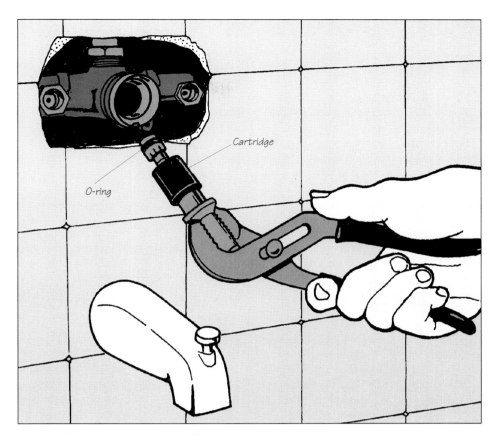

Figure 4. Grab the end of the cartridge and pull it out of the wall.

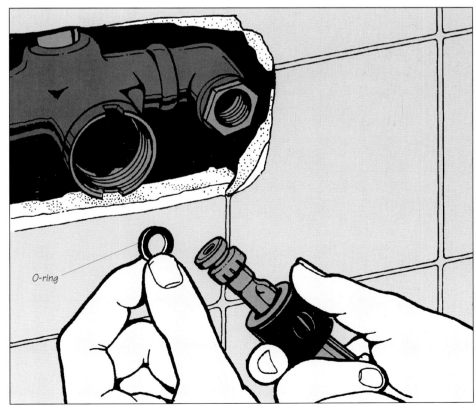

Figure 5. Remove the O-ring from the cartridge and replace with a new O-ring.

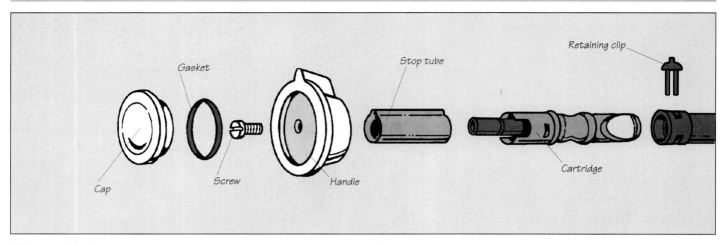

Figure 6. *After the handle and space tube are removed, the retaining clip of this cartridge design has to be pulled out to release the cartridge.*

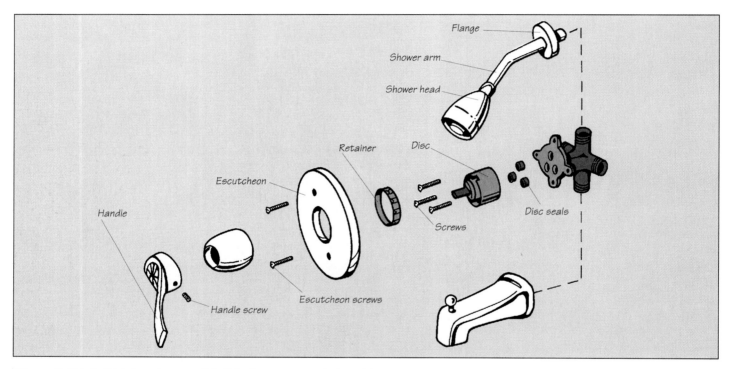

Figure 7. *This bathtub faucet uses a disk. If the faucet starts to leak and the spout drips, remove the screws to release the disc so you can replace the seals.*

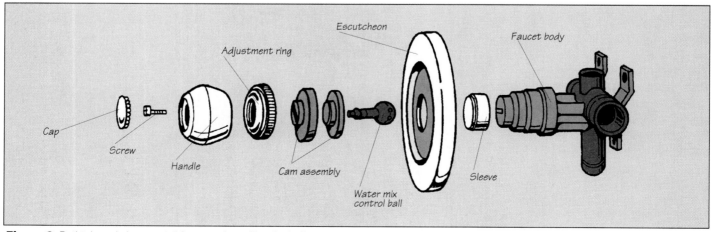

Figure 8. *Bathtub and shower-stall faucets also utilize the ball design. Replacing this type requires the same procedures that are described in the section on lavatories and sinks (see page 20).*

REPLACING A SPOUT
WITH A DIVERTER

Tools & Materials:
- ❏ Allen wrench
- ❏ screwdriver or hammer
- ❏ pipe joint compound
- ❏ spout with diverter
- ❏ plumber's putty or silicone caulk

Remember: *Turn off the water shutoff valve or the main valve (see Figure 1, page 8) before beginning work.*

Is the diverter characterized by a knob and stem on top of the bathtub spout as in Figure 1 or by a handle on the wall as shown in Figure 2?

If it is an in-the-spout diverter and that part fails, water will come out of the spout as well as the shower head when it's supposed to be coming out of the shower head alone, or the diverter won't stay in the raised position.

Repairing an in-the-spout diverter requires that you replace the spout.

Replacing a Spout

1. Check the underside of the bathtub spout. If a notch is present, the spout is held in place by an Allen screw. Insert different size Allen wrenches until you find the one that fits the screw (Figure 3). Remove the screw and pull the spout free from the pipe.

If the spot is stuck turn the spout off by using a screwdriver or the handle of a hammer (see step 2). Slide the new spout onto the pipe.

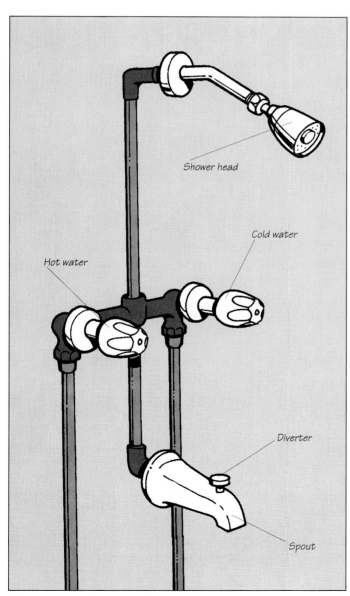

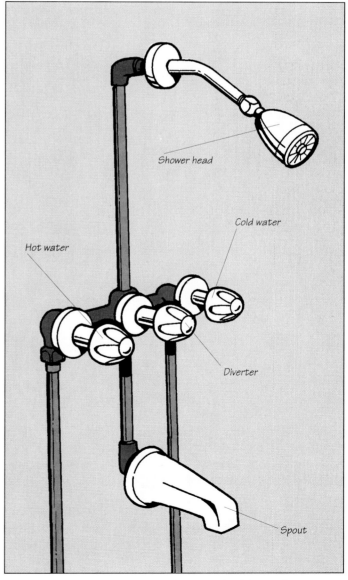

Figures 1 and 2. *Bathtub/shower diverters are part of the spout (Figure 1) or are located on the wall between the hot and cold water faucets (Figure 2). The information in this section concerns in-the-spout diverters. For guidance on how to repair a wall diverter, see page 80.*

2. If the underside of the spout is a solid case, with no notch, then the spout is screwed directly onto the water pipe. Insert the end of a large screwdriver or the handle of a hammer into the spout hole and turn counterclockwise (Figure 4). The spout will come free from the threads of the pipe.

Spread pipe joint compound on the threads of the pipe and screw the new spout onto the pipe (Figure 5).

If the spout hole lies off-center when the spout becomes too tight to turn by hand, insert the screwdriver or hammer handle and turn it slowly until the hole is centered over the tub.

➡PLUMBER'S TIP:

Take the old spout to a plumbing supply or home center store to make sure the replacement you get is of the same size. If the spout is threaded, for instance, the set-back distance of the threads inside the new spout have to match the length of the water pipe protruding from the wall.

Using plumber's putty or silicone caulk, seal the pipe at the point that it enters the wall. Apply the seal to the spout at the top, the back end and along the sides. This step is done to prevent any water that may back up from flowing out the rear of the spout around the water pipe and into the wall.

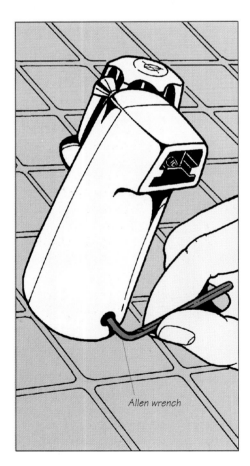

Figure 3. *Spouts are secured to the wall with an Allen screw, as here, or are screwed onto the water pipe.*

Figure 4. *If the spout is screwed to the water pipe, loosen it using a large screwdriver or handle of a hammer, then unscrew it.*

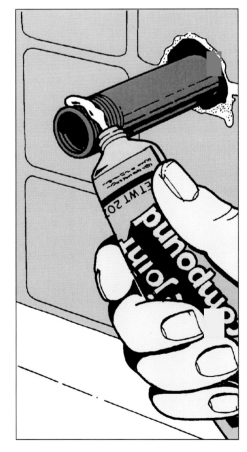

Figure 5. *Before installing a new spout, spread pipe joint compound around the threads.*

CLEANING A SHOWER HEAD

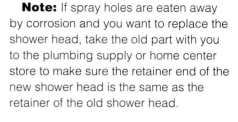

Tools & Materials:
- ❏ adhesive tape or electrical tape
- ❏ adjustable wrench or adjustable pliers
- ❏ awl or paper clip
- ❏ vinegar
- ❏ O-ring

Remember: *Turn off the water shutoff valve or the main valve (see Figure 1, page 8) before beginning work.*

If your shower head (Figures 1 and 2) gives forth an uneven spray, you can solve the problem easily.

Remove the Shower Head

Wrap adhesive tape or electrical tape around the shower head's retainer or around the jaws of the adjustable wrench or adjustable pliers you are using to remove the shower head.

Engage the retainer with the tool and turn counterclockwise (Figure 3) to free the shower head from the shower arm.

Note: If spray holes are eaten away by corrosion and you want to replace the shower head, take the old part with you to the plumbing supply or home center store to make sure the retainer end of the new shower head is the same as the retainer of the old shower head.

Clean the Shower Head

An uneven spray is caused by sediment settling in and clogging the spray holes. Use an awl or the end of a straightened paper clip to probe deposits from the holes (Figure 4).

There is probably a flow restrictor over the inlet side of the shower head. Remove any retaining device holding the flow restrictor and clean the holes from the backside (Figure 5). Flush with water.

If holes are badly plugged, fill a receptacle (large enough to hold shower head) with vinegar. Remove the O-ring on the inlet end of the shower head. Place the shower head in the vinegar. Vinegar may dissolve the deposits. Allow it to soak for several hours. Remove the shower head from the vinegar, flush it with water.

Reinstall the Shower Head

Reinsert the O-ring and screw the shower head back onto the shower arm. When you can no longer tighten the shower head by hand, turn the retainer about 1/2 turn with the wrench or adjustable pliers. Turn on the water and check for a leak. If water trickles from around the retainer, tighten it until the trickle ceases.

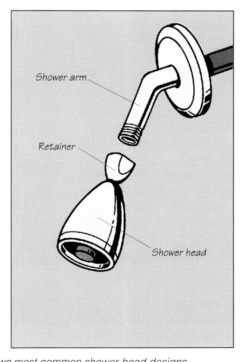

Figures 1 and 2. Shown are the parts of the two most common shower-head designs.

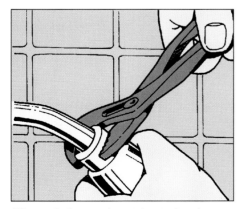

Figure 3. Loosen the retainer to free the shower head from the shower arm.

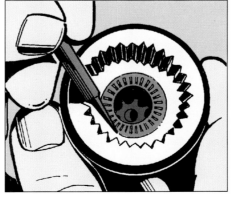

Figure 4. Clean sediment from the spray holes in shower head.

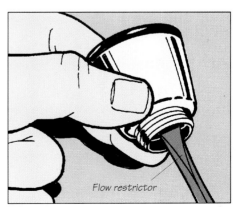

Figure 5. Remove flow restrictor to clean sediment in holes in rear of the shower head.

REPAIRING DRAIN STOPPERS
LEVER CONTROLLED

Tools & Materials:
❏ pop-up stopper O-ring
❏ screwdriver
❏ wire brush
❏ vinegar

When a lever-controlled bathtub drain stopper (called a tripwaste) works well, it's more convenient than a stopper you manually insert and remove each time you bathe. If a repair is necessary it is a lot easier to do than it seems.

Identifying the Problem
A tripwaste can malfunction in two ways:

1. The stopper won't seal the waste outlet. Water, therefore, will leak from the bathtub.

2. Drainage from the tub will be sluggish.

Identifying the Mechanism
There are two types of tripwastes: pop-up and plunger.

When the trip lever of a pop-up tripwaste (Figure 1) is moved up or down, a coil on the end of a linkage presses down against or releases itself from a rocker arm that is connected to the stopper. This allows the stopper to drop into or lift off the waste outlet.

A pop-up tripwaste is a two-component assembly. The trip lever and linkage/coil make up one component; the rocker arm and stopper make up the other.

A plunger tripwaste (Figure 2) is characterized by a strainer cover inserted into the waste outlet. This tripwaste is an all-in-one assembly made up of the trip lever, linkage, and a plunger on the end of the linkage.

The plunger resembles a weight. When you flip the trip lever to seal the waste outlet, the plunger drops into the waste pipe to close the pipe and keep water from flowing out of the tub.

Repairing Pop-Up Tripwaste
1. Pull the stopper/rocker arm assembly out of the waste outlet (Figure 3). If the problem you've been having is water leaking from the bathtub when the stopper is supposed to be sealing the waste outlet, slide the O-ring off the stopper and install a new O-ring.

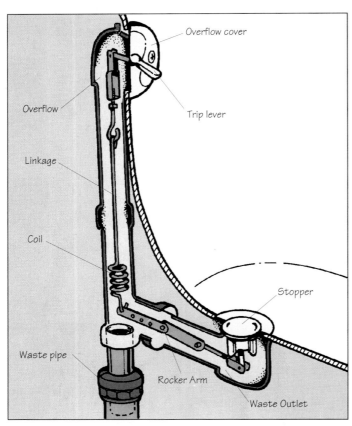

Figure 1. A pop-up tripwaste is a stopper in a bathtub that's raised and lowered by a trip lever on the cover over the overflow.

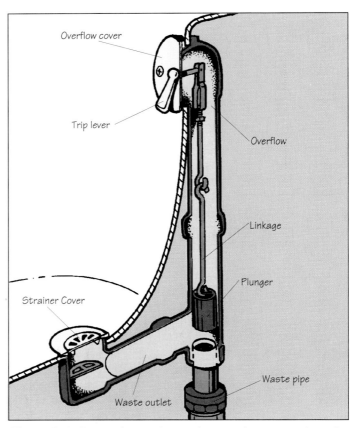

Figure 2. A plunger tripwaste is a strainer over the waste outlet and a lever that is moved up and down on the cover over the overflow.

Feed the assembly back into the waste outlet so the end of the rocker arm fits under the coil. You may have to wiggle it a bit to get it in place.

2. If the problem is sluggish draining, remove the stopper/ rocker arm assembly; then, undo the screws holding the cover over the overflow (Figure 4). Slowly pull the plate away from the bathtub. The trip lever and linkage/coil assembly will come with it (Figure 5).

3. Clean any hair and soap scum from all parts of the tripwaste mechanism (Figure 6). If parts are corroded, soak them in vinegar and scrub them with a wire brush.

➡ **PLUMBER'S TIP:**

If drainage from the tub isn't rapid enough because the stopper doesn't rise high enough off the waste outlet, now is the time to make an adjustment. Loosen the linkage locknut (Figure 9) and then turn the threaded end of the linkage so the linkage is lengthened about 3/16 inch. Tighten the locknut, reinsert the tripwaste, and check the result.

Repairing Plunger Tripwaste

If the problem is sluggish drainage, unscrew and clean the strainer before disassembling the tripwaste (Figure 7). Hair entwined in the slots is often the reason for this problem.

1. To remove the tripwaste mechanism, undo the screws holding the cover plate over the overflow and pull the cover plate away from the tub. The tripwaste assembly will come out of the overflow (Figure 8).

2. If the problem has been sluggish drainage and cleaning the strainer doesn't help, the tripwaste mechanism may be clogged with hair. Clean it.

If the problem has been that water leaks from the tub, lengthen the linkage so the plunger will drop further into the waste pipe. Loosen the locknut securing the linkage and screw the rod down about 3/16 inch (Figure 10). Check the result.

3. To reinstall a plunger tripwaste back into the overflow, you may have to maneuver the mechanism around a bit to get the plunger to fall into the waste pipe. Patience is required.

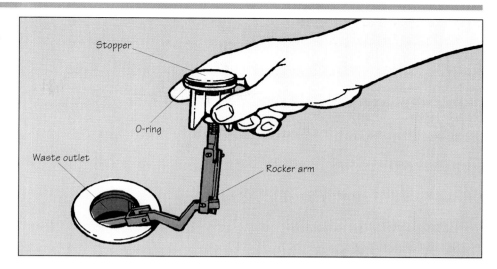

Figure 3. *To treat a pop-up tripwaste that is allowing water to leak from the tub, draw the stopper and rocker arm from the drain hole. Slide the O-ring off the lower end of the rocker arm and install a new O-ring.*

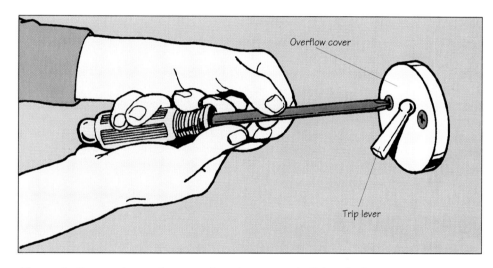

Figure 4. *Remove the overflow cover if you have to get the linkage/coil assembly out of the wall for servicing.*

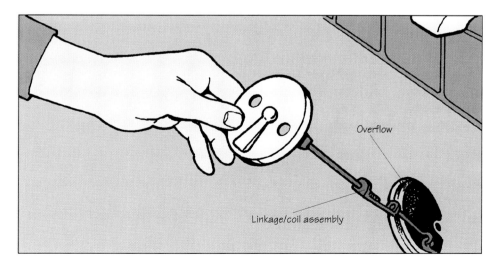

Figures 5. *Slowly pull the linkage/coil assembly out of the overflow .*

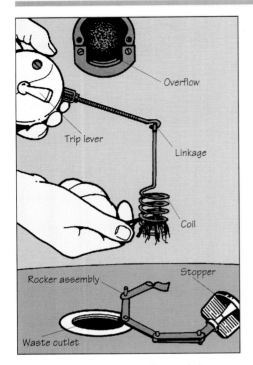

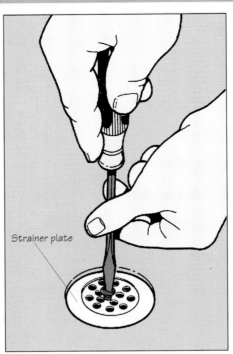

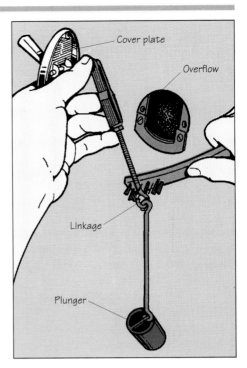

Figure 6. *Clean all parts. If a part is bent, replace the assembly.*

Figure 7. *If a plunger tripwaste is sluggish in draining, remove the strainer over the waste outlet, clean the strainer, and test results before removing the tripwaste.*

Figure 8. *Extract the plunger tripwaste through the overflow. Inspect it for bent parts. Then clean all parts.*

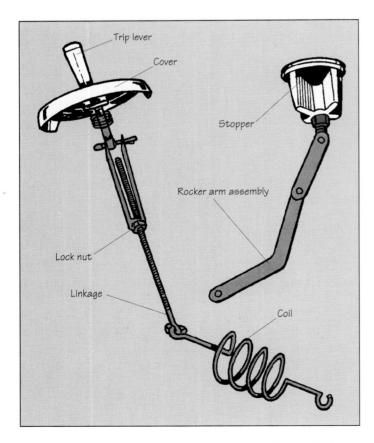

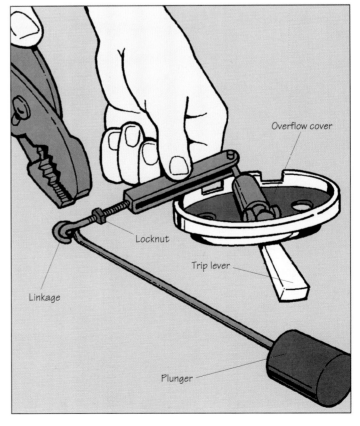

Figures 9 and 10. *A pop-up (Figure 9) or plunger (Figure 10) tripwaste is adjusted by loosening the locknut and lengthening the linkage.*

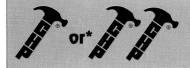

CLEARING CLOGGED DRAINS

Tools & Materials:
❑ screwdriver
❑ plumber's helper
❑ flashlight
❑ wire coat hanger
❑ paper towels
❑ awl
❑ auger

*1 for showers; 2 for bathtubs

Unclogging shower stalls and bathtubs are handled differently, which is why their difficulty rating is 1 and 2, respectively.

Clearing a Stall Shower
A clog in the drain of a shower stall is most likely hair mixed with soap scum. The part of the drain that receives the brunt is the strainer. Soap-coagulated hair twines itself around the slots, impeding the flow of water.

1. To regain forceful drainage, remove the strainer by undoing the screws or by twisting the strainer out of the waste outlet if there are no screws. Wearing rubber gloves to protect your hands from the gooey mess, use paper towels to clean the slots of the strainer. If necessary, use the tip of an awl or screwdriver to break entangled hair free.

2. Wash the strainer, but before returning it to the waste outlet, turn on the faucet and check the flow down the waste pipe to see if there's a problem other than a clogged strainer.

If water flows freely, return the strainer to the waste outlet. If water backs up, form a hook in one end of a straightened-out wire coat hanger. Shining a flashlight down the waste pipe to spot wads of hair in the pipe, use the hook to fish the blockage out of the pipe (Figure 1).

3. Hold the cup of a plumber's helper over the waste outlet, run the water until the cup is covered, and pump the tool

up and down vigorously a number of times (Figure 2). This will clear the trap. Finally, flood the drain with plenty of hot water.

Clearing a Bathtub
1. If servicing the tripwaste has no effect on drainage out of the bathtub (page 89), use a plumber's helper. Remove the cover over the overflow and stuff a cloth into the hole to seal it (Figure 3). Fill the tub so water will cover the cup of the plumber's helper. Now, plant the plumber's helper over the waste outlet and pump up and down as vigorously as you can. Test the result.

If the flow is now adequate, flood the drain with hot water. But if the stoppage persists, use an auger to clear it.

2. Take off the overflow cover and remove the pop-up or plunger tripwaste assembly (page 88). Then, insert the auger through the overflow to ream out the waste pipe and trap (Figure 4).

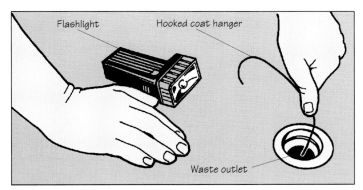

Figure 1. *After cleaning the strainer over the waste outlet of a shower stall, use a hooked coat hanger to fish scummy hair from the waste pipe.*

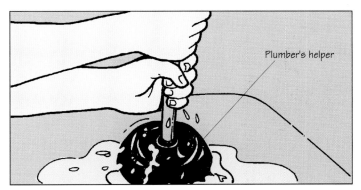

Figure 2. *Use a plumber's helper to clear a clogged trap of a shower stall. Finally, flood the drain with plenty of hot water.*

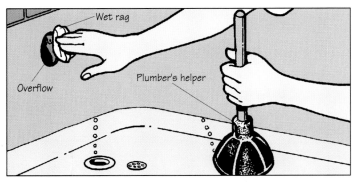

Figure 3. *Hair that is clogging a bathtub waste system can often be cleared away with a plumber's helper. Be sure to stuff a wet rag in the overflow to bring the full force of plunging against the clog.*

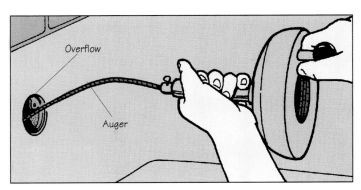

Figure 4. *If the clogging material resists the force of a plumber's helper, use an auger to ream out the waste pipe.*

Anatomy of a Water Heater

Water heaters are tanks equipped with energy devices that make water hot. Homes with gas or electric heating systems usually have water heaters with gas burners (Figure 1) or electric elements (Figure 2), respectively, to heat water in the tank. If a problem occurs, the tank can sometimes be repaired. These procedures are discussed below.

Many homes with oil-fired heating systems have a tankless hot water system, which is a coil that's part of the furnace boiler. Cold water flowing through this coil is heated by the boiler. If something happens to the coil, it or the boiler has to be replaced.

Making and Delivering Hot Water

When someone turns on a hot water faucet, water flows out the top of the tank through a hot water pipe. As water leaves the tank, the amount drawn off is replenished through a cold water pipe and an extension of that pipe called a dip tube. The dip tube extends down through the tank with its open end positioned 12 to 18 inches off the floor of the tank.

When a thermostat senses that the temperature of the water in the tank is not at the preset level, the thermostat causes the gas or electric heating unit to turn on. The heating unit stays on and heats the water until the thermostat senses that the temperature of the water has reached the desired level. It then turns the heating unit off.

Other Parts

A water heater has a temperature and pressure (T & P) relief valve and tube assembly to prevent excessive pressure from building up inside the tank and causing an explosion. If the temperature of the water inside the tank exceeds approximately 200°F, because a malfunctioning thermostat allows the heating source to remain on, the T & P relief valve opens to allow hot water or steam to pour out the relief tube. Pressure inside the tank is thereby reduced to a safe level.

A water heater also has a water drain to allow you to drain the tank. Furthermore, most water heaters are equipped with a magnesium anode (or sacrificial) rod. Its purpose is to attract elements in the water that would otherwise attack the tank's metal lining, causing it to corrode and leak. Once a tank leaks, it has to be replaced. The anode rod, therefore, extends the life of the tank.

Gas-fired water heaters have a flue to carry deadly carbon monoxide outside

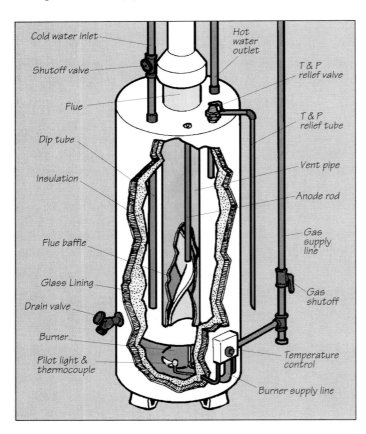

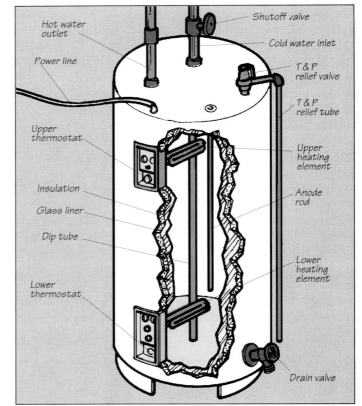

Figure 1. *A gas-fueled water heater has a burner at the bottom, much like that on a kitchen range. The flue in the center of the tank routes deadly carbon monoxide (a by-product of natural burning gas) outside the house.*

Figure 2. *An electric hot-water tank usually has two heating elements each with its own thermostat—one in the lower part of the tank and another in the upper part. The elements are wired directly to the home's fuse or circuit breaker panel. Smaller tanks (less than 40-gallon tank capacity) may have only one thermostat or heating element.*

the house. Carbon monoxide may be created by natural gas if it doesn't burn properly.

Heat Generation

Electric water heaters that hold 40 gallons or more usually have two elements that are wired directly to the home's fuse or circuit breaker panel. One element is in the lower part of the tank; the other is in the upper part of the tank. Each element is equipped with its own thermostat. Smaller electric water heaters have one element.

The parts involved in the production of heat in a water heater that uses natural gas include a control box that houses the burner control, temperature control dial, and pilot reset. The burner control lets you turn off gas when a repair is needed

or when the house isn't going to be occupied for a time.

There are three positions on the burner control: ON, OFF, and PILOT. When set to ON, gas can get to the burner and pilot. The pilot stays lit all the time. The burner comes on when the thermostat senses that water temperature is too low and opens a valve to allow gas to reach the burner.

When the burner control is set to OFF, gas can't get to the burner or pilot. The pilot is off.

When set to PILOT, gas can't get to the burner, but it can get to the pilot, which stays lit all the time.

The pilot reset, which is next to the burner control, is used to relight the pilot if you turn the burner control to OFF or the pilot is blown out by a gust of wind.

The discussion on page 96 explains how to use this part.

A thermocouple is a safety device that's part of the pilot. It automatically turns off gas flowing to the pilot if the flame goes out because of a gust of wind or a malfunction. Thus, gas won't escape into the house.

➡PLUMBER'S TIP:
If you experience a problem with the gas controls of your water heater other than having to relight a pilot every once in awhile (page 96), call the gas company serving your area. The gas company is responsible for seeing that gas-handling components perform safely and properly. This service is provided to gas company customers free of charge or at a nominal fee.

WATER HEATER TROUBLESHOOTING GUIDE

The following chart summarizes causes of and solutions for common problems that affect water heaters:

Problem	Cause	Solution
Not enough hot water	• Leaking hot water faucets • Long expanse of exposed pipe from water heater to hot water faucets • Sediment buildup in tank • Lower element is burned out (electric water heater) • Gas burner orifice blocked by dirt (gas water heater) • Tank is not large enough to meet needs of family	• Repair • Insulate pipes (page 94) • Drain and refill tank (page 94) • Replace element (page 98) • Call gas company for service • Install a larger tank (page 102 or 105)
No hot water or water is tepid	• Fuse blown or circuit breaker tripped (electric water heater) • Upper element is burned out (electric water heater) • Pilot is out (gas water heater) • Gas burner malfunction	• Replace fuse or reset circuit breaker (if trouble recurs, call an electrician) • Replace element (page 98) • Relight (page 96) (if condition recurs or you can't get pilot to light, call gas company for service) • Call gas company for service
Rumbling or hammering noise from inside tank	• Sediment buildup in tank	• Drain and refill tank (page 94)
Water leaks from T & P relief valve and tube assembly	• Tank thermostat set too high • Defective T & P relief valve	• Lower temperature setting of thermostat • Replace T & P relief valve (page 100)
Water leaks from bottom of tank	• Leaky tank	• Replace water heater (page 102 for gas water heater; page 105 for electric water heater)

MAKING MINOR ADJUSTMENTS & REPAIRS

Tools & Materials:
❑ pipe insulation
❑ pail
❑ garden hose
❑ matches
❑ screwdriver

Insulating Pipes and Heater

If there never seems to be enough hot water, insulating the water heater (Figure 1) and hot water pipes (Figure 2) may help. Hardware and home center stores sell several variations of insulation materials. Manufacturers claim insulation saves fuel and therefore reduces the cost of operation.

Draining the Tank

If there's not enough hot water, draining the tank completely to get rid of sediment may solve the problem. Also, there are several other reasons for partially or completely draining a water heater.

For example, draining a pail or two of water from the tank every month can help prevent noise that results when sediment builds up on the floor of the tank.

Furthermore, you may have to drain the tank completely to make a major repair or if the home is left unoccupied during cold weather. The combination of cold weather, no heat, and water leads to broken pipes and tanks from freezing water.

To drain the tank completely, follow these steps:

1. If it's an electric water heater, remove the fuse or turn off the circuit breaker that protects the circuit. If you're dealing with a gas water heater, turn the temperature (burner) control to OFF.

2. Close the shutoff valve on the cold water pipe (Figure 3).

3. Open all the hot water faucets in the house and leave them open.

4. Attach a garden hose to drain valve and extend the hose to a drain or sump, or outside the house (Figure 4). Hose spout must be lower than the drain valve.

5. Open the drain valve and allow water to drain entirely. This takes some time so be patient.

6. When the tank has been drained, try to tip it toward the drain valve, but don't exert pressure against the pipes. The purpose is to get as much water out of the tank without causing damage.

7. To fill the tank again, close the drain valve and open the valve on the cold water pipe. When the tank is full, water will flow from the open hot water faucets.

8. Turn off the faucets and restore electricity to an electric water heater. If you are dealing with a gas water heater, light the pilot according to directions on the instruction plate on the tank.

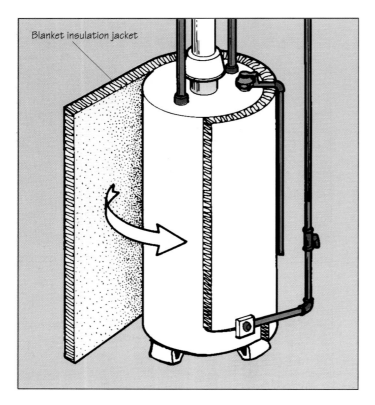

Figure 1. You can save energy by wrapping a water heater with a blanket of insulation made especially to fit.

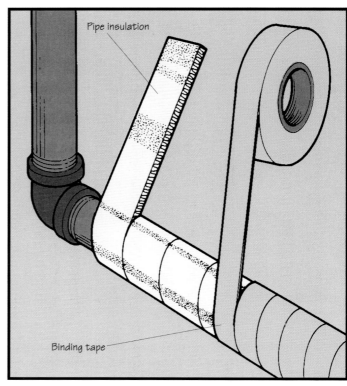

Figure 2. By wrapping hot water pipes with pipe insulation made for this purpose, you can keep water hot longer and save fuel.

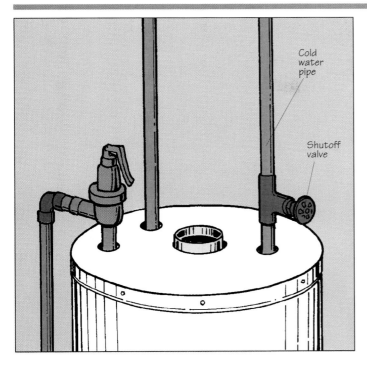

Figure 3. To drain a water heater, close the shutoff valve on the cold water pipe to keep water from flowing into the tank as water pours out of the tank.

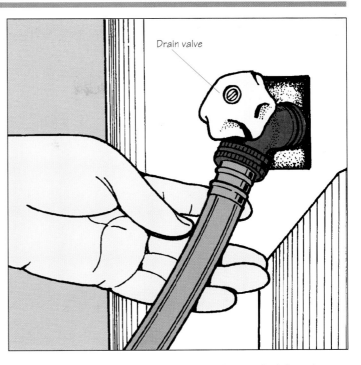

Figure 4. To drain a water heater, attach a hose to the bib and extend the hose to a drain that is below the level of the bib.

Figure 5. Remove the outer and inner covers over the burner box to get at the pilot.

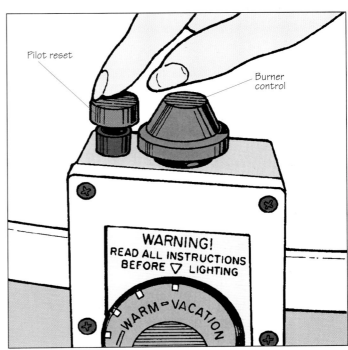

Figure 6. These are the controls you work with to relight a pilot. Turn the burner control to PILOT, then press the pilot reset as you hold a match to the pilot. Keep your finger on the pilot reset for one minute after the pilot is lit.

Relighting a Gas Pilot

If you turn the burner control of a gas water heater to OFF, the pilot will go out. A draft also can cause the pilot to flame-out. But if the pilot keeps going out after you relight it, the gas company should be informed.

Follow this procedure to relight a pilot:

1. Turn the burner control to PILOT.

2. Take off both the outside and inside covers over the burner and pilot. Both covers are usually removed by simply lifting them off (Figure 5).

CAUTION: If the burner was on just before the pilot light flamed out, the inner cover could be red hot.

3. Hold a lit match near the pilot and press the pilot reset (Figure 6). It's next to the burner control. The pilot should light. Extinguish the match, but keep your finger pressed down on the pilot reset for 60 seconds.

4. Then turn the burner control to ON and reinstall the covers.

Setting Temperature

The temperature at which to keep water is the lowest possible setting conducive with satisfactory results; usually 120°F.

Raising the temperature doesn't mean you're going to get a larger supply of hot water. It just means you'll get **hotter** hot water. If water creates steam as it comes out of the faucets, water is much too hot.

To set the temperature of water heated by gas to a desired level, hold a calibrated thermometer to record at least 160°F or more under a hot water faucet for two minutes. Then, note the reading.

If it's not to your liking, turn the temperature control dial (Figure 7) to the appropriate index mark — clockwise to raise the temperature or counterclockwise to lower the temperature.

The temperature control dial of a gas water heater is not usually marked numerically in degrees. Each index mark represents about a 10-degree increase or decrease.

Temperature controls of electric water heaters are usually marked numerically in degrees. These controls, however, are not exposed and therefore are more difficult to get at than a temperature control dial of a gas water heater.

If your water heater has two elements, each has its own temperature control. One or two covers screwed to the tank conceal them. Follow these steps:

1. Remove the fuse or turn off the circuit breaker protecting the electric circuit serving the water heater.

2. Remove the screws holding the cover(s) to the tank, and take off the cover(s).

3. If there's a panel of insulation under the cover(s), remove it. If insulation is fiberglass, wear gloves to protect your hands and spread apart the insulation to reveal the temperature controls (Figure 8).

4. Use a screwdriver to turn one temperature control, then the other, to the desired setting (Figure 9). Both should be set at the same temperature.

5. Replace the insulation and reinstall the cover(s).

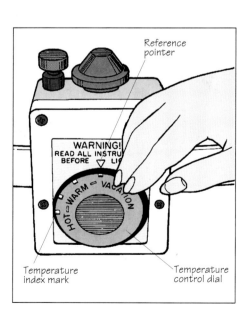

Figure 7. Set water to the desired temperature by turning the temperature control dial until the desired temperature index mark lines up with the reference pointer. Check water temperature with a thermometer.

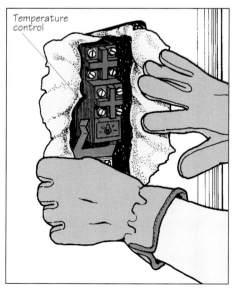

Figure 8. After turning off electricity, unscrew covers from the tank and fold back insulation to get at the temperature controls.

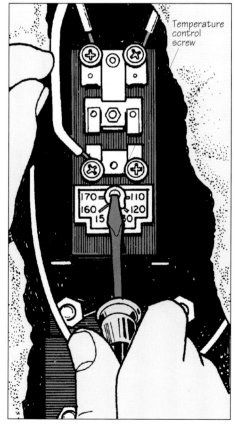

Figure 9. Before turning the temperature dial control screw to the desired number, be sure the power is OFF. The temperature control of an electric water heater is marked numerically in degrees.

MAKING MAJOR REPAIRS
THERMOSTATS & ELECTRIC ELEMENTS

Tools & Materials:
❑ pail
❑ screwdriver
❑ circuit tester
❑ masking tape or colored labels
❑ adjustable pliers
❑ pipe wrenches
❑ new thermostats and heating elements
❑ pipe joint compound

Remember: *Turn off the power and check with a circuit tester before beginning work.*

The most drastic major repair you'll ever have to make to a water heater is replacing the unit because it's leaking. That job is described on pages 102-106.

There are, however, two other repairs that may have to be made. They are replacing thermostats and heating elements of an electric water heater, described here, and replacing the temperature and pressure (T & P) relief valve of an electric or gas water heater, described on page 100-101.

Note: As mentioned in the guide to troubleshooting on page 93, if you encounter a problem with parts that supply gas to a gas water heater, call the utility company. A trained service technician will make the repair free of charge or for a nominal fee.

Troubleshooting Thermostats and Electric Elements

A problem of no hot water or insufficient hot water that's not resolved by doing one of the simple repairs described on page 94-96 is a sign that a thermostat or electric element of an electric water heater has failed.

Since they work as a team, it doesn't matter whether the guilty party is the element or thermostat. If one goes bad, replace them both.

If a water heater has two elements and

Figure 1. *It will save time if circuits are identified. Be sure you know which circuit breaker or fuse serves the electric water heater.*

Figure 2. *Measure the number of gallons drained from an electric water heater to ensure dropping the water level below the element that's being replaced.*

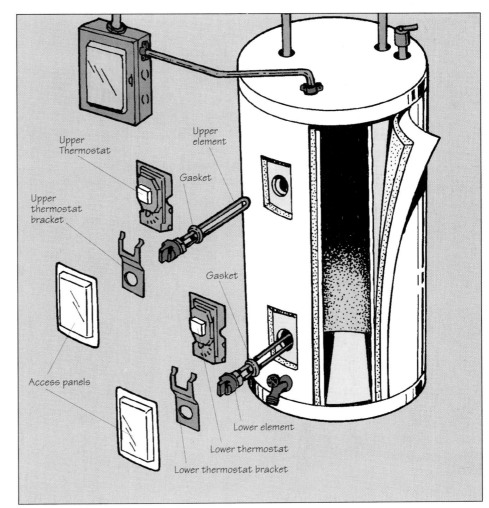

Figure 3. *The thermostats and elements of an electric water heater may have panels of insulation covering them (shown here) or fiberglass insulation as shown in Figure 4.*

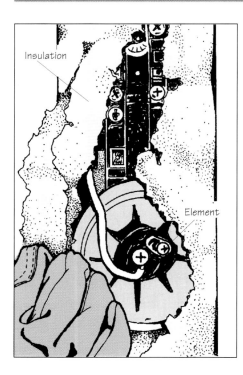

Figure 4. *If the thermostat and element are covered by billowy fiberglass insulation, fold insulation back away from those parts. Wear protective gloves.*

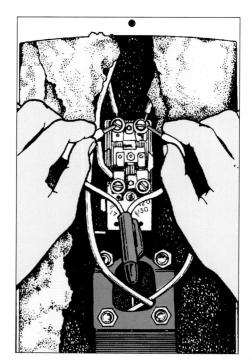

Figure 5. *Use a circuit tester to find out if electricity to the water heater is off. The one illustrated here has a neon light that glows if current is present.*

two thermostats, you can usually determine whether the fault lies with the upper assembly or lower assembly by testing at a hot water faucet.

If water is only warm, the upper assembly is at fault. If water is hot, but only for a short period, replace the lower assembly.

If the water is cold and the fuse or circuit breaker serving the water heater hasn't blown or turned off, respectively, both assemblies have failed.

Replacing Thermostats and Electric Elements

Here's how to proceed:

1. Remove the fuse or turn off the circuit breaker that services the water heater (Figure 1).

2. Close the valve on the cold water pipe.

3. Open hot water faucets throughout the house and drain water from the tank to a level below the element you'll be removing (Figure 2). If the tank holds 40 gallons and you're replacing an upper element and thermostat, drain 20 gallons. If you're replacing a lower element and thermostat, drain 35 gallons.

4. Remove the cover over the thermostat and element and remove or push aside the insulation covering these parts (Figures 3 and 4). Wear gloves to protect your hands if you're dealing with fiberglass insulation.

➡PLUMBER'S TIP:

Unless you're positive that the fuse you removed or circuit breaker you turned off is the one for the water heater, don't do this job. To avoid serious injury, check to see that electricity to the water heater has been turned off by using a circuit tester (Figure 5). Hold the probes across the main power terminals of the thermostat to which are attached the wires coming from the fuse or circuit breaker panel. If the circuit tester shows no current at the terminals, it's safe to continue.

5. Using colored labels or masking tape on which you scribe identifying marks, label each wire you disconnect and the terminal of the thermostat or heating element to which it attaches (Figure 6). Then, loosen terminal screws

and remove the wires from the thermostat and heating element.

6. Pull the old thermostat from its bracket.

7. Remove the protective collar around the element. Then, using adjustable pliers or an adjustable wrench, turn the heating element counterclockwise to remove it from the tank (Figure 7). Be sure to retrieve the old gasket.

8. Take the old thermostat and heating element to a store or company that sells your particular make of water heater to get replacements. You can find one by looking in the Yellow Pages of the phone book under "Water Heaters—Dealers."

9. Coat the threads and gasket of the new element with pipe joint compound, insert the new element into the tank, and tighten it. Install the collar.

10. Press the new thermostat into its bracket.

11. Using the identifying labels on wires and on the old element and thermostat as a guide, connect wires to the new element and thermostat (Figure 8).

12. Set the thermostat to the desired temperature using a screwdriver (Figure 9), press the thermostat reset switch (red button on the thermostat), refold insulation around the assembly, and reinstall the cover.

13. Make sure the drain valve is closed. Turn on the shutoff valve of the cold water pipe. When water runs from the hot water faucets, turn off the faucets and install the fuse or switch on the circuit breaker.

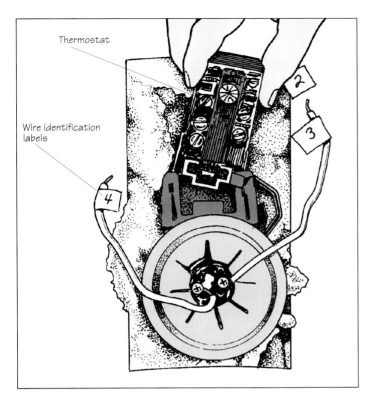

Figure 6. *Label wires so you'll be able to reconnect them to their correct terminal screws.*

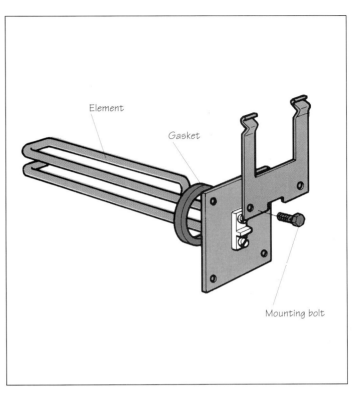

Figure 7. *Remove the element and gasket.*

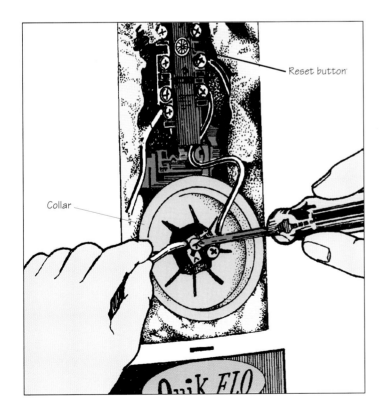

Figure 8. *When installing the new element and thermostat, reconnect the wires carefully following the labels.*

Figure 9. *Set the thermostat to the desired temperature using a screwdriver.*

All About Water Heaters

MAKING MAJOR REPAIRS
TEMPERATURE & PRESSURE RELIEF VALVE

Tools & Materials:
❏ pail
❏ pipe wrenches
❏ temperature and pressure relief valve
❏ pipe joint compound

Remember: *Turn off the gas or electricity before beginning work.*

The temperature and pressure (T & P) relief valve is the most important safety component on a water heater. This section describes how to know when the valve has malfunctioned and how to install a new valve. The valve is located on the side or in the top of the tank.

Signs of Trouble

Water dripping from the pipe connected to the T & P relief valve is a sign that the valve is weak and should be replaced. Make sure the water temperature is not too hot because of an improperly set thermostat.

Test the operation of a T & P relief valve every so often to make sure the valve is still operative. Place a pail under the T & P relief pipe and lift the lever of the valve (Figure 1). Water should flow out the pipe. If not, replace the valve.

T & P relief valve

T & P relief pipe

Figure 1. *Test the T & P relief valve by placing a pail under the T & P relief pipe and lifting the handle of the valve.*

Figure 2. *Use a pipe wrench to remove the T & P relief valve.*

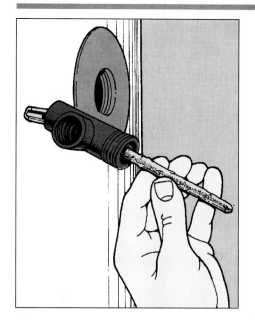

Figure 3. *When you take the T & P relief valve out of the tank, don't be surprised if you find it covered with sediment. Sediment is a common reason for T & P relief valve failure.*

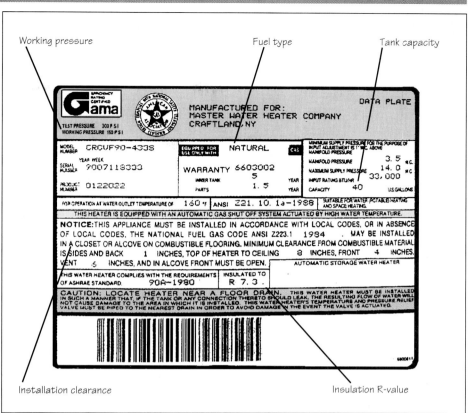

Figure 4. *When purchasing a new T & P relief valve, buy one that matches the working pressure rating of the tank.*

Replacing a T & P Relief Valve

Here's how to proceed:

1. With the gas or electricity to the unit turned off, close the shutoff valve of the cold water pipe.

2. Open a hot water faucet and drain off 10 gallons of water.

3. Using a pipe wrench to hold the T & P relief valve, turn the relief pipe out of the valve with another pipe wrench.

4. Remove the T & P relief valve from the tank by turning it counterclockwise with a pipe wrench (Figures 2 and 3).

CAUTION: Wear gloves; the valve may be very hot.

5. Buy a new T & P relief valve from a plumbing supply or home center store. The valve to get is one that has the same Btu/h (British thermal unit per hour) rating as the water heater. Check the data plate (Figure 4) attached to the water heater to find out what this rating is.

6. Coat the threads of the new T & P relief valve with pipe joint compound and screw the valve into the tank (Figure 5). Make sure it's tight.

7. Coat the threads of the relief pipe with pipe joint compound. Screw the pipe into the T & P relief valve (Figure 6).

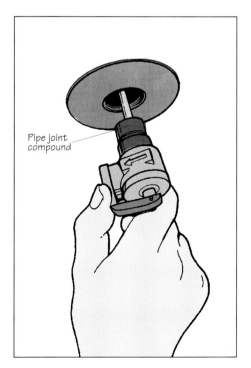

Figure 5. *Seal the threads and install the new T & P relief valve.*

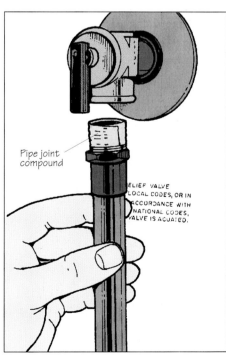

Figure 6. *Seal threads and attach the T & P relief pipe to the T & P relief valve.*

INSTALLING A GAS WATER HEATER

Tools & Materials:
❏ piece of glass or pocket mirror
❏ electrical tape
❏ garden hose
❏ pipe wrenches
❏ hacksaw or pipe cutter
❏ screwdriver
❏ appliance dolly
❏ carpenter's level
❏ hammer
❏ metal shims
❏ pipe joint compound
❏ hot and cold water nipples
❏ flexible copper water lines

Remember: *Turn off the shutoff valve on the gas pipe before beginning work.*

If there is a puddle under the water tank, first make sure it is from water dripping out of the tank and not condensation. Obviously, you do not need a new water heater if cool air hitting the tank's warm surface is condensing on the tank, causing moisture to drip onto the floor.

➡**PLUMBER'S TIP:**
To determine whether a water tank is leaking or if it's merely condensation, use electrical tape to tape a piece of glass or a pocket mirror to the underside of the tank. Wear gloves to keep from burning your hands. After a few hours, remove and inspect the glass. If there is condensation on the glass, the water on the floor is not the result of a leaking tank.

If a new water heater is needed, replace it as soon as possible. When shopping for one, pay attention to the yellow energy guide label pasted on the tank (Figure 1). This label lists the yearly operating costs of a particular unit based on national averages.

Replacing the Tank
To install a new gas water heater proceed as follows:

1. Turn off the shutoff valve on the gas pipe (Figure 2). This is **not** the burner control which is on the box attached to the tank. It's the valve that shuts off the flow of gas to the burner control. If you don't know where the valve is or how to close it, don't do this job.

2. Close the shutoff valve on the cold water pipe. Open hot water faucets throughout the house and attach a garden hose to the drain valve on the tank. Extend the garden hose to a drain or sump or outside the house. Open the drain valve and let the tank drain.

3. Remove the screws, if there are any, holding the flue to the tank (Figure 3). The flue may be sitting on the tank without being attached. In this case, disassemble the sections of the flue pipe. In either case, be careful! The flue may still be scalding hot.

4. Find the union nut that attaches the gas pipe to the nipple that is connected to

Figure 1. *When buying a new water heater, refer to the energy guide label for approximate yearly operating costs of the unit. Be sure to buy a hot water heater that will meet the needs of your home.*

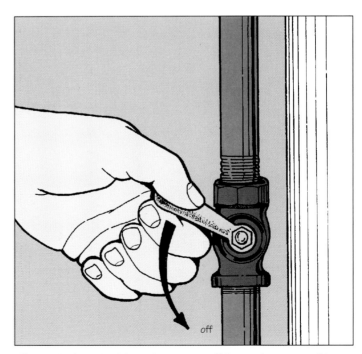

Figure 2. *If you don't know how to turn off the gas by means of the main shutoff valve, or you can't find that valve, do not attempt to replace a gas water heater.*

the burner control. Using two pipe wrenches—one for holding and one for turning—loosen the union nut so the gas pipe and nipple come apart. Then, using wrenches, unscrew the nipple from burner control (Figure 4). Save the nipple.

5. If hot and cold water pipes attached to the old tank are galvanized steel, they are connected with union nuts. Use two pipe wrenches to disconnect the nuts as illustrated in Figure 5.

If hot and cold water pipes are copper, use a hacksaw or pipe cutter to cut pipes about 3 inches below the shutoff valves (Figure 6). If there is no hot water shutoff valve, cut the hot water pipe the same distance up from the tank as where you cut the cold water pipe. The cuts must be straight, so take your time.

6. Move the old tank out of the way. It's much easier if you have someone helping. Also, a dolly used to move appliances from one place to another is really an aid.

7. After maneuvering the new tank into position, use a carpenter's level to make sure it's lying straight. If an adjustment is needed, place a metal shim under the appropriate legs of the tank to get the tank level (Figure 7).

8. Wrap Teflon tape around the threads of the T & P relief valve and pipe, and install the valve in the tank. Then, attach the T & P relief pipe to the valve.

9. If applicable, connect union nuts of galvanized steel hot and cold water pipes to hot and cold water nipples which you screw into the water heater (if the tank isn't already outfitted with them). These nipples are available from a plumbing supply or home center store.

They have arrows embossed on them. The arrow of the hot water nipple should face away from the water heater; that of the cold water nipple should face toward the water heater. Make sure threads are sealed with pipe joint compound. Tighten the union nuts. Use two pipe wrenches—one to hold the nipple and one to tighten the union nut.

10. If pipes are copper, one way to make the hookup is to solder copper pipes together using copper connectors.

Another way is to solder threaded male copper adapters to the ends of the water pipes and apply pipe joint compound to threads of cold and hot water copper nipples and screw them into the water heater.

Now, screw flexible copper water lines between the adapters on the pipes and the nipples on the tank (Figure 8). Tighten fittings with an adjustable wrench or adjustable pliers.

11. Connect the gas nipple to the burner control of the new tank (use pipe joint compound on threads). Then, connect the gas pipe to the nipple. Use pipe joint compound.

12. Attach the flue. That pipe must slope **upward** a minimum of 1/4 inch per foot.

13. Turn on the gas and test for gas leaks by spreading soapy water on joints of the gas pipe and nipple. Watch for bubbles, which indicate a gas leak. If soapy water does bubble, turn off the gas, tighten the fitting a little more and test again.

14. With hot water faucets open throughout the house, fill the tank. When water pours from the faucets, the tank is filled. Turn off the faucets, light the pilot (page 96) and turn on gas to the main burner.

Figure 3. *Remove the flue. It may or may not be attached to the tank with screws.*

Figure 4. *Disconnect the gas pipe from the nipple that extends to the burner control. Then, remove the nipple and lay it aside for use with the new water heater.*

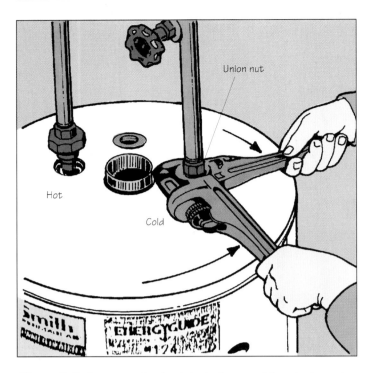

Figure 5. *If pipes are galvanized steel, disconnect them by loosening the union nut.*

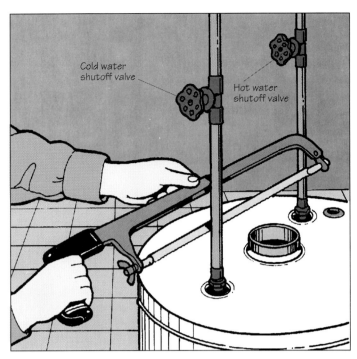

Figure 6. *If pipes are copper and there is no union nut, cut the pipes below the water shutoff valve. If there is no hot water shutoff valve, cut that pipe in line with the cut made to the cold water pipe.*

Figure 7. *Check that the new tank is plumb with a carpenter's level. If needed, place metal shims under legs to level.*

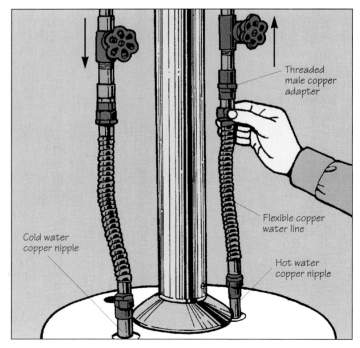

Figure 8. *When connecting a water heater to copper pipes, the cold water nipple should be on the right and the hot water nipple on the left when you face the unit.*

INSTALLING AN ELECTRIC WATER HEATER

Tools & Materials:
❏ piece of glass or pocket mirror
❏ electrical tape and wire connectors
❏ garden hose
❏ pipe wrenches
❏ hacksaw or pipe cutter
❏ screwdriver
❏ appliance dolly
❏ carpenter's level
❏ hammer
❏ metal shims
❏ pipe joint compound
❏ hot and cold water nipples
❏ flexible copper water lines
❏ circuit tester
❏ colored labels or masking tape

Remember: Turn off the power at the main circuit breaker or remove the fuse before beginning work.

With the exception of disconnecting electricity from a leaking water heater and connecting electricity to a new water heater, installing an electric water heater is done pretty much the same way as installing a gas water heater (page 102).

The only other exception is that there is no flue to contend with when you're replacing an electric water heater.

CAUTION: It is imperative for your safety that the first thing you do before tackling this job is to remove the water heater fuse or switch off the water heater circuit breaker in the fuse or main circuit breaker panel. Do not restore electrical service to the water heater until the new unit is in place and grounded (see below).

If you aren't sure which fuse or circuit breaker belongs to the water heater and you don't know how to use a circuit tester to verify that electricity to the water heater has been turned off, do not attempt to replace the water heater. The presence of high voltage can kill you.

Hooking Up An Electric Water Heater
Proceed as follows:

1. After establishing that water on the floor is the result of a leak and not condensation (page 102), turn off electricity.

2. Remove the cover from the spot on the old tank where the power cable from the fuse or circuit breaker panel enters the tank (Figure 1). Notice that wires of the power cable are color-coded. A bare copper or green wire is ground; a black or red wire is the hot wire; a white wire or a black-and-white wire is neutral.

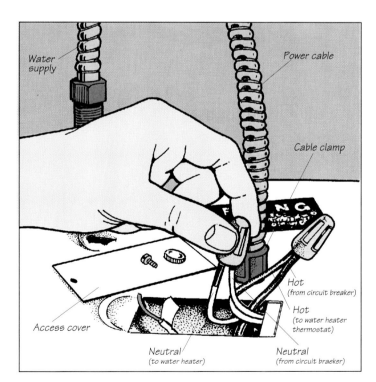

Figure 1. There is a cover on the top or side of an electric water heater that has to be removed to open the compartment where connections are made between the power cable and thermostats. Connections are made with wire connectors and wires are color coded to help prevent cross wiring.

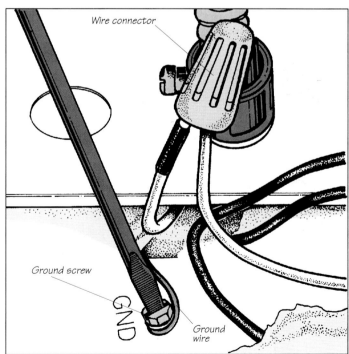

Figure 2. Make certain that the ground wire is connected securely to the ground screw, which here is identified by the initials GND.

3. The wires of the power cable are probably connected with wire connectors to the wires that are attached to the thermostats. Unscrew the wire connectors to disconnect the power cable wires from the thermostat wires.

4. Loosen the clamp holding the power cable to the tank and pull the power cable free of the tank. You can now proceed to disconnect pipes and cart the old tank away.

5. Position the new water tank, level it using a carpenter's level and metal shims, and hook up water pipes.

6. Remove the cover to open the power cable compartment. Push the power cable into this compartment

through the cable clamp that secures the power cable to the tank.

7. Using wire connectors, connect the hot and neutral wires of the power cable to their respective thermostat wires. Then, loosen the screw marked GRD or GND (for GROUND) and connect the ground wire to it (Figure 2). Be sure you tighten the screw so it grips the ground wire.

8. Tighten the cable clamp and install the cover over the power cable compartment.

9. Remove the covers over the thermostats and elements. Pull apart insulation to reveal the temperature controls.

10. Turn the temperature control to the desired temperature (Figure 3). Make sure both thermostats are at the same setting; then, press the red button on each thermostat (Figure 4). This is an overload reset button. Pressing it will complete the circuit when you turn on the power.

11. Fold the insulation back over the thermostats and install the both covers. Install the fuse or turn on the circuit breaker.

12. After one hour, turn on a hot water faucet to see if water is hot. If it isn't, you've done something wrong so **turn off electricity again** and check connections.

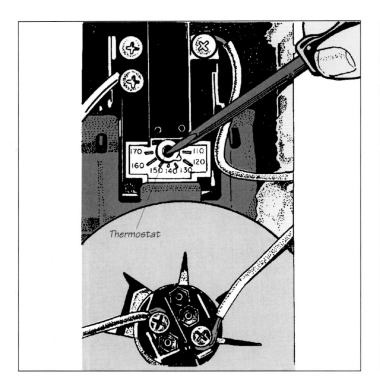

Figure 3. Set the temperature to the desired level using a screwdriver. Make sure both thermostats are at the same setting.

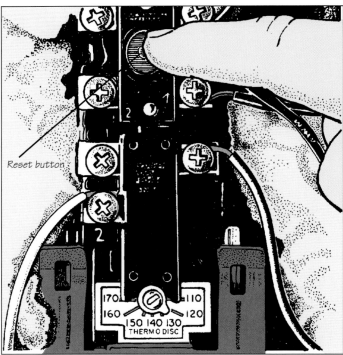

Figure 4. Press the red reset button on each thermostat to complete the circuit.

INSTALLING NEW INDOOR PLUMBING
FACTS TO KNOW BEFORE YOU BEGIN

As pointed out in Chapter I, pipes deliver potable water to plumbing fixtures and plumbing appliances (Figure 1) as well as dispose of soil and waste through a drainage network that empties into a municipal sewer or private septic system.

The network of drainage pipes is vented to the atmosphere so air pressure within the network is equalized, which prevents water in traps from being siphoned (drawn) from those traps. Every plumbing fixture and plumbing appliance in a house has a trap that should stay filled with water to block the passage of sewer or septic tank gases into the house.

The network of drainage pipes and vents is often referred to as the DWV system. **DWV** stands for **drain** pipe-**waste** pipe-**vent** pipe system (Figure 2).

The National Standard Plumbing Code states that the phrase "SWV system" is synonymous with the phrase "DWV system." **SWV** stands for **soil** pipe-**waste** pipe-**vent** pipe system.

In plumbing terminology, drain or soil pipes carry away solid as well as liquid matter. Waste pipes handle waste, which is defined by the National Standard Plumbing Code as liquid matter.

Pressure and Gravity

The delivery of potable water to plumbing fixtures and plumbing appliances is done by putting that water under pressure. The elimination of soil and waste through soil and waste pipes is accomplished by gravity.

All soil and waste pipes empty into a home's main drain pipe, which is the

largest pipe in the drainage network and the one that empties into the sewer or septic system. To maintain the required gravitational force, all pipes in the drainage network that lie horizontally should be sloped a minimum of 1/4 inch toward the sewer or septic tank.

Valuable Vents

Vent pipes are extensions of soil and waste pipes. They are placed above the level of traps and are directly or indirectly open to the atmosphere through the roof of the house so air can swoop into them and equalize pressure in the drainage network.

The effect of equalization is to prevent a vacuum effect that would siphon water from traps. Without this venting, the pipes serving toilets and the kitchen sink

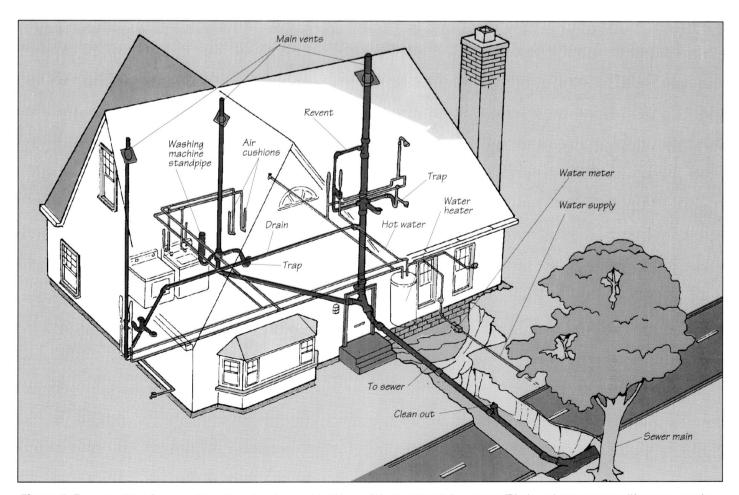

Figure 1. *Every plumbing fixture and appliance in a house should have: (A) pipes that deliver water, (B) pipes that transport soil/waste to a main drain pipe, which empties into a sewer or septic system, (C) water-filled traps that keep gases out and (D) vent pipes, and (E) cleanout plugs.*

107

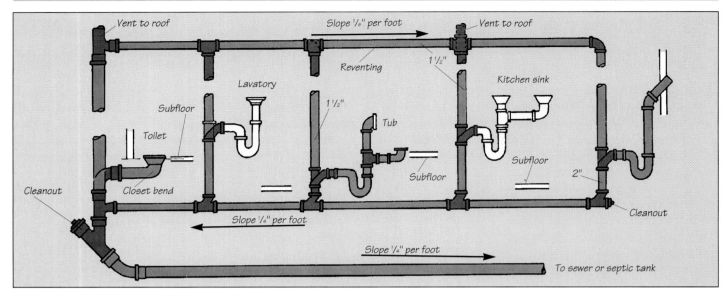

Figure 2. *A properly installed DWV system allows for venting of every trap. There should be a cleanout plug at least every 75 feet, and horizontally positioned soil and waste pipes should be pitched 1/4 inch per foot toward the sewer or septic tank.*

in particular would be a breeding ground for such diseases as diphtheria and cholera.

Every plumbing fixture and plumbing appliance should have a trap that is vented. You will usually see only two or three vent pipes extending above the roof of a house. The other vent pipes are tied into these two or three, which we call main vents. Several methods of tie-in are used. Wet venting and reventing are the most common for houses (Figure 3).

A wet vent is an extension of a waste pipe. It receives waste not coming from a toilet or kitchen sink. Check local building codes to determine if wet venting is allowed in your community.

According to the *National Standard Plumbing Code*, wet venting is permissible if a lavatory or sink is within 2$\frac{1}{2}$ feet of the stack or if a bathtub/shower is within 3$\frac{1}{2}$ feet of the stack.

Reventing is the tie-in of a branch vent pipe to a main vent. The branch vent rises vertically from a waste pipe serving a plumbing fixture or plumbing appliance and then turns horizontally to connect to a main vent below the roof. In extending itself horizontally, the branch pipe should slope upward a minimum of 1/8 inch per foot until it ties into the main vent.

You may be able to use reventing when you install a new plumbing fixture or plumbing appliance if you have an attic in the house that allows free access to main vents. If reventing isn't possible, the new plumbing fixture or plumbing

appliance will have to be installed individually with its own vent pipe extending through the roof.

Note: Consult the plumbing code applicable to your community for data concerning venting. In addition to stating what type of venting is allowed, the code stipulates what size vent pipe should be used in relation to its distance from the trap.

However, both the *National Standard Plumbing Code* and municipal codes agree that a toilet must have its own stack vented to the atmosphere.

➡ PLUMBER'S TIP:

If you get an occasional odor of sewage in the house, it may be the result of water in the trap of a little-used fixture or appliance having evaporated during a dry spell in the weather.

Run water into all traps to refill them. If the odor doesn't abate, a main vent pipe extending through the roof may be clogged. Maybe a bird made a nest over the opening. If that's not the case, there's the possibility that debris has fallen into and clogged a vent. Flush main vents with water from a garden hose. If this doesn't work, try an auger.

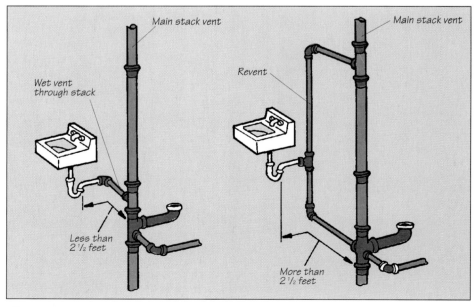

Figure 3. *Wet venting is tying the fixture to the main vent stack directly through the drain. Reventing involves a vent loop up past fixture height connecting with the main vent stack.*

INSTALLING NEW INDOOR PLUMBING
PREPARING A DETAILED PLAN

Tools & Materials:
- ❏ measuring tape
- ❏ graph paper
- ❏ pencil

If you are planning to make improvements that require installation of plumbing fixtures or plumbing appliances where there are no water and drainage facilities, draw up a detailed plan to scale before proceeding.

Once the plan has been prepared, along with a list of parts and materials, have someone with experience in doing a similar project check to see if anything has been overlooked. The plumbing supply store you do business with may have trained consultants on its staff who provide this service.

Follow these steps in preparing your project:

1. Get a copy of your local plumbing code from the office of the municipal plumbing inspector. You will find important information regarding such things as:

- ♦ The required size of DWV pipes.
- ♦ The slope required for horizontally positioned soil and waste pipes.
- ♦ Allowable venting methods.
- ♦ Placement of soil and waste pipe cleanout plugs. The National Standard Plumbing code, for example, requires a cleanout plug every 75 feet for a 4-inch main drain pipe.
- ♦ Recommended size for water delivery pipes.
- ♦ Types of pipe that are approved and prohibited.

2. After deciding where new fixtures and appliances are to go, make a drawing to show how you're going to get new water delivery and soil/waste pipes from here to there. Sketch in obstacles that are in the path and decide how you're going to outflank them.

Note: In planning the layout, leave ample clearance between fixtures (Figure 1).

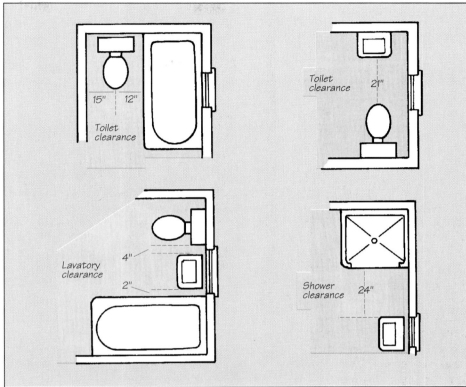

Figure 1. *In making the layout, be sure to allow ample clearance between fixtures. Shown is the minimum clearances recommended between bathroom fixtures.*

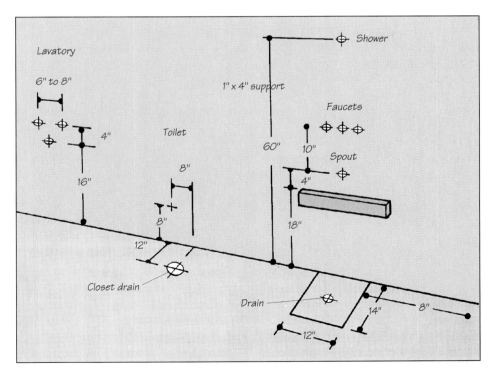

Figure 2. *When roughing-in plumbing for a new area, first establish the location of each fixture, noting the position of drains and faucets so stub-outs can be cut through walls and floors at the exact spots they're needed.*

109

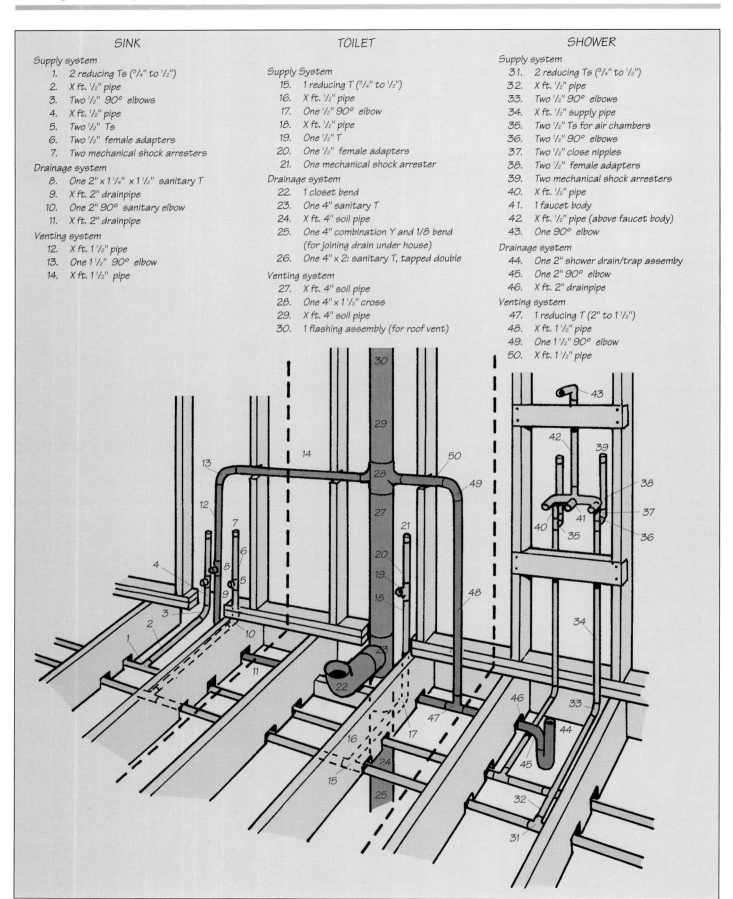

SINK

Supply system
1. 2 reducing Ts (³/₄" to ½")
2. X ft. ½" pipe
3. Two ½" 90° elbows
4. X ft. ½" pipe
5. Two ½" Ts
6. Two ½" female adapters
7. Two mechanical shock arresters

Drainage system
8. One 2" x 1¼" x 1½" sanitary T
9. X ft. 2" drainpipe
10. One 2" 90° sanitary elbow
11. X ft. 2" drainpipe

Venting system
12. X ft. 1½" pipe
13. One 1½" 90° elbow
14. X ft. 1½" pipe

TOILET

Supply System
15. 1 reducing T (³/₄" to ½")
16. X ft. ½" pipe
17. One ½" 90° elbow
18. X ft. ½" pipe
19. One ½" T
20. One ½" female adapters
21. One mechanical shock arrester

Drainage system
22. 1 closet bend
23. One 4" sanitary T
24. X ft. 4" soil pipe
25. One 4" combination Y and 1/8 bend
    (for joining drain under house)
26. One 4" x 2: sanitary T, tapped double

Venting system
27. X ft. 4" soil pipe
28. One 4" x 1½" cross
29. X ft. 4" soil pipe
30. 1 flashing assembly (for roof vent)

SHOWER

Supply system
31. 2 reducing Ts (³/₄" to ½")
32. X ft. ½" pipe
33. Two ½" 90° elbows
34. X ft. ½" supply pipe
35. Two ½" Ts for air chambers
36. Two ½" 90° elbows
37. Two ½" close nipples
38. Two ½" female adapters
39. Two mechanical shock arresters
40. X ft. ½" pipe
41. 1 faucet body
42. X ft. ½" pipe (above faucet body)
43. One 90° elbow

Drainage system
44. One 2" shower drain/trap assemby
45. One 2" 90° elbow
46. X ft. 2" drainpipe

Venting system
47. 1 reducing T (2" to 1½")
48. X ft. 1½" pipe
49. One 1½" 90° elbow
50. X ft. 1½" pipe

Figure 3. *An important step in the roughing-in process is to make a detailed drawing of how water delivery and DWV pipes will get to fixtures. Also, make a list of the plumbing parts that are needed.*

3. Write down on your plan the type of existing water delivery and DWV pipes—copper, PVC, CPVC, galvanized steel, cast iron, etc.

Consult your local code to determine whether new pipes and fittings have to be the same type as existing pipes and fittings, or whether it's permissible to switch to a different type that will be easier to work with.

Specifically, does the code permit integration of CPVC water delivery pipes into an existing copper or galvanized steel system (see page 115) and PVC DWV pipe into a cast-iron drain system (see page 116).

4. Do the roughing-in procedure (Figures 2 and 3), which is done to pinpoint the exact spots where water and soil/waste pipes will come into the room to hook up with a new fixture or appliance.

Don't take the term "roughing-in" literally. It should be a precise detailed layout of the arrangement or you'll pay a price later in lost time and money.

Figure 4 illustrates a new bathroom's water and DWV systems in action after careful planning.

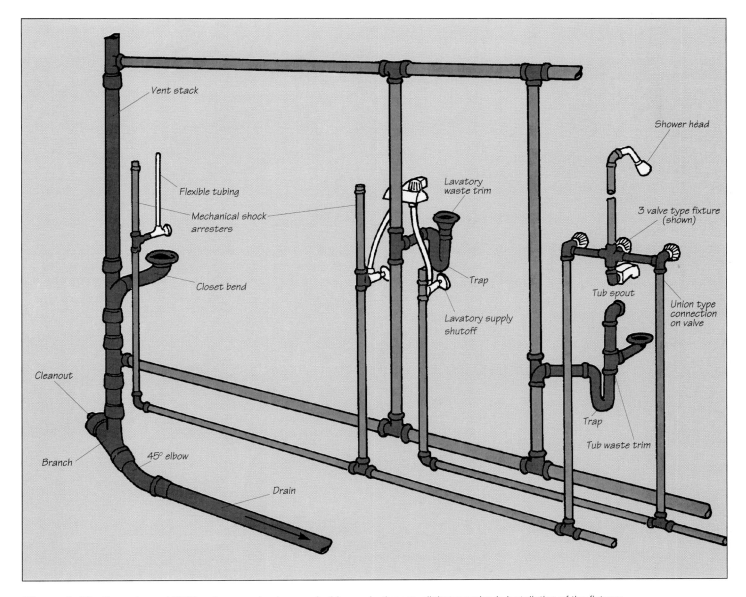

Figure 4. *After the water and DWV systems are in place, as in this new bathroom, all that remains is installation of the fixtures.*

INSTALLING NEW INDOOR PLUMBING
UNDERSTANDING & MEASURING PIPES

Tools & Materials:
❑ measuring tape
❑ specific materials and tools that are applicable to the type of pipe being installed: copper, gavalanized steel, brass, bronze, PVC, CPVC, or cast iron

Plastic Pipe

When extending existing plumbing for installation of new fixtures or appliances, two types of pipe are commonly used: polyvinyl chloride (PVC) for DWV and chlorinated polyvinyl chloride (CPVC) for hot and cold water delivery (Figure 1). Check that this concurs with your community plumbing codes.

As far as plumbing codes go, PVC is virtually universally accepted for DWV use and is easily obtained. Even if your home's main drain pipe is made of cast iron, a PVC soil or waste pipe extension can be spliced in using no-hub connectors also called hubless connectors or couplings (see page 117). In some areas plumbing codes permit the use of Acrylonitrile-Butadiene-Styrene (ABS), a material used before the development of PVC. Do not use ABS and PVC piping in the same system as each has a different resistance to thermal expansion.

There may be a problem in using CPVC. Some communities do not permit its use based on a premise that CPVC will not stand up under the heat and pressure that could possibly build up in hot water pipes. In spite of this premise, CPVC is rated to withstand a water temperature of 180°F and a pressure of 100 pounds per square inch, conditions that seldom, if ever, exist in the hot water delivery system of a home.

Be wary of a plastic pipe called polybutylene (PB). It is flexible and made for water delivery (Figure 2). However, its durability is in question.

Figure 1. *In areas where plumbing code allows, we suggest using CPVC piping for hot and cold water delivery to fixtures and appliances. It is easy to cut and connect, and can be joined to copper or galvanized steel pipe with transition fittings. PVC piping, used for the installation of the DWV system, is easy to install.*

Figure 2. *Polybutylene (PB) pipe, made of a flexible material, is used for hot and cold water delivery. However, the durability of the material has been questioned. It may be wiser to opt for CPVC where codes permit, even though its rigidness makes it more difficult to handle.*

Metal Pipe

Those who live in communities that do not allow the use of CPVC will have to make do with their existing pipe. More than likely, the existing pipe is made of copper (Figure 3), which is strong and long lasting. One of the disadvantages of using copper pipe is that it must be soldered. A little practice soldering, along with the suggestions on page 41, should help.

Prior to World War II, threaded galvanized steel was used to make water pipes.It is difficult to work with galvanized steel. Not only is it tricky to cut, it is also hard to disassemble existing sections in order to extend it even if the plumbing code allows tying the existing galvanized pipe to plastic or copper (Figure 4). If it does not, threading galvanized pipe together is difficult as well (Figures 5-7). Suggestions on how to handle this material are given on pages 46-50.

Water pipes made of brass or bronze are rare. Like galvanized steel, they have to be cut and threaded. Existing sections also must be unscrewed in order for the system to be extended.

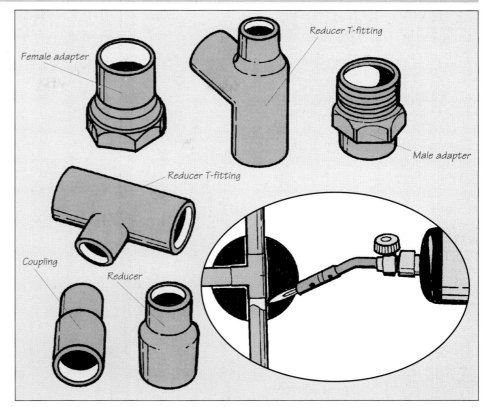

Figure 3. As with plastic and galvanized steel pipe, there are a range of copper connectors to help home plumbers meet different obstacles. Copper pipe is durable, relatively inexpensive and easier to work with than some might think. Soldering, however, requires patience and care.

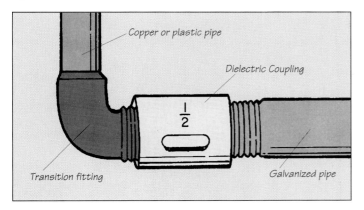

Figure 4. Galvanized steel pipe must be threaded together. For a simpler job, use copper or plastic with transition fittings if code permits.

Figure 5. Those working with galvanized steel pipe will need to learn the technique of threading. It begins with cutting the pipe to size.

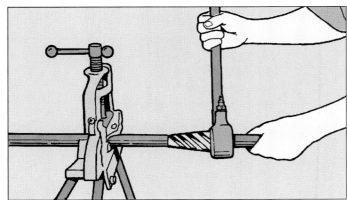

Figure 6. After galvanized steel pipe is cut, a reamer is used to remove burrs.

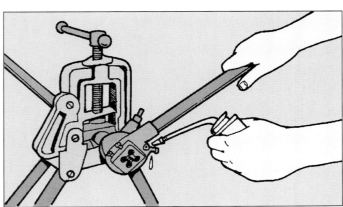

Figure 7. The galvanized steel pipe must be threaded with a die. Remember to oil the die frequently during this operation.

Measuring for What You Need

The pipe to be installed should be the same diameter as the pipe that exists within the home. To accurately measure the diameter of the pipe, cut a slice of the pipe at the point at which you intend to extend it. Then, take that slice and measure the inside diameter, rounding off that measurement to the nearest 1/8 inch (Figure 8). If it is not possible to get inside the pipe to take a measurement, use calipers to measure the outer diameter (Figure 9). Tell the salesperson whether you have measured the inside or outside diameter of the pipe.

When installing a length of pipe between two fittings, it is very important to take precise measurements. The best way to do this is to measure from the edge of one fitting to the edge of the other. This is called the face-to-face measurement.

Measure the distance of pipe required to reach the shoulder of the pipe fitting. This is the socket depth, also known as the assembly allowance. Pipes fitted in this way create a watertight, airtight joint. The length of pipe needed is determined by adding the socket depth to the face-to-face measurement (Figure 10).

PVC and copper pipe are available in lengths of 10 and 20 feet. CPVC is only available in 10-foot lengths. For those who must use galvanized steel, it is available in various lengths up to 21 feet.

Figure 8. *If it is possible to get inside the pipe, measure the diameter. When ordering, tell the salesperson that the measurement is the inner diameter of the pipe.*

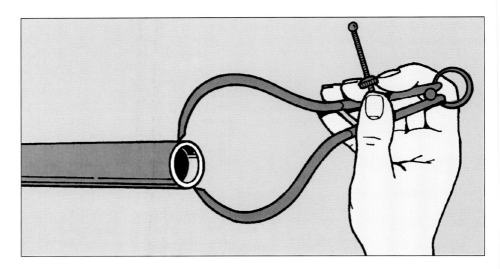

Figure 9. *If it is not possible to get inside the pipe to take a measurement, use calipers to measure the outer diameter. When ordering, tell the salesperson that the measurement is the outer diameter of the pipe.*

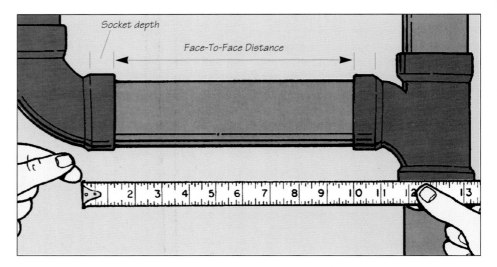

Figure 10. *The amount of pipe needed is determined by adding three measurements: the face-to-face distance, the left depth socket distance and the right depth socket distance (varies from 3/8 inch to about 1 inch).*

INSTALLING NEW INDOOR PLUMBING
EXTENDING WATER DELIVERY & DRAINAGE PIPES

Tools & Materials:
- ❏ CPVC and PVC pipe
- ❏ hacksaw
- ❏ adjustable pliers
- ❏ propane torch
- ❏ sandpaper or steel wool
- ❏ copper tee
- ❏ solder and flux
- ❏ threaded sweat adapter
- ❏ CPVC cold water transition fitting
- ❏ CPVC hot water transition fitting
- ❏ Teflon paste
- ❏ no-hub connectors (hubless couplings)
- ❏ PVC-DWV fitting
- ❏ snap cutter
- ❏ ratchet wrench
- ❏ pipe hangers

Remember: *Turn off the water shutoff valve or the main valve (see Figure 1, page 8) before beginning work.*

The installation of new plumbing fixtures or appliances usually requires an extension of the water delivery system as well as coordination with the existing drainage network.

Extending Water Pipes

Methods used for extending water pipes are described in previous sections of this book. Among the methods discussed are: soldering new copper pipe to existing pipe (page 41-43); solvent-welding new CPVC to existing CPVC (page 44-45); and renovating existing galvanized steel pipe (page 46-50).

When extending copper or galvanized steel water pipes in order to accommodate new plumbing fixtures or plumbing appliances, use the method described in this section if possible. It requires the use of CPVC.

Available in 3/8-, 1/2-, 3/4-, and 1-inch diameters, CPVC is purchased in lengths of 10 feet. The new pipe should be the same diameter as the piping that presently exists in your home. If the present pipe measures 1/2 inch, use 1/2 inch CPVC.

The CPVC pipe is joined to existing copper or galvanized steel pipe with copper-to-CPVC or galvanized steel-to-CPVC transition fittings (Figure 1), respectively. Solvent welding is the technique used to join plumbing fixtures and plumbing appliances to lengths of CPVC.

Installing the new pipe

To extend the existing copper pipe water system to a new plumbing fixture or plumbing appliance proceed as follows:

1. Turn off the water in the house and drain the system.

2. If tapping into the existing pipe at an elbow, rather than cutting the pipe, use a propane torch to heat the elbow until solder melts. Then, free the pipe from the elbow. Discard the elbow (Figure 2).

CAUTION: Wear thick gloves and use adjustable pliers to avoid burning your hands.

3. Use an abrasive, such as sandpaper or steel wool, to clean residue from the ends of the pipe.

4. Solder a copper tee between the two ends of the copper pipe using the techniques described on page 41-43.

5. Cold water pipes should be installed with a fitting called a threaded sweat adapter (Figure 3). Solder the adapter to the unoccupied opening of the copper tee. Then, thread a CPVC cold-water transition fitting to the threaded sweat adapter. Apply Teflon tape to the threads. Solvent-weld the new CPVC cold water pipe to the CPVC cold water transition fitting.

6. The installation for the hot water pipe is the same as for the cold water pipe, up to and including the installation of the threaded sweat adapter. Thread a CPVC hot-water transition fitting to the threaded-sweat adapter. A hot water transition fitting has an elastomeric seal that butts up against the threaded sweat adapter. This seal, which resembles a thick washer, won't lose shape when subjected to hot water and therefore it will not leak. Screw the two fittings together and seal the threads with Teflon paste. Connect the CPVC pipe by solvent-welding.

Use a galvanized steel-to-CPVC transition fitting (Figure 4) when tapping into an existing galvanized steel water system. The fitting can be screwed into a threaded part of the galvanized steel pipe. Spread Teflon paste on threaded joints. Solvent-weld the CPVC water pipe to the plastic end of the transition.

➡PLUMBER'S TIP
Water hammer, a shock wave caused by the build up of pressure within the pipes, can cause pipes to weaken and eventually to leak. In order to prevent water hammer, install mechanical shock arresters or make your own air chambers (page 142-143). This will provide a compressible cushion of air to absorb the pressure that results when faucets or appliance shutoff valves are turned off (Figure 5).

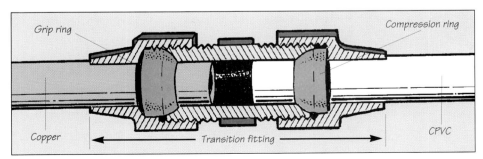

Figure 1. *Transition fittings allow you to join pipes made of two dissimilar materials—such as copper and CPVC shown here.*

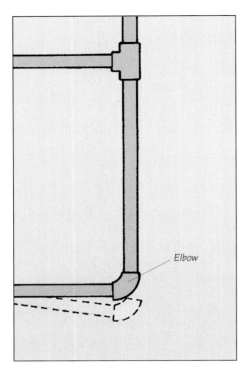

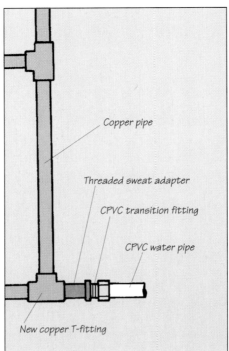

Copper pipe

Threaded sweat adapter

CPVC transition fitting

CPVC water pipe

New copper T-fitting

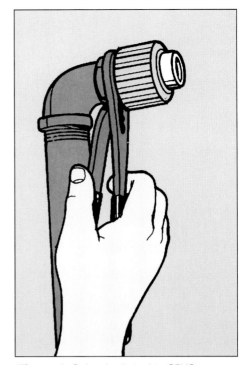

Figure 2. *When extending the water pipe, it may be necessary to tap into an existing copper pipe. If this is the case, melt the solder at an elbow. Then, break the elbow free and discard it.*

Figure 3. *Solder a copper tee between the pipes. Then, solder a threaded sweat adapter to the tee. Using Teflon paste to seal threads, thread a CPVC transition fitting to the adapter. Solvent-weld the new CPVC pipe to the transition fitting.*

Figure 4. *Galvanized-steel-to-CPVC transition fittings are threaded so they can be screwed into elbows or tees made of galvanized steel pipe.*

Air chambers

Figure 5. *Mechanical shock arresters or air chambers should be installed to prevent water hammer.*

The PVC DWV System

PVC is used to extend an existing DWV system. It is available in 10- and 20-foot lengths and in diameters of 1¹/₂-, 2-, 3- and 4-inch diameters and is cut with a saw or pipe cutter. Select the diameter that is in compliance with your community plumbing code.

Joining a DWV pipe to an existing cast-iron main drain pipe is among the toughest tasks home plumbers have had to face. The procedure used to involve cutting out a section of the cast-iron pipe, installing a new section of cast-iron pipe, and then sealing the joints with oakum and molten lead. However,the advent of no-hub connectors (hubless couplings) has made this obsolete.

A no-hub connector (Figure 6) consists of strong neoprene sleeves and a stainless-steel band. The band is outfitted with two screw clamps, that tighten and secure the connector to the cast-iron pipe and a PVC DWV fitting. The new DWV pipe is then solvent-welded to the fitting for extension to the fixture or appliance.

Tying a PVC DWV Pipe into a Cast-Iron Drain Pipe

To tie a PVC DWV pipe into an existing cast-iron stack or drain pipe, follow these guidelines:

1. Cut the cast-iron pipe to a length that equals the size of the PVC-DWV fitting. This is the most difficult part of the job. To make the job easier, rent a tool called a snap cutter (also called a chain cutter, Figures 7 and 8). A hacksaw will do the job if a snap cutter is unavailable but the task could take hours.

2. Two no-hub connectors are needed for this job. Slide a connector onto each end of the cast-iron pipe; the stainless-steel band and screw clamp assemblies go on first, followed by the neoprene sleeves. The sleeves should be folded back, leaving the opening between the two segments of pipe unobstructed.

3. Install the PVC-DWV fitting in the opening between the two ends of the cast-iron pipe. Roll the folds of the neoprene sleeves over the PVC-DWV fitting so that half of each sleeve covers the cast-iron pipe and half covers the fitting.

4. Slide the stainless-steel band and clamp assemblies into position and tighten the screw clamps with a ratchet wrench (Figure 9). Solvent-weld the new PVC pipe to the PVC DWV fitting. Make sure the pipes are adequately supported or they may buckle.

Note: The National Standard Plumbing Code requires horizontally run drain pipes to be sloped no less than 1/4 inch per foot if the pipe has a 3-inch diameter and no less than 1/8 inch per foot if the pipe has a 4-inch diameter. Consult the plumbing codes in your community.

Supporting Pipes

To prevent "bellying," water pipes should be supported with hangers (Figure 10) at the time they are installed. Hangers hold the pipe against basement joists. Place hangers at 32-inch intervals.

If copper or galvanized steel pipe is used to bring water to a new plumbing fixture or plumbing appliance, be sure the hangers are of the same metal to avoid a galvanic reaction.

To give water pipes maximum support, bore holes in joists and studs (preferred) or notch out joists and studs (Figure 11 and 12). Then, insert pipes through holes or notches.

> **CAUTION: Notching may weaken joists and studs. To prevent this, nail a metal mending plate over the cutout after the pipe has been inserted into the notch (Figure 12).**

DWV pipes should also be supported. Vertical runs of DWV pipe can be supported with riser clamps (Figure 13). Horizontal runs of DWV pipe, should be supported at intervals of 3 feet. Support also should be provided at the fittings. This can be done by bracing the pipe with cinder block, brick, or strap hangers nailed to a concrete or cinder block basement wall (Figure 14). If a DWV pipe runs overhead, parallel to the joists, it can braced with wooden supports nailed to joists (Figure 15). Provide some free play to allow for expansion so pipe will not bind and make noise.

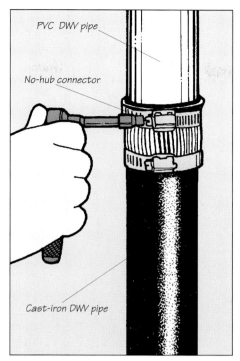

Figure 6. Use no-hub connectors and PVC DWV pipe when it is necessary to remove a section of cast-iron main drain pipe to extend the system.

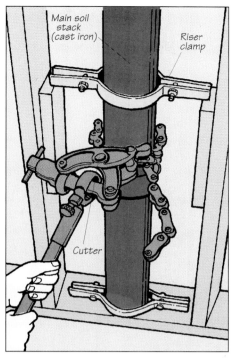

Figure 7. A snap or chain cutter makes cutting through cast-iron pipe a fairly quick job. A riser clamp supports the heavy weight of the cast iron. A hanger strap (Figure 8) is used to support the waste pipe, which drains into the main soil stack.

Figure 8. When extending a waste pipe to a new fixture, take out a 4-inch section of the cast-iron main soil stack. In this case, the existing waste pipe also has to be cut.

Figure 9. Three hub-connectors are used when splicing a sanitary cross into the existing cast-iron soil stack. A PVC spacer may be needed to tie the sanitary cross to the soil stack. Two no-hub connectors and a PVC spacer are used to reconnect the waste pipe.

Figure 10. *Hangers are used to support water pipe.*

Figure 11. *For support, you can notch the stud to accept pipe if you do not wish to drill a hole in the studs. However, add support (Figure 12).*

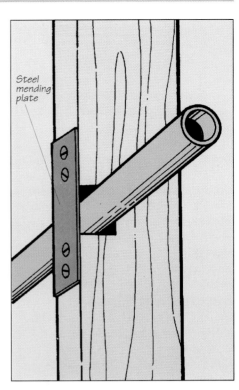

Figure 12. *The strength of a notched stud should be enhanced by placing a steel mending brace over the notch.*

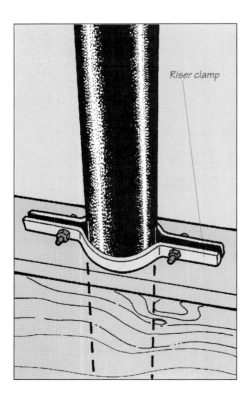

Figure 13. *Vertical runs of DWV pipe can be supported with riser clamps.*

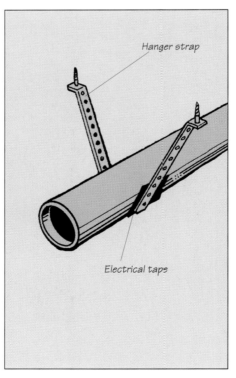

Figure 14. *Horizontal runs of DWV pipe can be supported with hanger straps. Place duct or electrical tape between pipe and hanger.*

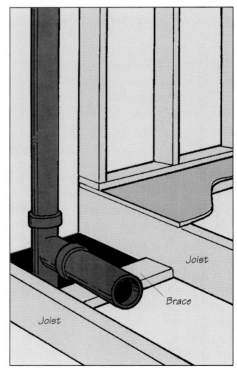

Figure 15. *Horizontal overhead lengths of DWV, which run parallel to joists, can be supported with wooden braces.*

WATER TREATMENT SYSTEM
SELECTING & INSTALLING

Tools & Materials:
❑ water treatment system
❑ wrenches
❑ pipe cutter

depends on repair needed

Is Filtration Necessary?

To find out whether or not you need a water treatment system in your home, have the water tested. The municipal health department can recommend a reputable agency to do this.

The test for bacterial content costs only a few dollars. Having a full test done, which includes an examination for organic compounds, pesticides, dissolved gases and solid particles, can cost several hundred dollars.

Consider the area in which your home is located. Are there or have there ever been gas stations in the vicinity? Is there or has there ever been manufacturing facilities? Is there or has there been a dump? Is your house on land that used to be a farm?

To figure out which tests to have done, ask municipal officials which tests should be made. In all likelihood, the water supply for your house is not the first in the region to be tested.

Selecting the Best Method

A single water treatment system will not be able to remove every contaminating agent. There are eight different types of systems. The three most commonly used are: activated charcoal filters, reverse osmosis (RO) filters and distillation units. Each eliminates more than one type of impurity. The remaining five systems—ultraviolet radiation, chemical treatment, ion-exchange, sediment filtration and aeration—have more narrowly defined roles.

Ultraviolet radiation and chemical treatment are effective against bacteria.

An **ion-exchange system** (or water softener) is effective if water has a heavy concentration of calcium, magnesium and/or iron. The phrase usually used to describe this kind of water is "hard water," but it does not fall into the "contaminated" category.

A **sediment filter** screens out particles that make water look cloudy. It is also effective if asbestos fibers are present in the water. Often this type of filter is used, in combination with an activated charcoal filter (Figure 1).

An **aeration unit** and **activated charcoal filter** are effective against radon gas and odor caused by gas (such as sulfur) present in the water. In addition, an activated charcoal filter eliminates organic chemicals and pesticides.

Activated charcoal filters are available in a variety of sizes and prices. Some smaller units are attached to the spout of the faucet. Large size tanks, which are connected to the water supply line at the entry point into the home, hold sizable quantities of charcoal. To maintain its effectiveness, an activated charcoal filter has to be replaced periodically.

Both **RO filters** (Figure 3) **and distillation units** remove a variety of heavy metals, such as lead, arsenic and mercury. They also remove sodium and nitrate. An RO unit, will often be combined with an activated charcoal filter to weed out organic chemicals, pesticides, odor and radon as well. Both units cost from hundreds to thousands of dollars.

A distillation water treatment system (Figure 2) does not filter the water. The unit boils the water. The steam is then condensed by a condensing coil and the impurity-free water collects in a storage tank, where it is drawn off by the faucet.

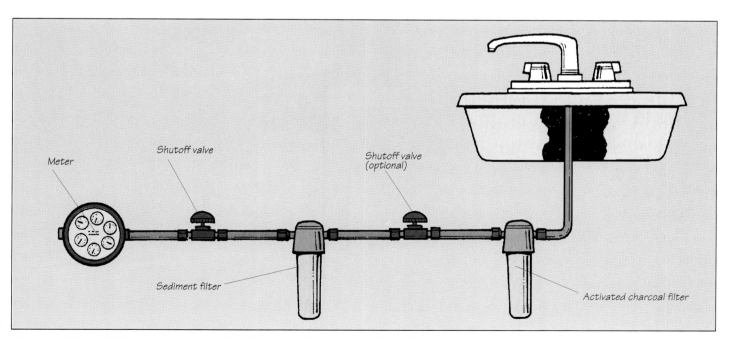

Figure 1. *This dual-filter arrangement consists of a charcoal filter and a sediment filter.*

Installing an Activated Charcoal Filter

Activated charcoal filters (Figure 4) represent the most common type of water treatment system. Installing a charccal filter can be as simple as screwing the unit into the spout of the kitchen sink, or as complex as tying a floor-mounted tank into the pressure tank of a private well system.

One disadvantage of using a filter that is connected to the spout of the sink is that the filter must be changed every three months.

Many homeowners install units in the cabinet beneath the kitchen sink by splicing the filter into the cold water supply line.

The manufacturer's instructions will show how to make the installation. Generally, the job involves cutting the water supply line in order to splice the filter into the pipe. Compression fittings are used often, but if this is not possible, solder the pipe to the fittings of the filter.

➡PLUMBER'S TIP:

A shutoff valve can be installed on the intake side of the filter so that the water can be turned off at that point when the filter needs to be replaced. Otherwise, the water can be turned off at the main water shutoff valve (located near the water meter if water is supplied by a utility company) or by switching off the submersible pump (if the water supply comes from a private well).

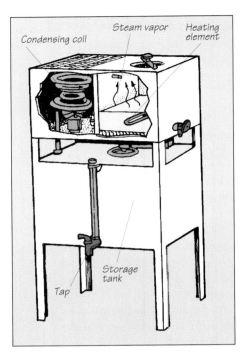

Figure 2. *A distillation system is tied to the water pipe. The unit boils the water. Then, a condensing coil condenses the impurity-free water that is collected in the storage tank. That water is then drawn off through the tap.*

Figure 3. *The reverse osmosis unit, shown here, combines an RO membrane to filter out heavy metals and an activated charcoal filter to trap organic chemicals, pesticides, radon and odor. It also contains a sediment filter and a large tank to store the filtered water.*

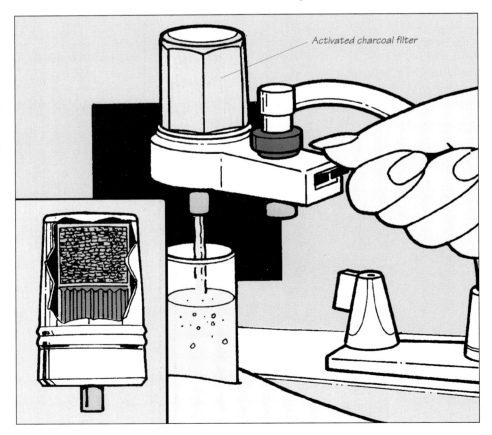

Figure 4. *A common, effective and inexpensive type of filtration is the charcoal filter. When attached to the spout of the sink, a lever allows the user to switch between filtered and regular tap water. A disadvantage is that the filter has to be changed frequently.*

INSTALLING A LAVATORY

Tools & Materials:
❏ adjustable wrench
❏ basin wrench
❏ spud wrench or adjustable pliers
❏ screwdrivers
❏ pail
❏ rags
❏ drywall knife
❏ 2 x 4
❏ rope
❏ brick
❏ silicone caulking
❏ basin clips
❏ eye protection

Remember: *Turn off the water shutoff valve or the main valve (see Figure 1, page 8) before beginning work.*

The information in this section pertains to those who are making a one-for-one lavatory exchange. This means that the old lavatory (either as part of the vanity, or a wall-hung unit) is being replaced with a similar size lavatory. Those who are installing a lavatory that is larger than the one being replaced should refer to page 58. Those who are installing a lavatory where there was none before must extend pipe and should refer to page 115.

Removing the Old Lavatory from the Vanity

1. Turn off the water before beginning work.

2. Using an adjustable wrench or basin wrench, loosen the nuts holding hot and cold water risers to the faucet.

3. Place a pail under the trap and use a spud wrench or adjustable pliers to loosen trap coupling nuts. Remove the trap and stuff a rag in the drain stub-out to block the permeation of sewer gases into the house.

4. Release the stopper.

5. If you are removing a rimmed lavatory, look for basin clips under the vanity top (Figure 1). These clips secure the lavatory to the vanity by locking into tabs. The tabs are slotted so they can be easily loosened or tightened with a screwdriver. Remove the basin clips by turning the bolts counterclockwise.

6. Apply pressure from below to loosen the lavatory from the vanity. If the lavatory is stuck in place, use a drywall (gypsum wallboard) knife to scour the plumber's putty or silicone seal between the lavatory and vanity.

7. If the existing hardware (faucet, drain, tailpiece and stopper) is to be reused, remove them from the old lavatory.

Installing a New Lavatory in a Vanity

1. Install the faucet.

2. When installing a rimmed lavatory, turn it upside down and use a screwdriver to push rim tabs (if they are used) inward until each is at a 90-degree angle to the rim (Figure 2). This is a good time to hook up the faucet assembly as well. Do not put too much pressure on the wrench when you assemble the faucet, as it could crack the lavatory.

3. A 1/8-inch-wide bead of silicone caulking should be applied around the edge of the opening of the vanity (do this for both rimmed and non-rimmed lavatories).

4. Press the lavatory down into the silicone caulking. With a rimmed lavatory, it will be necessary to maintain the pressure while installing all the basin clips. To accomplish this, tie a length of rope around a 2x4. Then, place the 2x4 across the lavatory and fish the rope through the drain hole. Tie a brick around the end of the rope (Figure 3). The basin clips can be installed. Be sure they lock with the rim tabs. Remove the brick, rope and 2x4.

5. Connect the hot and cold water risers; drain tailpiece, trap, and stopper. Run the water and check for leaks.

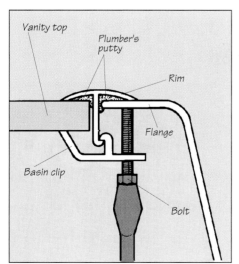

Figure 1. *A rimmed lavatory is held to the vanity with clips. To release the clips, loosen the bolts.*

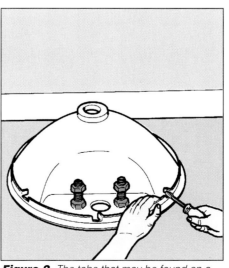

Figure 2. *The tabs that may be found on a new rimmed lavatory should be pushed in until they form a 90-degree angle.*

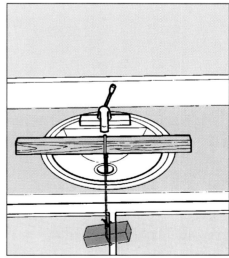

Figure 3. *Use this setup to keep a newly installed rimmed lavatory secure while you install basin clips.*

Replacing a Wall-Hung Lavatory

Inspect the wall-hung lavatory that is to be replaced. Determine how it has been mounted by checking the underside of the unit at both rear corners. If the lavatory was installed with bolts (Figure 4), put something under the unit to support it. Then release the fixture by removing the bolts.

You may find slots cut into each corner of the rear edge of the lavatory (Figure 5). The slots intersect with tabs that are connected to a bracket and screwed into the wall. This type of unit must be lifted off the bracket.

The lavatory may have been installed with self-contained lugs (Figure 6). In this

case, it must be lifted off the bracket.

If the new lavatory uses the same type of retention method as the old lavatory, mount it the same way. However, if retainers are different, remove the existing and install the new one (Figure 7).

Use these guidelines when mounting a wall-hung lavatory:

1. Notice the holes left in the wall by the existing retainer. They are probably spaced 16 inches apart. If the screws that held the retainer to the wall were screwed into the studs, the new retainer can be attached the same way. However, if the screws do not reach the studs, you will have to use toggle bolts. Be sure they are long and strong enough to support the weight of the new lavatory.

2. Lavatories are normally positioned 31 to 34 inches floor to rim. Be sure to allow for the distance between the slots or lugs of the lavatory and the top of the lavatory rim when deciding upon the height at which the lavatory will be hung. Otherwise, the lavatory will be hung too high.

3. Hold the retainer up to the wall at the correct height and secure one end of it to the wall.

4. Place a carpenter's level across the retainer. An assistant will have to hold the carpenter's level steady to keep it from slipping as you maneuver the retainer up or down until the carpenter's level shows that it is straight. At this point, screw the other end of the retainer to the wall and mount the lavatory.

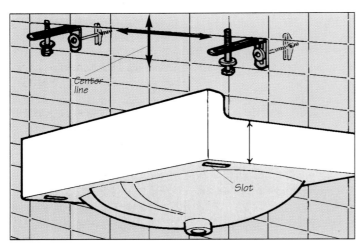

Figure 4. If lavatory has slots at bottom of the back, it is supported with this type bracket. The holding bolts are adjusted for level with a wrench.

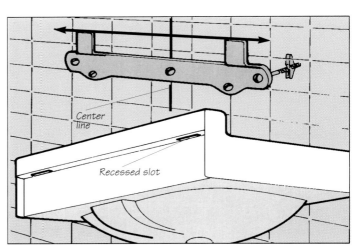

Figure 5. In this lavatory recessed slots also are used for bracket assembly. The bowl is simply set down over the bracket assembly.

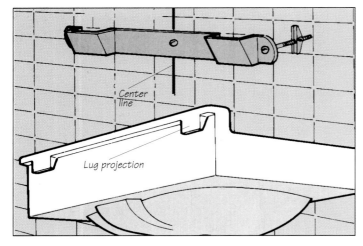

Figure 6. The lug-style bracket is similar to brackets shown above. In this setup, the bowl lugs slip into the bracket assembly to make the connection.

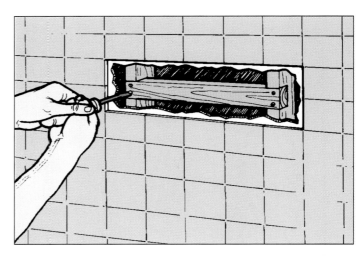

Figure 7. To secure a bracket that cannot be attached to the studs with screws, a 1x3 or 1x4 horizontal framing piece can be mortised into the studs.

RELOCATING A TOILET
INSTALLING A BIDET

Remember: *Turn off the water shutoff valve or the main valve (see Figure 1, page 8) before beginning work.*

The following guidelines demonstrate how to move an existing toilet from one location to another or installation in a new bathroom. Previous sections discuss replacing damaged floor- and wall-mounted toilets with new units (pages 74 and 76).

The Preliminaries

1. Turn the water off.

2. Before you begin, consider how the toilet will be vented. Consult plumbing codes for the allowable distances of the closet bend and soil pipe to the vent. For example, the same DWV setup can be used if placing the toilet less than six feet away from a vent.

3. Flush the toilet. Then, use a large sponge to remove water left in the bowl and in the tank.

4. Remove the caps that cover the bowl hold-down bolts. Use a wrench to remove the nuts from the bolts.

5. Working at the water supply line (riser), use pipe and/or adjustable wrenches to remove the riser and the water shutoff valve.

6. The tank and bowl of a two-piece toilet must be decoupled (page 74). Wiggle the bowl until it breaks free from the floor. Stuff a rag into the closet bend. Place the toilet aside, handling it carefully. If it is dropped, the bowl and tank may crack (Figure 1).

7. Cut the water supply line so its end is beneath the floor or inside the wall. Cap the end of the pipe. Then, trace the line back to the place it intersects the water pipe and remove it at this point. The water supply line for the relocated toilet should be spliced in at this point.

8. Undo the screws holding the closet bend flange to the floor and remove the flange (Figure 2).

9. Determine whether the new location for the toilet will allow you to tie a closet bend into the existing soil pipe. Otherwise, the existing soil pipe has to be sealed and a new setup installed. If this is the case, use a hacksaw to cut off the existing closet bend and as much of the soil pipe as necessary. To install a new DWV setup, first cap the old soil pipe, cut into the home's main drain pipe and connect a fitting. Then, extend the new soil pipe from where the toilet is going to be to the main drain, and extend the soil pipe up through the house and through the roof for venting. The area where the pipe goes through the roof must be sealed with roof cement and flashing.

10. Cover the hole in the floor with underlayment in preparation for laying new floor covering. If the new floor covering is not going to be installed right away, a piece of plywood should be placed over the hole to prevent an accident.

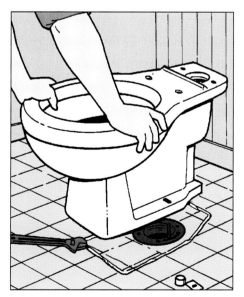

Figure 1. *Handle the tank and bowl with care. Place them in a safe spot while preparing for installation. If dropped, the toilet may crack.*

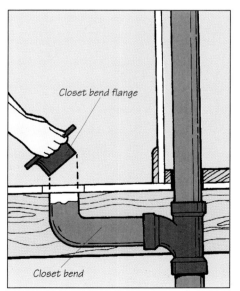

Closet bend flange

Closet bend

Figure 2. *Remove the closet bend flange. Cut the closet bend and either seal the opening or attach and extend a new closet bend for the relocated toilet.*

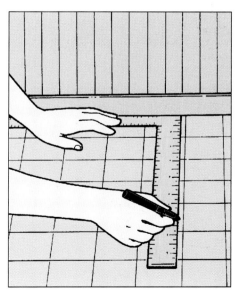

Figure 3. *Draw a baseline.*

Setting Up the New Location

1. Indicate the location for the new toilet. Use a framing square to draw a baseline on the floor at a 90° angle to the wall in the place where the toilet is to go (Figure 3). Center the bowl over this baseline and draw an outline of the base of the bowl onto the floor (Figure 4). Remove the bowl and measure to make sure the baseline is equidistance between the end lines of the outline.

2. Lay the toilet on its side. Measure the distance from the rear or front of the bowl to the center of the horn (Figure 5).

Transpose this measuremen: onto the baseline (Figure 6).

3. Measure the diameter cf the pipe tailpiece of a new closet bend flange and transpose that onto the floor. Check and double-check the measurements before cutting a hole in the floor .

4. Drill a pilot hole in the floor (Figure 7). Use this as a starting point for cutting the hole for the closet bend (Figure 8).

5. Install the new flooring (this may already have been done).

6. Insert the closet bend through the hole so the flange rests on the floor (Figure 9). Screw the flange to the floor.

Install hold-down bolts and place a wax seal around the flange (Figure 10). Then, mount the toilet (page 115).

7. Use a carpenter's square to make sure the bowl is level (Figure 11). If it is off kilter, place a small metal shim under the segment of the bowl that makes the bubble of the carpenter's level center itself, thereby indicating that the bowl is straight and true. Tighten the nuts to the hold-down bolts. Seal the rim with silicone caulking.

8. Connect the closet bend to the soil pipe (Figure 12). Extend the water supply line (page 115), seal connections, turn on the water and check for leaks.

Figure 4. *Draw an outline of the base of the bowl onto the floor.*

Figure 5. *Determine the position of the center of the horn.*

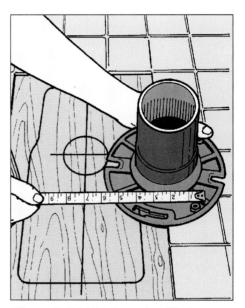

Figure 6. *Establish the center of the horn on the floor. The closet bend will fit into this space.*

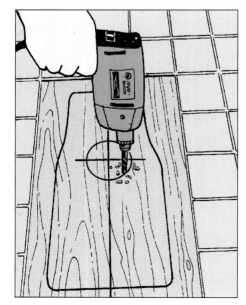

Figure 7. *Drill a pilot hole.*

Figure 8. *Saw the hole for the closet bend and flange.*

Figure 9. *Insert the flange and its extension so that the extension drops into the basement.*

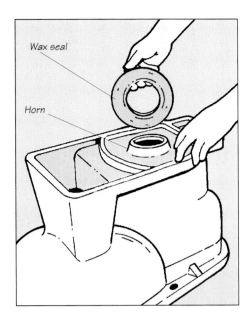

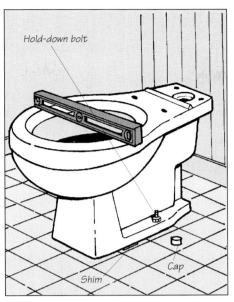

Figure 10. *In order to seal the bowl, turn it upside down. Press the wax seal to the horn of the bowl so it sticks. Then, hold the bowl right-side-up and place it into position on the closet bend flange.*

Figure 11. *Make sure the bowl is level. Then, tighten the nuts to the hold-down bolts. Seal around the rim with silicone caulking.*

Figure 12. *Extend the pipe to tie the toilet into the most convenient soil pipe.*

Installing a Bidet

Installing a bidet is similar to installing a toilet. Both cold and hot water pipes will be necessary. Follow the directions for extending these pipes as described on page 115. When positioning the bidet in the bathroom, allow two inches between the back of the bidet and wall it is going up against (Figure 13). A closet bend is not necessary; instead use an ordinary lavatory or sink trap. Cut and insert a tee in an existing waste pipe and extend the bidet drain pipe to it.

Figure 13. *This diagram illustrates the typical DWV requirements for a bidet.*

125

REPLACING A BATHTUB

Tools & Materials:
❑ wallboard knife
❑ hammer
❑ cold or brick chisel
❑ adjustable and pipe wrenches
❑ pliers
❑ screwdrivers
❑ drywall knife
❑ 2 x 4s
❑ saw
❑ carpenter's level
❑ shims

Remember: *Turn off the water shutoff valve or the main valve (see Figure 1, page 8) before beginning work.*

Replacing a bathtub is not easy. Most likely, the job will require cutting into a wall to reach the pipes. You may even have to remove a wall in order to take out the old tub and and fit the new tub into the room.

Removing the Old Tub
1. Turn off the water. Remove faucets, spout and diverter. In order to expose the pipes, a wall (in the adjacent room or closet behind the bathtub) may have to be removed (Figure 1). If this cannot be done, remove the ceramic tile or the plastic panel and cut away the plaster or drywall (gypsum wallboard) subwall.

2. Disconnect the waste pipe, overflow and water pipes serving the tub (Figure 2).

3. Chip out one course of ceramic tile around the perimeter of the tub or remove the plastic panels along the walls (Figure 3).

4. Move the tub away from the wall. This may be difficult. If the tub will not budge, it may be held to the wall framing with retaining clips. Remove as much of the wall as is necessary (Figure 4) to reach and remove the clips (Figure 5 and 6).

5. The tub may fit through the doorway. Try standing it on end. To

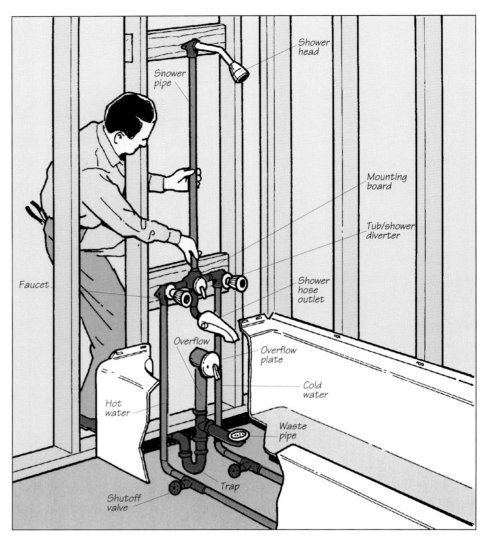

Figure 1. *This drawing shows tne plumbing arrangement for a bathtub/shower.*

move the tub across the floor place a few 2x4s or left-over carpeting or flooring (if of suitable size) under it for use as skid strips (Figure 7). This will help protect floor while making it easier to move tub.

6. The alternative to getting the tub through the doorway is to cut down a wall (Figure 8). This involves cutting away studs. If the wall is loadbearing, nail 2x4s and 2x6s to the studs to help shore up the framing.

Installing the New Tub
When the new tub is moved into place, make sure it is level, using shims if necessary. Attach retaining clips, if necessary (the tub may or may not require clips depending upon the manufacturer). Use tub caulk (Figures 9 and 10). Then, connect the plumbing, check for leaks and perform the necessary carpentry and wall-finishing work to get the room back into shape.

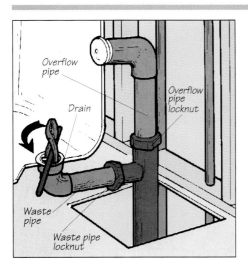

Figure 2. *Disconnect drain, waste and overflow by loosening locknuts.*

Figure 3. *If the walls are tiled, chip out a course of ceramic tile around the perimeter of the tub.*

Figure 4. *It may be necessary to remove more tile than shown in Figure 3. It may also be necessary to remove floor tiles.*

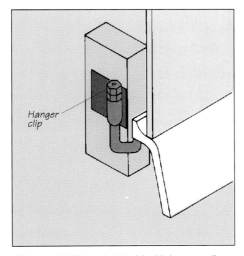

Figure 5. *If the tub is held with hanger clips, they must be loosened or removed before the tub can be taken out.*

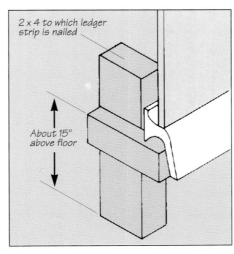

Figure 6. *The tub may rest on a ledger strip, as shown here. If so, simply take off the strip when removing the old tub.*

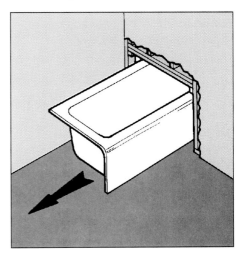

Figure 7. *If the bathtub won't fit through the doorway, it will have to be taken from or brought into the bathroom through a wall.*

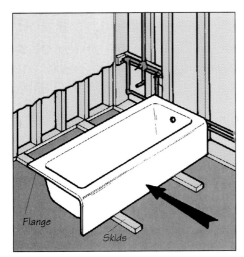

Figure 8. *Use skid strips to move the tub.*

Figure 9. *With the new tub in place, install Sheetrock. Then, tile , grout and finish the job by squeezing a bead of tub caulk in the joint formed by the rim of the tub and the tile.*

Figure 10. *Smooth the caulk with a wet finger. Then, using a damp cloth to wipe off any excess that may have ended up on the tub and/or tile.*

INSTALLING A SHOWER
IN AN EXISTING BATHTUB

Tools & Materials:
- ❏ hammer
- ❏ cold or brick chisel
- ❏ drywall knife
- ❏ drop cloth
- ❏ tub/shower faucet body
- ❏ pipe extension
- ❏ shower head
- ❏ spout pipe
- ❏ spout and diverter
- ❏ greenboard
- ❏ tile or plastic panels
- ❏ Teflon tape or pipe joint compound

Remember: *Turn off the water shutoff valve or the main valve (see Figure 1, page 8) before beginning work.*

Installing a Permanent Fixed Shower

Installing a permanent shower in an existing bathtub is a complex project. In order to gain access to the water pipes, the wall board or subwall must be removed. Then, new pipe must be installed and finally, a wall must be rebuilt and protectively covered.

The installation of a less permanent, hand-held shower head is discussed later in this section.

1. Turn off the water.

2. Disassemble the bathtub's faucets and remove the spout (pages 80-86).

3. Gain access to water pipes by removing the wallcovering (ceramic tile or plastic panel) and the wallboard or plaster subwall. Lay a drop cloth over the tub to prevent damage from falling debris.

4. After the wall has been taken down, remove all nails and debris from the studs in preparation to take the new subwall.

5. Loosen and remove the hot and cold water supply lines. Use whatever method is appropriate for the materials used (for example, use a propane torch on copper pipes). They "elbowed" at a 45-degree angle from the water pipes. Also, remove the line that held the spout.

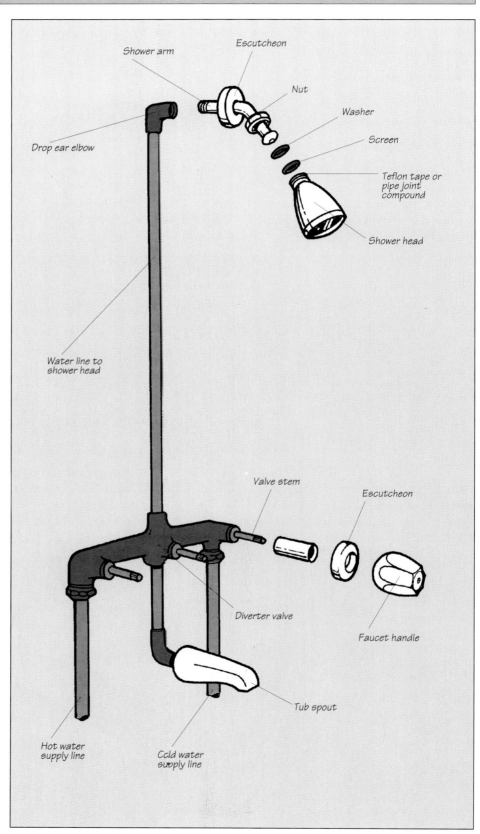

Figure 1. *This illustration shows the plumbing for a two-handle tub and shower control with a diverter valve.*

6. The shower pipe is usually located about 48 inches up the wall from the rim of the tub, but you can set it at any height that accomodates the tallest person that will use the shower. Nail a 1x4 across the studs at the height of the pipe. Notch the lumber to support the 1/2-inch shower pipe.

7. Buy a tub/shower faucet body that will fit and connect it to the water pipes. Also, buy the pipe extension for the shower, pipe for the spout, a new spout and diverter and the necessary elbows to turn the pipes toward the bathtub.

8. Connect all the pipes as shown in Figures 1-3. Then, connect the faucets, bathtub spout and shower head. Turn the water on and check for leaks. Do not disregard any sign of leakage. Even the slightest "weep" will cause a problem. If you close the wall and then discover a leak, you will have to reopen the wall.

Note: Cap the shower arm at the drop ear elbow when you test for leaks. This is especially important if you are installing a flow-restricting or pulsating shower head, which puts a heavy load on soldered joints.

9. Turn the water off and carefully remove the faucets, spout and shower head. Build a subwall using greenboard, a water-resistant drywall.The greenboard should be covered with tile or plastic paneling. Do not simply paint the greenboard, as moisture will cause it to deteriorate in time.

➥PLUMBER'S TIP:
Mark the location of the pipes onto the greenboard. Then, cut the greenboard to accept the pipes. Do not be too concerned with cutting neat holes for the faucet and shower-head lines. Escutcheon plates can be used to cover them.

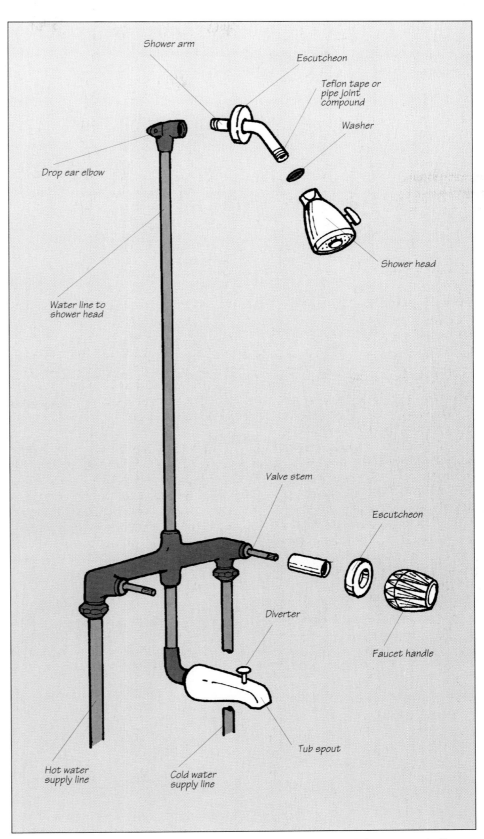

Figure 2. *This illustration shows the plumbing for a two-handle tub and shower control with a gate diverter.*

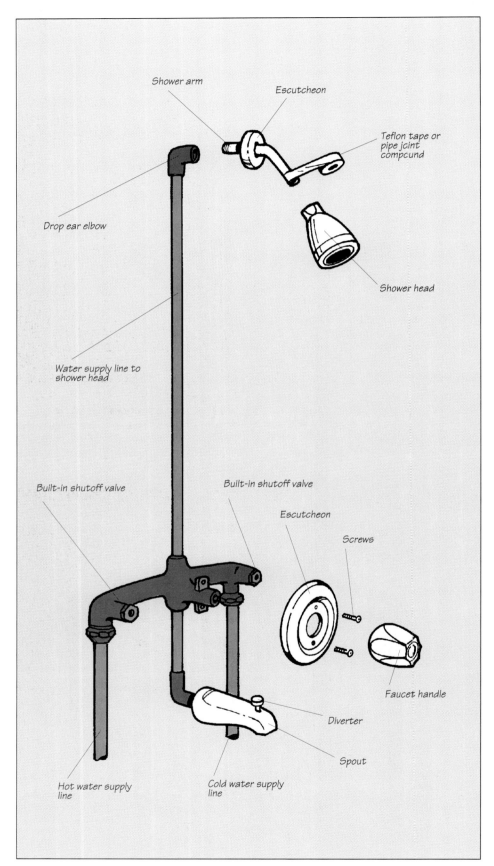

Shower arm

Escutcheon

Teflon tape or pipe joint compound

Drop ear elbow

Shower head

Water supply line to shower head

Built-in shutoff valve

Built-in shutoff valve

Escutcheon

Screws

Faucet handle

Diverter

Spout

Hot water supply line

Cold water supply line

Figure 3. *This illustration shows the plumbing for a one-handle tub and shower control.*

Figure 4. *This illustration shows an adjustable shower arm that lets you choose just the right shower height for you.*

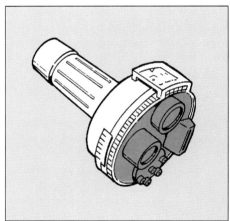

Figure 5. *This illustration shows a massage shower head that lets you select different sprays.*

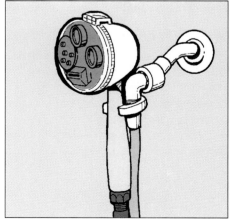

Figure 6. *This illustration shows a hand-held shower head connected to shower arm.*

Installing a Tub Spout Hand-Held Shower

A hand-held shower head and hose can be connected to the bathtub spout in bathtubs that don't have an existing shower. Shower modification kits are available at your local hardware or home center supply store. These kits provide a new bathtub spout with the adapter for the shower hose and a diverter to switch between the bathtub spout and shower head. Installation can be accomplished in several easy steps (Figures 1 through 6).

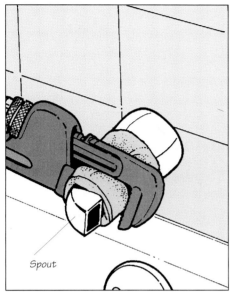

Figure 1. *Remove the tub's present spout and install the new spout that has a adapter for the shower hose.*

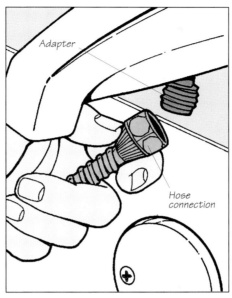

Figure 2. *Connect the shower hose to the adapter. The adapter and hose connection are threaded together and can be permanently installed if you wish.*

Figure 3. *Judge where the shower-head holder should be placed, and mark the location with a felt marker.*

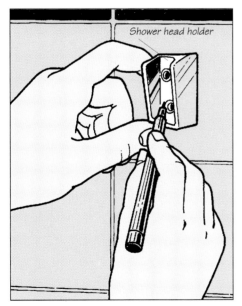

Figure 4. *Place the holder on the wall and mark the position of the holes. Use an electric drill with a carbide-tipped bit to drill holes in tile. Be sure to buy the correct size drill bit (take the holder to the hardware store with you). Purchase masonry anchors and screws if they are not provided with the shower kit.*

Figure 5. *Tap the masonry anchors carefully into the holes with a rubber or wooden mallet—not a hammer. Try not to strike the tile, which may crack.*

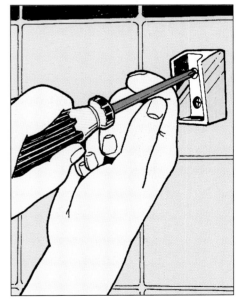

Figure 6. *Hold the holes in the shower-head holder over the anchors. Insert and tighten the masonry screws.*

131

INSTALLING A SHOWER
WHERE NO BATHTUB EXISTS

Tools & Materials:
- ❏ lumber for framing
- ❏ carpentry tools
- ❏ pipes and fittings
- ❏ greenboard
- ❏ ceramic tile or
  prefabricated shower enclosure kit

There are three steps involved in building a shower where no bathtub exists. They include building a frame for one of several type stalls (Figures 1 and 2); installing plumbing; and finishing off the enclosure.

Building a Stall Frame

1. The dimensions illustrated (Figures 3 and 4) can be used as guidelines. As long as the dimensions don't exceed the dimensions of the floor pan, the shower enclosure can be built to any size.

2. Erect the frame.

Installing the Plumbing

1. Rough-in the plumbing (Figure 5). If the shower is being placed on a concrete floor, a recess must be cut into the floor. However, if a prefabricated shower enclosure kit is being used, the openings in the floor pan will hold molded-in drains that are supplied. Depending on whether the floor is wood or concrete, the openings and their sizes will vary. Extend the waste line 1/2 inch above the subfloor or concrete slab.

2. Install the floor pan and drain. Level the pan, using cedar shingles where necessary. Then, nail the pan to the studs with No. 6 x 1½ inch large-headed roofing nails.

Note: Those installing the shower on a concrete slab may wish to hire a professional to install the pan and drain system.

3. Install the necessary piping to hook up the faucets and shower head. Then, connect the pipe to the main water delivery pipes. Turn the water on at this point and check for leaks. Then, remove the faucets and shower head.

4. Cover the framing members with greenboard. Tile the walls or install the panels of a prefabricated shower enclosure kit (Figure 6).

Installing a Prefabricated Shower Enclosure Kit

Tips to aid in the installation of a prefabricated shower enclosure kit follow:

1. If the unit is one-piece, leave off the two outer studs on the frame until the unit is put into place. This extra room will make it easier to maneuver the enclosure into position.

2. Before installing the enclosure kit,

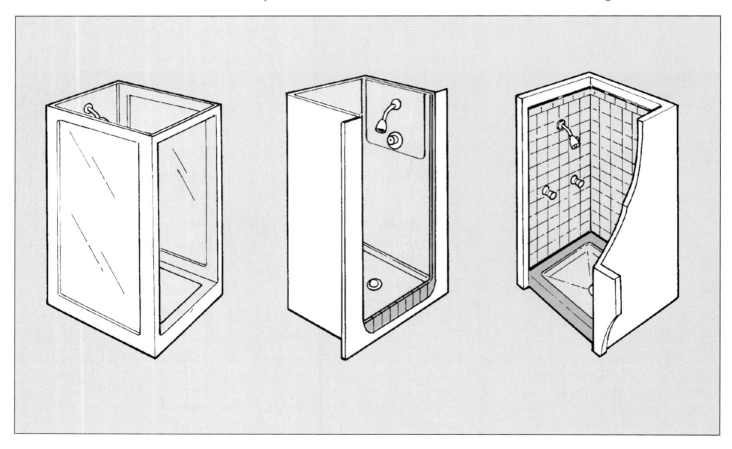

Figure 1. *There are several style options for a shower stall from which to choose. They include (A) a coated or stainless-steel enclosure, (B) a plastic enclosure or (C) a tiled-wall unit.*

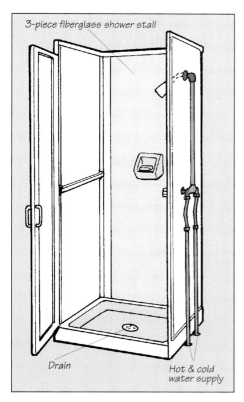

Figure 2. *There are prefabricated shower stalls that are designed as freestanding units.*

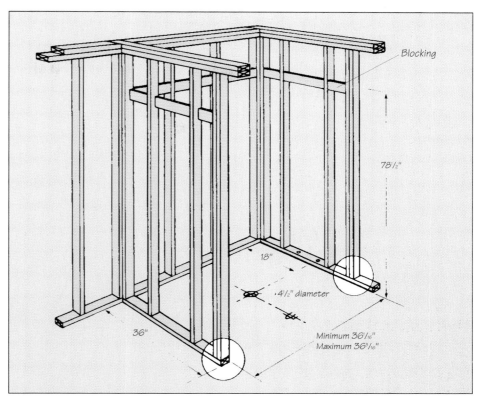

Figure 3. *This drawing illustrates details necessary for installing a shower.*

place foil-faced insulation batts between the studs (Figure 7). When water pounds on panels that are not insulated, a knocking sound results. The insulation will soften the noise to an acceptable level. After the insulation is in place, use a drywall knife to slice the foil in several places so that moisture can escape.

3. If the plumbing wall of the shower enclosure is not pre-drilled to fit the faucets and shower pipe, mark the panel at the proper places. Then, drill holes where the faucets and shower pipe will project. Be careful, the panels are brittle and can crack if too much force is applied (Figure 8).

4. When the shower enclosure is in place, use a carpenter's level to see that it lies straight and true. If not, correct the problem with shims. Then, if necessary, drill holes along the flanges and use roofing nails to fasten the enclosure to the studs through the subwall.

5. Caulk joints with waterproof sealant.

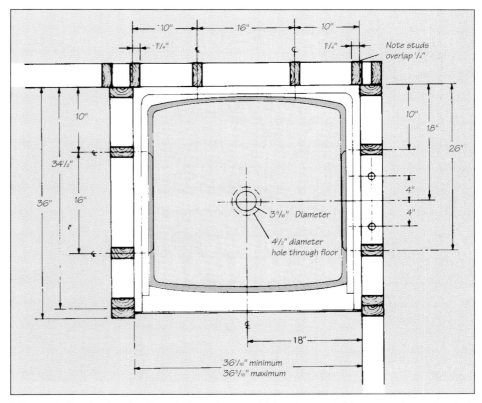

Figure 4. *The framing details and dimensions to which a shower stall is commonly constructed are shown in this illustration.*

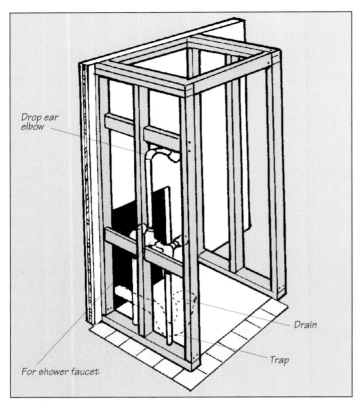

Figure 5. Rough-in the plumbing for the drain, shower faucet and shower arm.

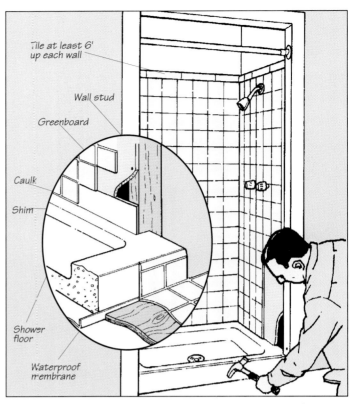

Figure 6. Install pan or waterproof membrane to protect subfloor. Attach waterproof gypsum board (greenboard) to studs with nails or screws. Greenboard should be raised about 1" off the pan with metal shims. Then install tile.

Figure 7. To help soundproof a plastic or metal shower enclosure, install foil-faced insulation between the studs. This will reduce the sound level of water pounding on panels.

Figure 8. Although the panels have sufficient "give" to enable you to get faucet and shower hardware into their respective holes, do not use excessive force.

INSTALLING A FOOD WASTE DISPOSER

Tools & Materials:
- ❑ pipe wrenches or adjustable pliers
- ❑ hacksaw
- ❑ adjustable wrench
- ❑ screwdrivers
- ❑ hammer
- ❑ putty
- ❑ knife
- ❑ kitchen cleanser
- ❑ plumber's putty or silicone sealer
- ❑ on-off switch
- ❑ cable
- ❑ wire connectors
- ❑ insulation stripper
- ❑ cable clamp
- ❑ P-trap
- ❑ gaskets

Before purchasing a food waste disposer, determine the restrictions, if any imposed by the plumbing code in your municipality. Most plumbing codes follow the National Standard Plumbing Codes:

1. The sink waste hole must be a minimum of 3½ inches in diameter.

2. The drain pipe from disposer to trap tailpiece must be no less than 1½ inches in diameter.

3. The disposer must be installed in a double sink, and each basin must drain into its own trap.

Preparing for the Job
1. Remove the doors of the cabinet.

2. Use a pipe wrench or adjustable pliers to remove the trap (Figure 1) and tailpiece (Figure 2).

3. Take the trap arm off the stub-out (Figure 3). Then, stuff a rag into the stub-out to prevent sewer gases from entering the room.

4. Remove the locknut, washer, and gasket holding the strainer to the sink (Figure 4). Push the strainer up and out. If it is stubborn, tap it with a hammer to get it loose.

5. Using a putty knife, remove any plumber's putty that sticks to the strainer hole. Then, clean the area with a kitchen cleanser.

Mounting Disposer Hardware
1. Spread a 1/4-inch wide bead of plumber's putty or silicone sealer around the underside flange of the sink sleeve. The sink sleeve comes with the disposer (Figure 5).

2. Clean the opening of the sink with steel wool. Push the sleeve through the strainer hole from the topside of the sink (Figure 6). Press down hard and twist so the bead of putty spreads beyond the edge of the sleeve and onto the surface

of the sink 1/16 to 1/8 inch.

3. Working inside the cabinet, install the parts of the disposer mounting assembly on the sleeve. Begin with the gasket, followed by the backing ring, and the mounting ring and set screws (Figure 7). To secure components, slip the snap ring in place and tighten each set screw a few turns at a time. Repeat the tightening step, going from one screw to another, tightening each a little, until parts are secured (Figure 8). Do not tighten one screw fully and then another. The backing ring could become distorted and a leak may result.

CAUTION: Hire a licensed electrician if you do not have advanced electrical experience.

Initial Electrical Work
1. Choose a place for the on-off switch. It can go inside the cabinet near the disposer or on the wall near the sink. It is easier to mount the switch inside the cabinet. If the switch is to go on the wall, the wires will have to be fished through the wall (Figure 9).

2. Check the manufacturer's specifications to determine the type of cable to use for the disposer. The building department in your community can tell you what is required by code.

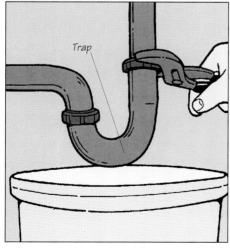

Figure 1. Remove the trap.

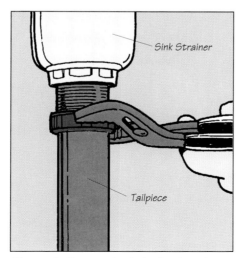

Figure 2. Remove the drain pipe from the sink strainer.

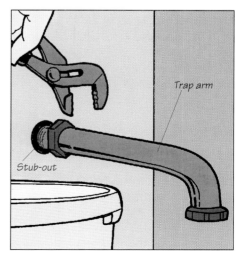

Figure 3. Remove the trap arm from the stub-out.

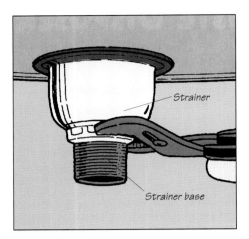

Figure 4. *Release and remove the strainer.*

Figure 5. *Apply a liberal amount of plumber's putty to the bottom lip of the sink sleeve (found on the food waste disposer).*

Figure 6. *Use steel wool to clean the sink opening . Press the sink sleeve into the hole. Wiggle the sleeve back and forth until an even bead of the putty forms around the rim.*

Note: The National Electrical Code requires a food waste disposer to be on its own circuit. Most disposers can get by with a 15-amp circuit, while some manufacturer's instructions recommend a 20-amp circuit.

3. Unscrew the protector plate from the bottom of the disposer and pull out the electric leads (they are probably white and black).

4. Install a cable clamp through the hole in the base of the disposer. Then, push the end of the cable through the clamp into the disposer.

5. Strip off cable insulation and connect wires of same color: the two white (neutral) and the two black (hot) . Use appropriate size wire connectors.

6. Strip the insulation off the third (green) wire, which is the ground wire. (It may not be insulated). Bend the end of this wire around the green-colored grounding screw that is found in the base of the disposer. Tighten the screw securely to ground the disposer.

7. Push wires into the disposer base, tighten the cable clamp and install the protective cover.

Mounting the Unit

1. Slide the mounting plate into position on the drain tailpiece (the drain tailpiece comes with the disposer). Hold the gasket in place while inserting the screws through the mounting plate and gasket holes. Then, attach this assembly to the disposer (Figure 10).

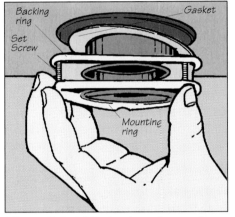

Figure 7. *Install the hardware for securing the food waste disposer to the sink.*

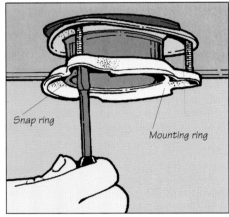

Figure 8. *Secure the mounting assembly by turning each screw a few turns at a time. The snap ring is under the lip of the mounting ring.*

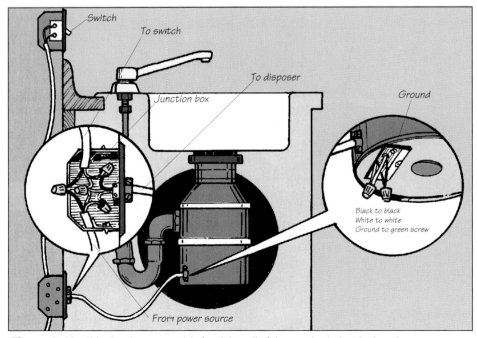

Figure 9. *Use this drawing as a guide for doing all of the required electrical work.*

2. Lift disposer up to the mounting ring and turn the lug ring until the lugs engage the mounting ring (Figure 11). A wrench should be included with the disposer. Use this wrench to tighten the lug ring.

3. Screw an extension tailpiece onto the drain tailpiece that is attached to the disposer. Be sure to seal the join with a slip-nut gasket.

4. Install the P-trap to the end of the extension tailpiece and tighten the slip nut until it is hand-tight.

5. Measure the distance from the open end of the trap to the stub-out. Use a hacksaw to cut the drain pipe to this size. Be sure to allow 1½ inches more than the face-to-face measurement. This is the amount that the end of the drain pipe sets into the stub-out.

6. Install the drain pipe to the trap on one end and to the stub-out on the other (Figure 12). Insure positive sealing at joints to prevent leaks.

Final Electrical Work

Make the connection at the on-off switch. Extend and connect the cable to the circuit breaker or fuse panel.

Operational Problems

➡PLUMBER'S TIP:

If a food waste disposer stops running, it may be overheated. Wait several minutes before pressing the reset button (Figure 13). See the owner's manual for other ways to free a jammed unit.

➡PLUMBER'S TIP:

If a problem is caused by drain clogs, do not use chemical cleaners. Disconnect the current, place a pail under the trap, remove the trap and clear the waste pipe with an auger (Figure 14).

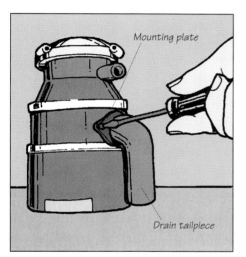

Figure 10. Attach the drain tailpiece and mounting plate to the garbage disposer.

Figure 11. The mounting unit projects from the sink strainer hole. Attach the food waste disposer to this unit.

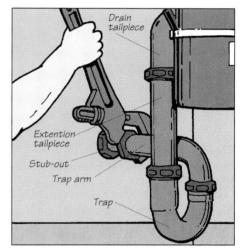

Figure 12. Extend the drain to the drain stub-out, completing the plumbing hookup.

Figure 13. If the disposer becomes overheated, it will shut off. Wait several minutes before resetting it.

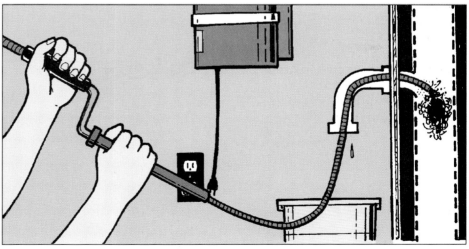

Figure 14. If the drain becomes clogged, do NOT use chemical cleaners. Disconnect the current, put a pail under the trap, remove the trap, and clear the waste pipe with an auger.

INSTALLING A DISHWASHER

Tools & Materials:
❏ 3/8-inch copper water supply pipe
❏ 1/2-inch copper or PVC drain pipe
❏ copper tube cutter
❏ copper tee
❏ solder and flux
❏ propane torch
❏ drain line fitting

Remember: *Turn off the water shutoff valve or the main valve (see Figure 1 page 8) before beginning work.*

The installation of a dishwasher requires carpentry skills, electrical skills and plumbing skills. The best place to install a dishwasher is in a cabinet by the kitchen sink (Figure 1).

Check the manufacturer's instructions concerning the plumbing rough-in and electrical requirements. The following guidelines will help you accomplish this project.

Note: The recommendations offered here are meant to augment the manufacturer's instructions—not supersede them.

Guidelines
Consult the municipal plumbing code before beginning work. Some regulations are practically standard. Two such regulations are: The use of minimum 3/8-inch copper pipe for the water supply line and the use of 1/2-inch copper pipe or PVC pipe for the drain.

Restrictions concerning vents, traps and types of piping vary from municipality to municipality.

Similarly, electric work should be done in accordance with the National Electric Code and the modifications to that code enacted by local authorities (Figure 2).

Installation
1. Although it may not be suggested by the dishwasher manufacturer, it is wise to have the dishwasher on its own circuit.

2. An average-size dishwasher needs a 24-inch-wide by 21-inch-long space. Modify a cabinet near the kitchen sink to accept the unit.

3. Turn the water off. Cut the sink's hot water pipe below the shutoff valve which serves the sink's hot water faucet. Solder a copper tee to the pipe.

4. Use 3/8-inch copper pipe to extend the water supply from the tee to the dishwasher.

Note: A shutoff valve built into the water pipe of the dishwasher is required by code. When a repair must be made, you turn off the water to the dishwasher without turning off water to entire house.

5. The dishwasher can drain directly into the sink's drain. A tee fitting with a 1/2-inch branch is made especially for this purpose.

6. If a food waste disposer unit exists, have the dishwasher drain into the disposer (Figure 4). Usually this requires the removal of a plug, covering an inlet, located on the disposer unit. A fitting to secure the disposer to the 1/2-inch drain pipe can be obtained from an appliance or plumbing supply store. Also, a kit containing all necessary drainage parts, may be available for your appliance.

7. If the municipal plumbing code requires, extend the drain pipe from the kitchen drain or garbage disposer to an air gap and from the air gap to the dishwasher (Figure 5). The purpose of the air gap is to prevent water from siphoning in from the kitchen drain to the dishwasher.

8. Connect the water supply line, drain line and power supply to the dishwasher (Figure 6).

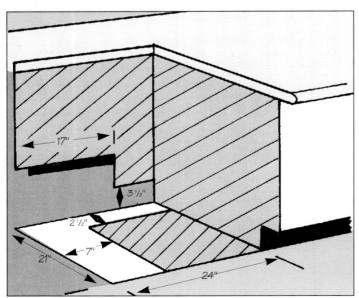

Figure 1. *Using this drawing as a guide, modify a cabinet to accept the dishwasher. Areas not shaded are available for dishwasher piping and drain.*

Figure 2. *Bore a hole (large enough to accomodate the drain and water supply lines) into the lower rear of the sink cabinet side panel. Shut off electricity and run a cable from a 20-amp grounded circuit.*

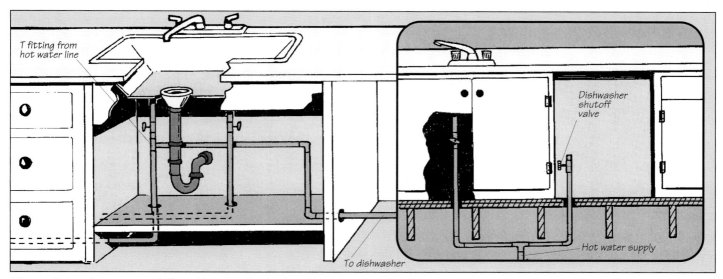

Figure 3. Install a water supply line with a shutoff valve (two alternative hookups are shown), then run copper tubing into the cabinet space.

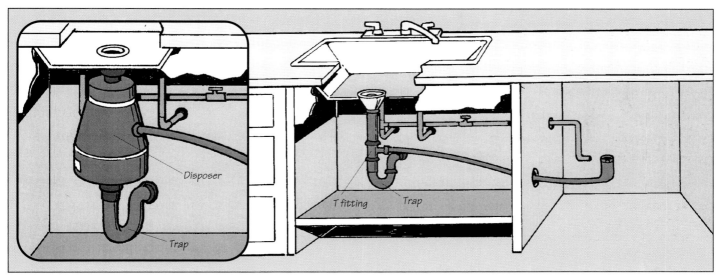

Figure 4. The dishwasher can drain either through a food waste disposer or directly into the sink drainage network.

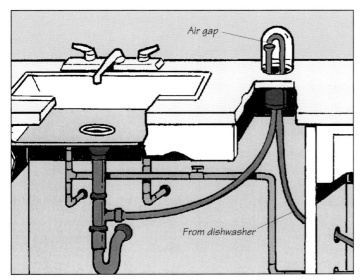

Figure 5. An air gap may be required to prevent sink water from backing up into the dishwasher.

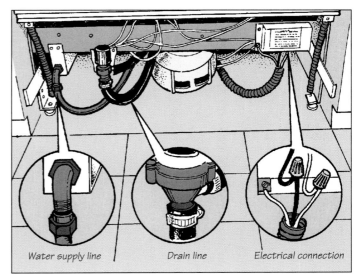

Figure 6. Final installation includes hookups for the water supply line, the drain line and the electrical power.

KEEPING PIPES FROM FREEZING

During the cold-weather season, water pipes may freeze. This section outlines preventive measures to follow in order to avoid this problem.

Preventing Frozen Pipes

In an occupied house, there are several ways to keep the temperature of the pipes above the freezing point (Figure 1).

1. If the basement or crawl space is not heated and therefore may drop below freezing, wrap insulation jackets or batts around sections of pipe. Basement sills, crawl spaces and cantilevered floor joists are primary locations.

You also could install a space heater, an electric, thermostatically controlled unit that hangs from a joist, which is most effective.

2. If water pipes pass through the weather walls (the outside walls) of the house, heat delivered by the home heating system will not protect them from freezing. In this case, there are four options: (1) during cold snaps, allow water to run from faucets at a low-to-moderate stream; (2) have insulation blown into the outside walls where pipes

are located; (3) provide heat from an external source; (4) cut and reroute pipes to take the them out of the weather walls.

Draining a System

If the home is not going to be occupied during cold weather, and therefore the heating system will be turned off, the plumbing system should be drained to prevent frozen pipes. Use the following guidelines to help you:

1. Turn off the water at the main shutoff valve or switch off the submersible pump (Figure 2).

2. Turn off the water heater's energy source, which is either electric (Figure 3) or gas (Figure 4).

3. Flush all toilets; open all faucets and drain valves (including outdoor faucets, Figure 5). Leave them open.

4. Drain the water heater.

5. If you have a private water system, drain the water holding tank as well as any water treatment equipment.

6. If there is a hot-water heating system, turn off the furnace and open radiant equipment drain valves to drain the water. Then drain the furnace.

7. Use a large sponge or syringe to empty toilet bowls. Bale out the remaining water lying in toilet tanks.

8. To get at the pumps of the washing machine and dishwasher, some panels will have to be removed from these appliances. Once this is done, remove the drain hoses so that the water will drain from the pumps.

CAUTION: Be sure the electricity to the appliances is turned off.

9. Examine the pipes, especially near the valves, for small circular knobs that contain tiny holes in them. These knobs act as drains. Loosening them with the valve closed allows trapped water to drain (Figure 5).

10. Antifreeze can be purchased for home use at hardware stores or home supply outlets. Depending on the lowest temperature anticipated in the home, mix the solution for the appropriate potency level. Pour about 8 ounces into every trap, including all toilet bowls, sink, lavatories, showers, bathtubs and the washing machine standpipe (Figure 5).

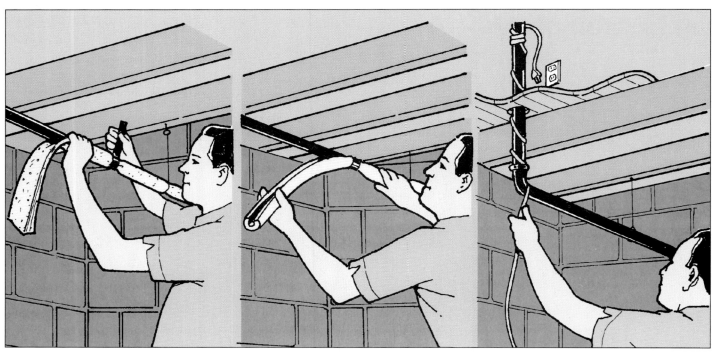

Figure 1. Prevent pipes from freezing by applying batt insulation or insulation jackets. You can wrap pipes with electric heating tape, but this solution won't be any help during a power outage.

Figure 2. *The first step in draining a home's water system is to close the main shutoff valve or switch off the submersible pump.*

Figure 3. *If the water heater is electric, remove the fuse in the main electric service panel or flip off the circuit breaker.*

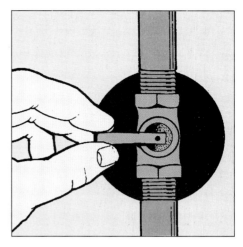

Figure 4. *If the water heater is gas, turn the main gas valve off.*

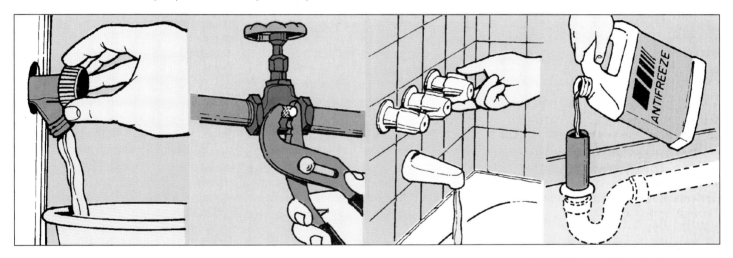

Figure 5. *Open all faucets and let pipes drain. Drain the water heater. Check for circular knobs near the valves of the pipe; these knobs act as drains and should be loosened to dislodge trapped water. Every sink, toilet and plumbing appliance in the home has a trap into which antifreeze should be poured. Traps may be hidden.*

Thawing a Frozen Pipe

A diminished flow of water from the faucet indicates a frozen pipe that has not burst. Heat the frozen section with a heat gun or hair dryer (Figure 6).

CAUTION: Do not touch the pipe while proceeding with this step. Also, be sure the heat gun or hair dryer is grounded.

Move the heat gun or hair dryer back and forth so the heat is not concentrated in one spot. You will need an assistant to stand over the faucet and monitor the flow of water. When the water flows at a normal rate, the obstacle is cleared.

If you are not sure which section is frozen, feel along the pipes with your hand. Do this gingerly with hot water pipes. Usually a frozen section will feel colder than the rest of the pipe.

Figure 6. *Use a heat gun or hair dryer to thaw a frozen section of pipe.*

SILENCING NOISY PIPES

Tools & Materials:
❏ pipe hangers
❏ insulation
❏ tee
❏ reducer
❏ air chambers or shock arresters

*depends on repair needed

Remember: *Turn off the water shutoff valve or the main valve (see Figure 1, page 8) before beginning work.*

A loud noise heard after a faucet is shut or the washing machine or dishwasher turns off is most likely caused by water hammer. Depending upon the method that's needed to solve the problem, the job is given a 1 or 3 rating on the difficulty scale. If the sound is caused by a pipe hanger that has come loose, the repair for this problem is easy to do. However, if that is not the case, a more extensive repair may be necessary.

Drain and Pray
Examine water pipes that are exposed, such as those going to the washing machine. Look for extensions on pipes that are capped and rise above or fall below shutoff valves. These are air-cushioning chambers. If the exposed pipes have them, it is an indication that all water delivery pipes in the house have them, so lack of air chambers is not the problem.

Every so often, however, one or more air chambers becomes waterlogged. When this happens, air is no longer present to absorb the shock resulting from the water when the flow is turned off. Alleviate the condition this way:

1. Turn off the home's main water shut-off valve or switch off the submersible pump.

2. Open all faucets and allow the system to drain. Given enough time, water trapped in the air chambers may drain as well.

3. Turn the water back on. Water will fill the water delivery pipes without filling the air chambers.

Note: Even if all of the water pipes in your home are concealed, and you cannot tell whether or not pipes are outfitted with air chambers, take the time to perform the above procedure.

Treat It Like a Rattle
If the previously described treatment does not alleviate the noise, assume that the noise is coming from a pipe, because the pipe is vibrating against a wooden framing member of the house. With water pipes that are exposed, there is little trouble in securing them.

Inspect pipes from one end to the other, looking for those that lie right up against a joist. Place insulation between the pipe and joist. The insulation acts as a cushion (Figure 1).

Check the metal pipes that hang from joists. There may be an insufficient number of hangers or a hanger may have loosened. Hangers used for metal pipes should be made of the same metal as the pipe to prevent a galvanic reaction. The pipe should be held solidly so there is little or no movement. Make sure metal pipes are held by a hanger at every joist.

CPVC water pipe must be treated differently to allow for thermal expansion and contraction. Therefore, see that the

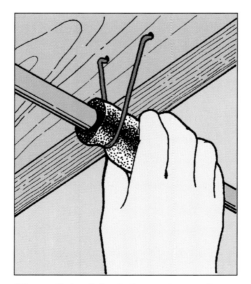

Figure 1. *Insulation between pipes and wood framing acts as a cushion to reduce noise.*

CPVC water pipe is supported every 32 inches (on center); that is, to every other joist. Use special plastic hangers made for CPVC. They allow it to slide back and forth as the temperature inside the pipe changes. Hangers are available at plumbing supply stores.

Time for Drastic Action
If the above treatments have not resolved the problem, air chambers or shock arresters will probably have to be installed into the system. Each hot and cold water pipe going to faucets and appliances should be equipped. The task will not be too difficult if pipes are exposed. However, concealed pipes will require the removal of walls.

Note: There are two ways to do this job: (1) Install air chambers as described here (the less expensive way). Air chambers must be a size larger than the pipe. (2) Install shock arresters, which are mechanical devices work by means of pistons or bellows. Shock arresters (available at plumbing supply stores) are easier to install, but are more costly. Installation instructions are included.

Installing Air Chambers
1. Turn off water; drain the system.

2. Cut copper or CPVC pipe to accept a copper or CPVC tee as close to the faucet or water intake valve as possible.

3. Solder or solvent weld the tee to the cut pipe (Figure 3).

4. Solder a copper nipple or solvent weld CPVC nipple to the tee (Figure 4) and a copper or CPVC reducer to the nipple (Figure 5). If the water pipe is 1/2 inch, use a 3/4- to 1/2-inch reducer. If the water delivery pipe is 3/4 inch, use a 1- to 3/4-inch reducer.

5. Solder or solvent weld (whichever is applicable) the air chamber to the reducer (Figure 6). If the water pipe is 1/2 inch, the air chamber should be at least 12 inches long. If the water pipe is 3/4 inch, the air chamber should be at least 18 inches long.

6. Solder or solvent weld a copper or CPVC cap to the air chamber (Figure 7).

Figure 2. *Turn off water, drain the system and cut the water pipe.*

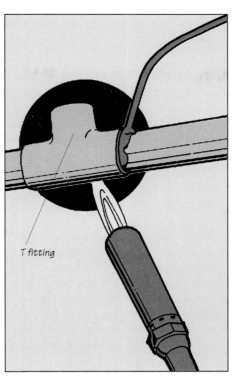

Figure 3. *Solder a copper tee to cut copper water pipe. Solvent-weld a CPVC tee to the CPVC pipe.*

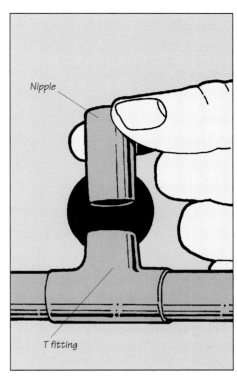

Figure 4. *Attach a nipple to the tee.*

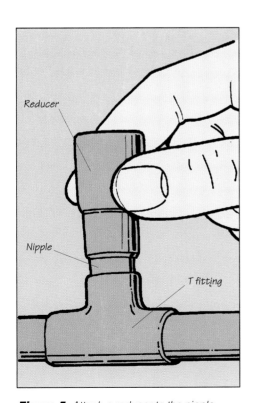

Figure 5. *Attach a reducer to the nipple.*

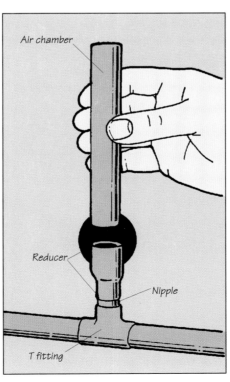

Figure 6. *Attach air chamber to the reducer.*

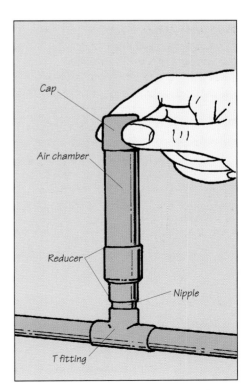

Figure 7. *Attach a cap to the air chamber.*

INSTALLING A SUMP PUMP

Tools & Materials:
- ❏ sledge hammer
- ❏ cold chisel
- ❏ masonry drill
- ❏ jackhammer
- ❏ shovel
- ❏ concrete
- ❏ concrete tools
- ❏ sump pump
- ❏ sump liner
- ❏ sump cover

A sump pump is necessary in basements that flood. It keeps water away from the heating system and other appliances in the basement, thereby preventing damage to the equipment. It also will keep you from having to swab the floor every time it rains.

Choosing the Right Type

There are two styles of sump pumps. A vertical unit (Figure 1) and a submersible unit (Figure 2). The vertical unit consists of a raised motor that does not come in contact with water. The motor sits on top of a vertical stand several feet above the top of the sump. On the other hand, the entire pump in the submersible unit lies in the sump so it gets covered by water.

Since a submersible pump must be sealed, it is more expensive than the vertical pump. The disadvantage of a vertical pump is that it is noisier than a submersible unit. After deciding whether to buy a vertical or submersible pump, determine the capacity needed and the current draw needed to meet the requirements posed by the flooding problem. In general, a sump pump equipped with a 1/3-horsepower motor meets the requirements in most basements, but horsepower is a nebulous rating. Therefore, discuss pump capacity and current draw with the sump pump expert at the plumbing supply house.

Look for a pump that will deliver the greatest capacity for the least amount of current draw. Pump capacity, which is measured in gallons per minute or gallons per hour, is a measure of how much water the pump will discharge from the basement. Current draw (watts = volts x amps) indicates how much electricity a pump requires to run.

A sump pump operates automatically. It is not necessary to switch it on when the first drops of rain begin to fall. This is especially reassuring when you are away from home. The pump will not work during a storm that causes a power failure. If this is a concern, the pump can be equipped with backup batteries or a generator.

Digging a Sump

Pinpoint the lowest part of the basement floor. This will be the part toward which water flows when the basement floods. If you are not sure, stand about 10 feet away from each corner of the basement and pour a few buckets of water onto the floor. The lowest part of the floor is at the corner toward which the water flows.

Scribe a circle on the floor 6 inches larger than the diameter of the pump. Next, break through the concrete floor and dig out the earth to make the sump (Figure 3). It should be about 24 inches deep, but check with the manufacturer's instructions to be sure.

Those who have time, energy and patience can start the excavation using a masonry drill and then continue the job with a cold chisel and sledge hammer. Eye protection should be worn.

To make life easier, a jackhammer can do the job (Figure 4), but do not forget to wear eye protection.

When the sump is dug, line the hole so dirt cannot get into and damage the

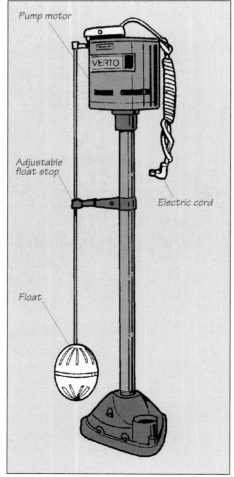

Figure 1. *Vertical sump pump.*

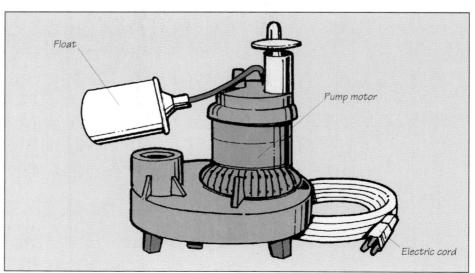

Figure 2. *Horizontal sump pump.*

pump. There are two ways to do this: (1) line the bottom and sides of the sump with concrete; (2) fill the bottom of the sump with gravel and install a store-bought sump liner to cover the sides (Figure 5). Then, place concrete around the edge of the sump and bevel it so that it slopes down toward the hole (Figure 6).

Install the Discharge Pipe

The discharge pipe can be directed from the pump in two ways.

1. Remove a basement window and run the discharge pipe through the opening to the outside. Close off the window area around the pipe with plywood.

2. Make a hole in the cinder block or concrete wall about a foot or so above ground level. Then, run the discharge pipe through the hole to the outside of the house and seal the hole with concrete. Place a splash block under the outlet of the hole, since it will receive the flow from the discharge pipe. Slope the block away from the foundation.

No matter how it is connected, the discharge pipe should contain a one-way check valve in to prevent water from outside the house backing up and flowing into the pump.

Note: Never allow sump discharge (ground or rain water which doesn't need to be treated) into the sewer line or your septic tank. This is prohibited by most plumbing codes.

Install the Pump

Place the pump into the sump and connect the discharge pipe (Figure 7). Then, cover the sump. You can buy a cover or make one from a piece of 3/4-inch plywood (Figure 8).

Plug the pump into a nearby outlet. If there is none, install one or have one installed by an electrician.

CAUTION: To test the pump, pour water into the sump. It should automatically begin to work when the sump is about half full. Never test a sump pump when there is no water in the sump. It may result in damaging the unit. Check the discharge pipe connections for leaks.

Figure 3. *Break through a concrete floor with a masonry drill; then excavate using a sledge hammer and cold chisel.*

Figure 4. *To reduce the amount of work involved in digging a sump, rent a jackhammer.*

Figure 5. *The easiest way to keep dirt out of the pump is to place a sump liner in the hole.*

Figure 6. *Finish the edge of the sump liner with concrete. Bevel the concrete so that the water will flow toward the hole.*

Figure 7. *Place the pump into the sump, connect the discharge pipe and plug into electric outlet.*

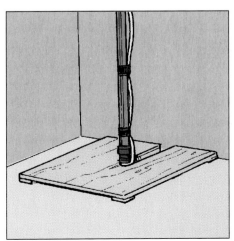

Figure 8. *Make or buy a cover for the sump.*

INSTALLING A FREEZE-PROOF SILLCOCK

Tools & Materials:

- ❏ freeze-proof sillcock
- ❏ copper tube cutter
- ❏ screwdriver
- ❏ pipe wrenches
- ❏ galvanized coupling and transition fitting
- ❏ Teflon paste or pipe joint compound
- ❏ copper pipe
- ❏ CPVC pipe
- ❏ steel wool or emery cloth
- ❏ flux and solder
- ❏ propane torch,
- ❏ solvent welding chemicals
- ❏ carpenter's level
- ❏ copper coupler
- ❏ CPVC coupler

Remember: *Turn off the water shutoff valve or the main valve (See Figure 1, page 8) or the submersible pump before beginning work.*

Most homes have outdoor sillcocks (also called hose bibs and outdoor faucets). If the homeowner forgets to close the shutoff valve on the pipe inside the house, the sillcock can freeze and crack. A freeze-proof sillcock is designed to drain itself so this won't happen.

The self-draining feature is characterized by a small opening in the sillcock called a vacuum break (Figure 1). When a freezer-proof sillcock is turned off, air rushes into the sillcock through the vacuum break to break the "seal" of water. This allows the residual amount to drain.

Choosing the Right Unit

In order to accommodate the variety of ways in which sillcocks can be mounted, a number of freeze-proof sillcock kits are available. Most likely, the sillcock on the side of your house is installed in one of the following ways (Figure 2):

1) between open joists in the basement (this is the most common type of installation).
2) through a cantilevered floor.
3) through an interior wall (found most often in homes with concrete slab foundations).
4) across or through joists.

Installing the Unit

1. Determine the type of material (copper, CPVC, galvanized steel pipe) that was used to install the present sillcock. Turn off the water to the sillcock by closing the home's main water valve or by switching off the submersible pump. Open the sillcock and let water drain.

2. Copper or CPVC pipe should be cut on the backside of the sillcock shutoff valve (behind the valve). Then, remove the screws that hold the sillcock to the house (Figure 3) and pull the sillcock and piece of cut pipe out through the foundation (Figure 4). Discard the sillcock, cut pipe and shutoff valve. Since the new sillcock is freeze-proof, a shutoff valve is not needed.

3. When dealing with galvanized pipe, remove the screws that hold the sillcock to the house. Then, inside the house, use pipe wrenches to remove the shutoff valve from the pipe. To unscrew this portion of pipe from the valve, grasp the pipe between the valve and sillcock with one wrench and grasp the valve

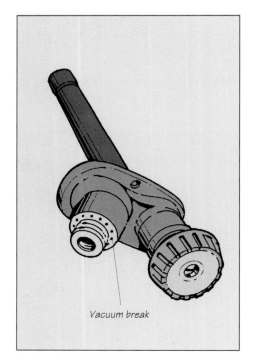

Figure 1. *This freeze-proof sillcock has a vacuum break that allows trapped water to drain.*

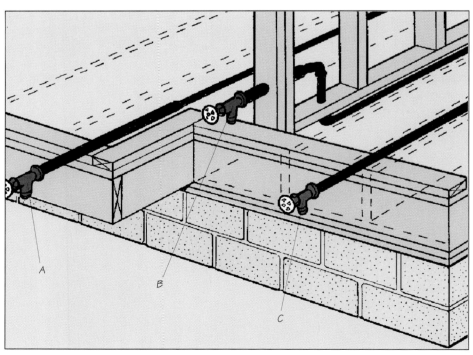

Figure 2. *In order to choose the correct freeze-proof sillcock for your home, determine what type of hose bib installation is on the house: (A) through cantilevered floor; (B) through interior wall; (C) between or through joists.*

with another wrench. Do the same thing to remove the valve from the water pipe that remains. Discard the sillcock, the piece of pipe and the valve.

Screw a galvanized coupling to the end of the water delivery pipe and thread a galvanized-to-copper transition fitting to that. Be sure threads that are in contact with plastic are well-sealed with Teflon paste. Use pipe joint compound to seal metal pipe to metal.

Note: The remainder of the installation procedure is the same whether working with copper or galvanized water pipe. If using CPVC, the pipes should be solvent-welded rather than soldered.

4. There will be a hole in the foundation where the old sillcock was installed. Place

the freeze-proof sillcock and attached pipe into the hole (Figure 5) , but do not screw it to the foundation yet.

5. Measure the diameter of the water pipe. Then, measure the distance from the galvanized fitting or the end of the copper or CPVC water pipe, to the sillcock. Add the socket depth to this measurement and cut a piece of copper or CPVC pipe (of the same diameter as the water pipe) to this length.

6. Clean the ends of the pipe with steel wool or emery cloth and apply flux or CPVC primer to the ends that will be joined.

7. The piece of pipe that comes attached to the sillcock is of a smaller diameter than the piece of copper or CPVC pipe you have cut. Push the two joints together so that the amount

allowed for the socket depth is inside the new piece of pipe. It is not necessary to use a coupling (Figure 6).

8. The run of pipe extending to the sillcock should slope slightly downward to the sillcock. If it does not, use hangers to attach the pipe to joists so that the pipe slopes. Solder or solvent-weld the two ends together.

9. Working outside at the sillcock, use a carpenter's level to get the sillcock straight (Figure 7). Then, attach it to the house with the mounting screws provided in the kit.

10. Working inside the house again, use a coupler to push the two unsecured ends of pipe together. Treat the ends with flux or CPVC primer and solder or solvent-weld them together (Figure 8).

Figure 3. Remove screws that hold the existing sillcock to the house.

Figure 4. After removing the shutoff valve, pull the sillcock, pipe and shutoff valve from the house.

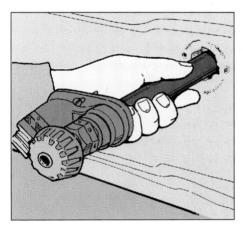
Figure 5. Install the freeze-proof sillcock and attached pipe.

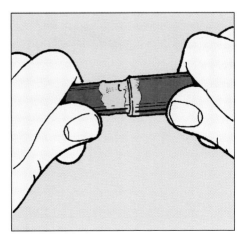
Figure 6. Join the sillcock pipe to the water pipe and extension.

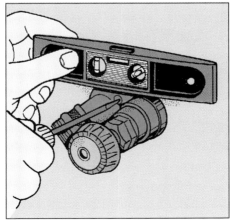
Figure 7. Level and secure the sillcock to the house.

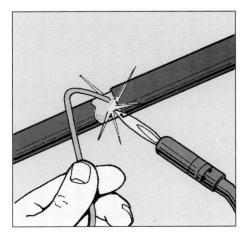
Figure 8. Complete the job by attaching the water pipe extension to the water pipe.

INSTALLING A LAWN SPRINKLER SYSTEM

Tools & Materials:

- ❑ water pressure gauge
- ❑ tape measure
- ❑ adjustable wrench
- ❑ wood stakes
- ❑ hammer
- ❑ miter box and back
- ❑ saw
- ❑ flat shovel
- ❑ spade
- ❑ try square
- ❑ pipe
- ❑ control valves
- ❑ stop waste and drain valve
- ❑ rolled plastic
- ❑ tube cutter
- ❑ utility knife
- ❑ sandpaper

Remember: Turn off the water shutoff valve or the main valve (see Figure 1, page 8) before beginning work.

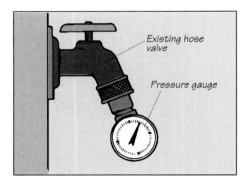

Figure 1. *Use a water pressure gauge to measure the water pressure at each hose bib. It is important to know the water pressure in order to select the best pipe size.*

Getting Started

1. Check the municipal plumbing code to determine applicable regulations.

2. Most manufacturers provide a design-layout booklet for sprinkler systems. It should include a grid with a scale of about 1 inch equal to 10 feet.

3. Attach a water pressure gauge to a sillcock (Figure 1). The dealer who sells you the system may have a gauge to lend you. Otherwise, it will be necessary to purchase one.

4. Turn the water on and record the static water pressure showing on the gauge. The pressure is given in psi (pounds per square inch). Repeat the process until all exterior sillcocks are tested. The highest reading is the important one.

Determine Gallons Per Minute (GPM)

1. In order to determine the size of the water meter, open the meter access and inspect the pipe connected to the meter on the house. The size may be stamped on the meter stem. If not, wrap a string around the pipe, measure the string, and record the measurement and the type of pipe used (copper, steel or PVC). Match this size to Figure 2. If the pipe size used is not shown in Figure 2, ask the sprinkler system dealer to determine the size. The water company should be able to help, if all else fails.

2. Determine the size of the main water pipe used in the home. If the pipe is smaller in the house than at the meter,

measure the outside of the pipe and compare this measurement to Figure 2 to determine its size. The control valve of the sprinkler system must be the same size as the water pipe.

3. Match the water meter size, the water delivery pipe size and water pressure reading to Figure 3 to determine the GPM (gallons per minute). Compare readings of different days and different times to determine the best watering schedule.

Plotting Patterns

1. Draw the house, garden and lawn on a scaled grid. Mark structures not to be sprayed.

2. Plot the spray pattern using the design-layout booklet provided by the manufacturer (Figure 4). Shift the pattern accordingly to minimize overspray onto walks, drives, patios, and other areas that should not be watered.

3. On the plan, locate a point between the house and meter to place the cut-in tee from the sprinkler kit. Draw lines connecting water pipes to control valves.

4. Count the number of sprinkler heads and control valves, and measure the pipe runs. Take this information to the dealer for his evaluation.

Choosing Materials

When it comes to choosing the type of pipe to be used, ask the plumbing dealer for advice. The most popular type of pipe used for this project is Schedule 40 PVC and flexible polybutylene (PB). Both are

APPROXIMATE PIPE SIZE

Outside Measures	Size & Material
4 - ³/₈"	1" Galvanized pipe
3 - ¹/₂"	³/₄" PVC SCH.40
2 - ³/₄"	¹/₂" Galvanized pipe; ³/₄" Copper

Figure 2. *Use this table to select the best pipe size for the main water supply pipe. The size will be based on the diameter of the pipe connected to the water meter.*

SAMPLE GPM

Water pressure	Meter	Pipe size	GPM
50	1"	1"	19.5
50	1"	3/4"	15
50	3/4"	3/4"	12

Figure 3. *Based on water meter size water pipe size, and water pressure reading at the hose bib, this table will help establish the delivery of water (in GMP) to the sprinkler system. Be sure to check your findings with the dealer who supplies the materials for this job.*

easily cut and joined by solvent welding or mechanical couplings, respectively. The plastic pipes will require supports for added strength. Use Teflon tape at the connecting points for sealing.

If you live in an area subject to freezing temperatures, positive drain valves should be used. These valves are similar to freeze-proof sillcocks (page 146). They prevent freezing by allowing water in the pipe to drain. Make sure the main control valve is equipped with a positive drain as well. Use anti-siphon sprinkler heads to prevent contamination of drinking water. The valves should prevent water from backwashing into the general water supply in the case that a line ruptures.

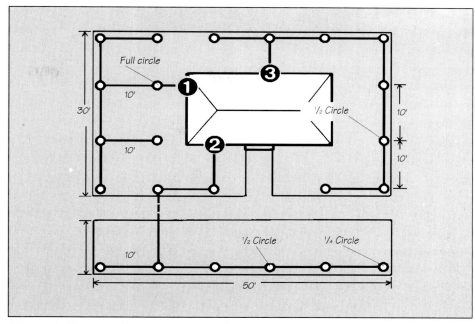

Figure 4. Plot the landscape and location of sprinkler heads. Note those that are to make a half or a quarter circle so overspray is minimized. Lines 1, 2 and 3 are main distribution lines.

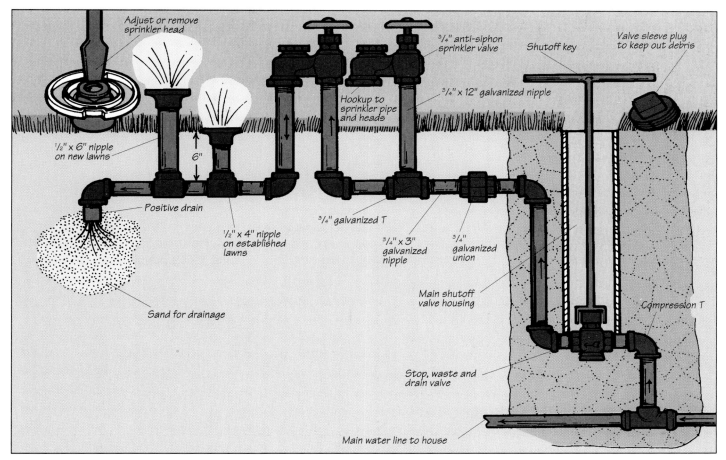

Figure 5. This drawing illustrates the plumbing for a section of the sprinkler system. Galvanized pipe was used here. Be sure to refer to installation guidelines from the manufacturer of your particular system. The instructions found here are general in nature and may not be appropriate for your specific design.

Installing the System

1. Before beginning work, refer to Figure 5 and turn the water off.

2. Measure and cut the main water delivery pipe.

Slip the compression nuts over each end of the cut pipe. Then, slip the tee onto the line. Connect the tee with the compression nuts on the tee.

Note: Be careful when connecting the tee; too much force may strip the threads or rupture the tee. Start with hand-tight pressure and then add 1/2 turn. Check for leaks. If there is a leak, tighten nuts another 1/2 turn at a time until the problem no longer exists.

3. Insert and connect a length of pipe into the free end of the tee and connect the main control valve (Figure 6).

4. With the main control valve OFF, turn on the water and check for leaks.

5. Assemble the other control valves and place them on pipe stems. Stems should be 6 to 12 inches above ground. If plastic is used, stake each stem for support. Galvanized steel pipe does not require supports. Valves and stem assemblies should be spaced 8 inches apart.

6. At the end or low point of each supply line, install a tee with the threaded end facing down. Install a positive drain valve at this low point. Then, cap the ends of the other tees.

7. Dig a shallow trench from the main

control valve to the other control valves and splice in the water supply line. Then, install the main water delivery line between the main control valve and other control valves.

8. Turn the main control valve on slowly and inspect all lines for leaks. Then, turn the main control valve off and inspect the positive drain action.

9. Install a pipe run to each sprinkler.

10. When pipe runs are completed, remove the heads of all sprinklers. Commonly used are brass fittings, which can be unscrewed.

11. To check the connections for leaks, turn on each run and flush the heads of dirt and debris. Also, check the positive drain.

12. With the system off, reinstall the sprinkler heads. To check the spray pattern, turn on each run. If a pattern is not satisfactory, adjust the pipe run before digging the trench.

13. Stake sprinkler heads into position.

Guidelines for Digging Trenches

1. Leave the stakes in place, marking where each sprinkler head is located and move the pipe slightly to either side. Be careful not to put stress on pipes.

2. Lay a plastic sheet near the pipe run to collect sod and soil.

3. With a hoe or flat shovel, cut the sod in strip about 12 inches wide parallel to the pipe run. Roll up the sod and lay it on the plastic.

Note: It is important to keep the sod that you dig up moist so that it will not suffer damage. Always place the sod "roots side" facing down to minimize exposure to air and sunlight.

4. Dig a V-shaped trench about 8 inches deep along the entire length of the run. Place the soil on the plastic.

5. To assure proper drainage, place about 2 inches of sand and gravel mix at the bottom of the trench.

6. Remove any obstructions from the trench. Slide the pipe run into the trench and repack the soil around the pipe.

Note: To place the head flush with the sod level you must take into account the depth of the sod. For a new lawn you need to determine how thick the sod will eventually grow and set the heads at the appropriate height above the existing dirt, usually 2 inches.

7. Remove sprinkler heads and flush each line to remove soil. Replace the heads, test the pattern and make any necessary adjustments.

8. Replace the sod. Then, water the area to help the sod regain stamina.

➡PLUMBER'S TIP:
Trenching under drives and walks is done by attaching a garden hose to a length of galvanized pipe with a hose bib-to-pipe thread adapter. This produces a sluiced tunnel (Figure 7).

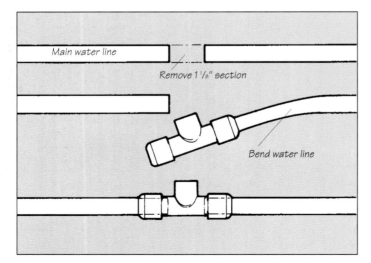

Figure 6. Connect the main water supply pipe to the home's water supply with a tee and compression nuts. Attach the tee to the main control valve.

Figure 7. Slice a trench under driveways and walks by attaching a garden hose to a length of galvanized pipe with a hose bib-to-pipe thread adapter.

MAINTAINING A SEPTIC SYSTEM

* This job should be performed by a professional serviceman.

According to the U.S. Public Health Service: "The purpose of a septic system is to treat household wastes, including soapy water from the laundry and bath, discarded food scraps and body wastes. A septic system will serve a home satisfactorily only if it is properly located, designed, constructed and adequately maintained. To obtain satisfactory service, the homeowner must know something about the design, operation, and maintenance of the septic system."

How a Septic System Works

A septic system consists of three main sections. One is the watertight septic tank; the second is the distribution box(es); the other is the drainfield, frequently referred to as the leaching area or leaching field (Figure 1).

Sewage from the house flows through the main drain pipe into the septic tank (Figure 2). As sewage enters the tank, solids and liquid separate; however, finer particles remain suspended in liquid and flow out of the tank with liquid to a distribution box. From there, liquid and fine particles enter several lines leading to the drainfield where they percolate into the ground (Figure 3).

Solids that remain in the septic tank are broken down into a sludge by bacteria. Eventually, this sludge must be cleaned out of the tank so it doesn't build up and clog the system. The only maintenance necessary for a septic system is the periodic cleaning of the tank.

Indications of Trouble

A homeowner can detect a problem with the septic system by observing the following indications.

1. Toilets and pipes back up, indicating that the septic tank is filled. Call a serviceman to pump out the tank.

2. Grass takes on a darker hue, growing more vigorously above the septic tank. This indicates that the tank is cracked and has to be replaced because the sewage is escaping.

3. The ground above the drainfield erupts, due to a buildup of gas. This indicates that the system was not properly installed. If this should happen, report the occurrence to community officials, such as the town engineer. Municipal ordinances governing the installation of septic systems are strict and the contractor may be held responsible.

The Importance of Periodic Maintenance

A problem with the septic system occurs most often when a homeowner disregards periodic maintenance. As mentioned earlier, the septic tank must be pumped out periodically.

Depending upon the number of people in the family, a septic tank requires maintenance every two to four years (unless a home has a food waste disposer—then, the job usually has to be done once every year or two). The serviceman hired to do the job can advise whether more or less frequent cleaning is needed.

To facilitate the cleaning of a septic

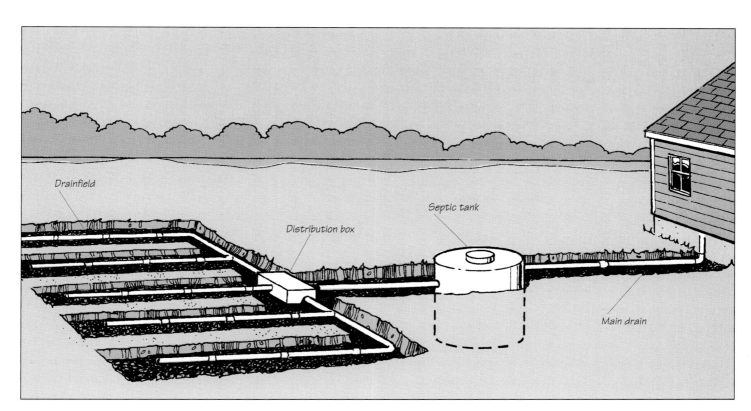

Figure 1. *A septic system is made up of a drainfield, which includes the distribution box, and a septic tank.*

tank and to prevent possible damage to that system, provide the serviceman with a diagram of the system in relation to the house (Figure 4). This diagram should have been given to you by the contractor who built the house or by the previous owner of the house. If you do not have a diagram, check with the town engineering department. Often times, a copy is kept on file.

The diagram will help the serviceman pinpoint the location of the tank so he does not have to do a lot of digging. It also will help him avoid driving heavy equipment over the septic tank and drainfield. Heavy weight bearing down on the tank and drainfield can damage them.

If the serviceman is a true professional, he will cut the sod into large chunks so that it can be replaced without unduly disturbing the lawn. When the top of the tank is revealed, he will remove the cover and insert the hose of his special pumping equipment into the sludge (Figures 5 and 6). He will turn on the pump and keep it on until a shallow layer of sludge remains. During the process, he will occasionally stir sludge with a long shovel to keep it in suspension. Then, he will reinstall the cover, fill the hole and replace the sod. If the job is done properly, you will hardly be able to see where the soil was disturbed.

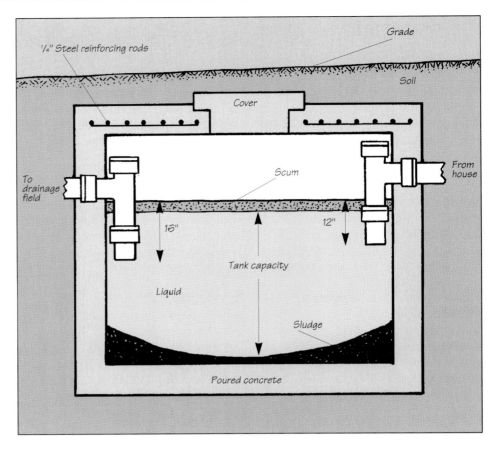

Figure 2. The above illustration shows a cross-sectional view of a typical poured concrete septic system. The soil and waste enter from the right and remain in the tank while the bacterial action breaks down the solids into liquid that flows out the left. The material that doesn't break down remains as sludge at the bottom of the tank.

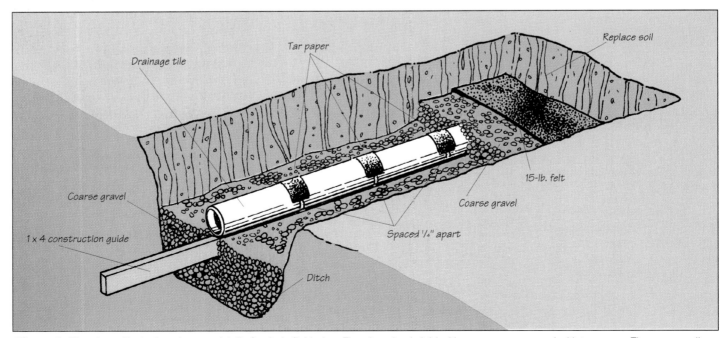

Figure 3. The above illustration shows a detail of a drain field pipe. The clay pipe is laid with open gaps covered with tar paper. These gaps allow the liquid to seep into the ground.

Clearing the Air

There are several questions that homeowners often ask concerning septic systems:

Will grease harm a septic system? Grease causes no more harm to a septic system than it does to a sewer system.

Is it necessary to bypass the septic tank with a drain line from a washing machine, so detergent-laden water from the machine flows directly to the drainfield? No! Feeding a drain line directly into the leaching area so detergent-ladened water does not enter the septic tank can have just the opposite effect. Detergents can cause the drainfield to clog. On the other hand, detergent scum flowing into and staying in the septic tank will be cleaned out with sludge when the tank receives its periodic cleaning.

Is it true that store-bought chemicals help dissolve sludge that builds up in a septic tank? According to the Public Health Service: "There are no known chemicals, yeasts, bacteria, enzymes or other substance capable of eliminating or reducing the sludge in a septic tank so that periodic cleaning becomes unnecessary."

Can you install a food waste disposer in a home served by a septic system? As long as the size of the septic tank is adequate, no harm can be done by having a disposer. However, the U.S. Public Health Service and Federal Housing Authority recommend minimum standards for septic tanks. The chart below outlines these standards.

Dwelling Size	Gallon-Size Tank Without Disposer	Gallon-Size Tank With Disposer
One or two bedroom	750	1,125
Three bedroom	900	1,400
Four bedroom	1,000	1,500
Five bedroom	1,250	1,875
Each additional bedroom	250	375

Figure 4. *A diagram of the layout of the septic system allows the serviceman to locate the tank immediately, reducing the amount of digging and lowering the cost of service.*

Figure 5. *Maintaining a septic system involves periodically pumping out sludge.*

Figure 6. *A thin layer of sludge should remain in the tank in order to maintain the bacteria that act upon and break down solids.*

Selected Relevant Sections of the National Standard Plumbing Code (NSPC)

Important: *Check sections of the plumbing code applicable to your municipality before applying any of the following sections of the NSPC. Municipal codes take precedence.*

2.3 CHANGE IN DIRECTION OF DRAINAGE PIPING

2.3.3 Horizontal to Vertical
Horizontal drainage lines, connecting with a vertical stack, shall enter through 45 degree wye branches, 60 degree wye branches, combination wye and one-eighth bend branches, sanitary T or sanitary tapped T branches, or other approved fittings of equivalent sweep. No fitting having more than one branch at the same level shall be used unless such fitting is constructed so that the discharge from any one branch cannot readily enter any other branch.

2.3.4 Horizontal to Horizontal
Horizontal drainage lines connecting with other horizontal drainage lines shall enter through wye branches, combination wye and one-eighth bend branches, or other approved fittings of equivalent sweep.

2.3.5 Vertical to Horizontal
Vertical drainage lines connecting with horizontal drainage lines shall enter through wye branches, combination wye and one-eighth bend branches, or other approved fittings of equivalent sweep.

2.9 PROTECTION OF PIPES

2.9.1 Breakage
Pipes passing under or through walls shall be protected from breakage. Any plumbing pipe passing under a footing or through a foundation wall shall be provided with a relieving arch.

2.9.3 Cutting or Notching
Any structural member weakened or impaired by cutting, notching, or otherwise, shall be reinforced, repaired, or replaced, so as to be left in a safe structural condition.

2.13.1 Strainer Plates
All strainer plates on drain inlets shall be designed and installed so no opening is greater than 1/2 inch in least dimension.

2.13.3 Openings for Pipes
In or on buildings where openings have been made in walls, floors, ceilings, for the passage of pipes, they shall be closed and protected by the installation of approved metal collars securely fastened to the adjoining structure.

2.22 WATER CLOSET CONNECTIONS

a. Three-inch bends may be used on water closet or similar connections provided; a 4-inch by 3-inch flange is installed to receive the closet fixture
b. Four-inch by three-inch closet bends shall be permitted.

4.2 TYPES OF JOINTS FOR PIPING MATERIALS

4.2.4 Soldered
Every soldered joint shall be made with approved fittings. Surfaces to be soldered shall be cleaned bright. The joints shall be properly fluxed and made with approved solder. Joints in copper water tube shall be made by the appropriate use of approved cast brass or wrought copper fittings. Joints for potable water used in copper, brass, or wrought copper fittings shall be made with a solder containing not more than 0.2 percent lead.

4.2.14 Plastic
Every joint in plastic piping shall be made with approved fittings by either solvent cemented or heat joined connections, approved elastomeric gaskets, metal clamps, and screws of corrosion resisting materials; approved insert fittings; approved mechanical fittings; or threaded joints according to approved standards.

5.1 SEPARATE TRAPS FOR EACH FIXTURE

Each plumbing fixture shall be separately trapped by a water seal trap, except as otherwise permitted in this code, placed as close as possible to the fixture outlet. The vertical distance from the fixture outlet to the trap weir shall not exceed 24 inches. No fixture shall be double trapped. Exceptions to the separate trapping requirements are as follows:
a. Fixtures that have integral traps.
b. A combination plumbing fixture may be installed on one trap provided the waste outlets are not more than 30 inches apart.
c. One trap may be installed for a set of not more than three single compartment sinks, laundry trays or lavatories immediately adjacent to each other in the same room, and the trap is centrally located when three such fixtures are installed.
d. No clothes washer or laundry tub shall be discharged to a trap serving a kitchen sink.

5.2 SIZE OF FIXTURE TRAPS

Fixture trap size (nominal diameter) shall be sufficient to drain the fixture rapidly.

No trap shall be larger than the drainage pipe into which it discharges. Integral traps shall conform to appropriate standards.

5.3.5 Prohibited Traps The following traps are prohibited:
a. Traps which depend upon moving parts to maintain their seal.
b. Bell traps.
c. Crown vented traps.
d. Separate fixture traps which depend on interior partitions for their seal.
e. "S" traps of uniform internal dimension.
f. Drum traps.

5.4 DRAINAGE PIPE CLEANOUTS

5.4.1 Location
Cleanouts shall be not more than 75 feet apart, including the developed length of the cleanout pipe in horizontal drainage lines of 4 inch nominal diameter or less, and not more than 100 feet apart, including the developed length, of the cleanout pipe for larger pipes.

7.4 INSTALLATION OF FIXTURES

7.4.1 Access for Cleaning
Plumbing fixtures shall be so installed as to be readily accessible for cleaning both the fixture and the area about it. Where practical, all pipes from fixtures shall be run to the nearest wall.

7.4.2 Water-Tight Joints
Joints formed where fixtures come in contact with walls or floors shall be sealed.

7.4.3 Securing Floor-Mounted Fixtures
Floor-mounted fixtures shall be rigidly secured to the structure and to their mounting flanges by corrosion resisting screws or bolts.

7.4.4 Securing Wall-hung Water Closet Bowls
Wall-hung water closet bowls shall be rigidly supported by a concealed metal hanger which is attached to the building structural members so that no strain is transmitted to the closet connector or any other part of the plumbing system.

7.4.5 Setting
Fixtures shall be set level and in proper alignment with reference to adjacent walls.

7.5 WATER SUPPLY PROTECTION

The water supply for every plumbing fixture, fixture fitting, appliance, or appurtenance shall be installed to prevent backflow.

7.11 LAVATORIES
7.11.1 Lavatory Waste Outlets
Lavatories shall have waste outlets not less than 1¼ inches in diameter. A strainer, pop-up stopper, crossbars or other device shall be provided to restrict the clear opening of the waste outlet.

7.12 BATHTUBS
7.12.1 Bathtub Waste Outlets and Overflows
Bathtubs shall have waste outlets and overflows at least 1½ inches in diameter and the waste outlet shall be equipped with an approved stopper.

7.13 SHOWERS
7.13.1 Shower Waste Outlet
Waste outlets serving showers, except showers over bathtubs, shall be at least 2 inches in diameter and shall have removable strainers no less than 3 inches in diameter having strainer openings not less than 1/4 inch in minimum dimension.

7.13.3 Shower Floors or Receptors
Floors or receptors under shower compartments shall be laid on or be supported by a smooth and structurally sound base. Floors under shower compartments, other than those laid directly on the ground surface or where prefabricated receptors have been provided, shall be lined and made watertight by the provision of approved shower pans of durable material. Such pans shall turn up on all sides at least 2 inches above the finished threshold level. Pans shall be securely fastened to the waste outlet at the seepage entrance making a watertight joint between the pan and the outlet. Floor surfaces shall be constructed of smooth, non-corrosive, non-absorbent, and waterproof materials.

7.13.4 Water Supply Riser
Every water supply riser from the shower valve to the shower head outlet, whether exposed or not, shall be secured.

7.14 SINKS
7.14.1 Sink Waste Outlets
Sinks shall be provided with waste outlets not less than 1½ inches in diameter. A strainer, crossbar, or other device shall be provided to restrict the clear opening of the waste outlet. Sinks on which a food waste grinder is installed shall have a waste opening not less than 3½ inches in diameter.

7.15 FOOD-WASTE-GRINDER UNITS
7.15.1 Domestic Food-Waste-Grinder Waste Outlets
Food waste grinders for domestic use shall be connected to a drain of not less than 1½ inches in diameter.

7.17 DISHWASHING MACHINES
7.17.2 Separate Trap
Each unit shall discharge through an approved air gap fitting and be separately trapped or discharge indirectly into a properly trapped and vented fixture.

7.17.3 Residential Sink and Dishwasher
The discharge from a sink and dishwasher may discharge through a single 1½ inch trap. The discharge from the dishwasher shall be increased to a minimum of 3/4 inch and be connected with a wye fitting between the sink outlet and the trap inlet.

7.17.4 Residential Sink, Dishwasher, and Food Waste Grinder
The discharge from a sink, dishwasher, and food waste grinder may discharge through a single 1½ inch trap. The discharge from the dishwasher shall be increased to a minimum of ¾ inch and be connected with a wye fitting between the discharge of the food waste grinder and the trap inlet, or to the head of the food waste grinder.

10.4 PROTECTION OF POTABLE WATER SUPPLY
10.4.1 General
A potable water supply system shall be designed, installed, and maintained to prevent contamination from the nonpotable liquids, solids, or gases into the potable water supply through cross connections.

10.5 PROTECTION AGAINST BACKFLOW AND BACKSIPHONAGE
10.5.2 Minimum Required Air Gap
a. How measured—The minimum required air gap shall be measured vertically from the lowest end of a potable water outlet to the flood level rim or line of the fixture or receptacle into which it discharges.
b. Size—The minimum required air gap shall be twice the effective opening of a potable water outlet unless the outlet is a distance less than three times the effective opening away from a wall or similar vertical surface in which cases the minimum required air gap shall be three times the effective opening of the outlet.

10.14.7 Water Hammer
All building water supply systems in which quick acting valves are installed shall be provided with devices to absorb high pressures resulting from the quick closing of these valves. These pressure absorbing devices shall be either air chambers or approved mechanical devices. Water pressure absorbers shall be placed as close as possible to the quick-acting valves or installed also at the ends of long pipe runs or near batteries of fixtures. All devices shall be accessible for repair, replacement, or replenishing of air.

12.2 PROTECTION OF TRAP SEALS
12.2.1 Protection Required
The protection of trap seals from siphonage, aspiration, or back-pressure shall be accomplished by the appropriate use of soil or waste stacks with adequate venting in accordance with the requirements of the Code. Venting systems shall be designed and installed so that at no time shall trap seals be subjected to a pneumatic pressure differential of more than 1 inch of water pressure under design load conditions. If a trap seal is subject to loss by evaporation, means shall be provided to prevent the escape of sewer gas.

12.4 VENT TERMINALS
12.4.1 Extension Above Roofs
Extension of vent pipes shall terminate 6 inches above the roof, measured from the highest point where the vent intersects the roof.

12.4.2 Waterproof Flashings
Each vent terminal shall be made watertight with the roof by proper flashing.

12.4.4 Location of Vent Terminal
No vent terminal shall be located directly beneath any door, window, or other ventilating opening of the building or of an adjacent building nor shall any such vent terminal be within 10 feet horizontally of such an opening unless it is at least 2 feet above the top of such opening.

12.5 FROST CLOSURE
Where frost closure is likely to occur, each vent extension through a roof shall be at least 3 inches in diameter. When it is found necessary to increase the size of the vent extension to meet this requirement, the change in diameter shall be made inside the building at least 1 foot below the roof.

12.8 FIXTURE VENTS
12.8.1 Maximum Length of Trap Arm
Each fixture trap shall have a protecting vent so located that the developed length of the trap arm is within the requirements set forth in Table 12.8.1.

**Table 12.8.1
MAXIMUM LENGTH OF TRAP ARM**

Diameter of Trap Arm	Distance — Trap to Vent
1¼ inches	3 feet 6 inches
1½ inches	5 feet
2 inches	8 feet
3 inches	10 feet
4 inches	12 feet

A copy of the National Standard Plumbing Code may be purchased from the National Association of Plumbing-Heating-Cooling Contractors, P.O. Box 6808, Falls Church, VA 22046. Illustrated or non-illustrated versions are available.

GLOSSARY

Adapter A fitting that connects two pipes of different sizes or materials.

Aerator The diverter/screen unit that is screwed onto the end of a faucet to control splashing.

Air chamber A vertical, air-filled pipe that prevents water hammer by absorbing pressure when water is shut off at a faucet or valve.

Air gap A device used in a dishwasher's drainage system that prevents waste water from backing up and contaminating clean dishes in the dishwasher. This term is also used in referring to the space needed between the source of potable water (a faucet outlet) and the rim of the sink or lavatory it discharges into.

Backflow A reverse flow of water or other liquids into water supply pipes, caused by negative pressure in the pipes.

Backflow preventer A device or means that prevents backflow.

Ballcock A toilet tank water supply valve, which is controlled by a float ball.

Braided stainless steel Flexible steel lines outfitted with connecting nuts, easier to handle and install than conventional metal lines.

Branch Any part of a pipe system other than a riser, main or stack.

Branch vent A vent pipe that runs from a vent stack to a branch drain line.

Bushing A device that permits reduction of one pipe size to another and/or male to female connections.

Calipers A tool used to measure the diameter of pipes.

Caulking A waterproofing compound used to seal plumbing connections.

Check valve A special valve that allows water to flow in only one direction.

Cleanout A removable plug in a trap or a drainpipe, which allows easier access for removing blockages inside.

Closet bend A curved section of drain pipe that is located beneath the base of the toilet.

Closet flange The rim on a closet bend by which that pipe attaches to the floor.

Coupling A fitting used to connect two pipes.

CPVC Chlorinated polyvinyl chloride; a plastic pipe used for hot water lines.

Cross connection A physical connection between the potable water supply and any nonpotable water source.

Diameter The nominal inside pipe diameter as designated in the commercial sizing of pipes.

Diaphragm Used instead of a stem washer, this cap is found on compression faucets.

Diverter valve A device that changes the direction of water flow from one faucet or fixture to another.

Drain Any pipe that carries waste water through a drainage network into the municipal sewer or private septic system.

Drainage network All the piping that carries sewage from a house into the municipal sewer or private septic system.

DWV Drain-waste-vent; a term applied to the system of piping and fittings used to carry away drainage and waste ; also applied to the pipe and fittings used for the same purpose.

Elastomeric seal Found in a hot-water transition fitting; made of material that does not lose shape when subject to hot temperatures.

Elbow A fitting used for making directional changes in pipelines.

Escutcheon A decorative plate that covers the hole in the wall in which the stem or cartridge fits.

Female thread The end of a pipe or fitting with internal threads.

Fitting Any device that joins sections of pipe or connects pipe to a fixture.

Flapper valve A valve that replaces a tank stopper in a toilet.

Float ball The hollow ball on the end of a rod in the toilet tank, which floats upward as the tank fills after flushing and closes the water inlet valve.

Flush valve A device at the bottom of a toilet tank for flushing.

Flux A material applied to the surfaces of copper pipes and fittings to assist in the cleaning and bonding processes.

Galvanic action An electrical process by which corrosive elements are leached from one metal substance and attracted to another.

Gasket A device used to seal joints against leaks.

Grade (also known as pitch) The slope of a line of pipes in reference to the horizontal. It is expressed in fractions of an inch per foot of pipe length—for example, 1/4 inch per foot.

Hanger A device used to support suspended pipe.

Inlet valve A valve in a toilet tank that controls the flow of water into the tank.

Joint Any connection between pipes, fittings or other parts of a plumbing system.

Joint compound A material applied to threaded connections to help prevent leaks.

Lavatory A wash basin that is located in a bathroom or powder room.

Lift-rod Device that opens and closes popup stoppers.

Main Principal drain pipe to which all branches connect, directly or indirectly.

Main vent (or stack) Principal vent to which branch vents may be connected.

Male threads The end of a fitting, pipe or fixture connection with external threads.

No-hub (hubless) connectors A fitting that connects two pipes by means of neoprene sleeves and stainless-steel clamps.

Nominal size The designated dimension of a pipe or fitting; it varies slightly from the actual size.

Nonpotable water Water that is not safe to drink.

O-ring A ring of rubber used as a gasket.

Overflow tube A tube in a toilet tank into which water flows if the float arm fails to activate the shutoff valve when the tank is filled.

Pipe sleeve A clamp used to patch pipe leaks.

Pipe support Any kind of brace used to support pipe.

Plumber's putty A material used to seal openings around fixtures.

Pop-up valve A device used to open and close drains.

Potable water Water free from impurities in amounts sufficient to cause disease or harmful physiological effects.

PVC Polyvinyl chloride; a plastic used to make cold-water pipe.

Reducer A fitting used to join two pipes of different diameters.

Relief valve A safety device that automatically releases water due to an excessive buildup or pressure and temperature; used on a water heater.

Revent A pipe installed to vent a fixture trap that connects to a main vent.

Riser A water supply pipe that extends vertically.

Roughing-in The planning for parts of the plumbing system before installation of fixtures or appliances.

Septic tank A water-tight receptacle into which raw sewage is deposited for dissolution by bacterial action.

Shims Used to level or add support.

Shutoff valve A device set into a water line to allow for interruption of the flow of water to a fixture or appliance.

Slope In reference to a horizontal plane, the fall of a line of pipe; a fraction of an inch per foot of pipe.

Soil stack A vertical pipe that carries wastes to the sewer drain; also, the vertical main pipe that receives both human and nonhuman wastes from a group of plumbing fixtures including a toilet or from all plumbing fixtures in a given installation.

Soldering/sweating The process used to join copper pipe.

Solvent welding The technique used to join plumbing fixtures and appliances to CPVC.

Stack Any vertical main that is a part of the DWV system.

Stub-out The termination of water delivery or drainage network pipe extended into a room through a wall or floor to which a fixture or appliance is to be connected.

Sump pump A special pump used to remove accumulations of water from a sump or shallow pit.

T (tee) A pipe fitting with three points of connection that is T-shaped.

Tap A faucet or hydrant that draws water from a supply line.

Temperature and Pressure relief valve (T & P) Device that prevents temperature and pressure from building up inside the tank and exploding.

Thermocouple A safety device that automatically turns off gas flowing to the pilot if the flame goes out.

Threaded sweat adapter Used to install cold-water pipes.

Toggle bolts A bolt used to fasten brackets to the wall; distinguished by two hinged wings.

Trap The water-filled curved pipe that prevents sewer gas from entering the house through the drainage network.

Tripwaste Lever-controlled bathtub drain stopper; two kinds, pop-up or plunger.

Valve seat The part of the valve into which washer or other piece fits, stopping the flow of water.

Vent stack A vertical vent pipe.

Washer A disc (made of soft material) that provides a seal against the flow of water.

Waste Discharge from plumbing fixtures or plumbing appliances that does not contain fecal matter.

Water closet Toilet.

Water drain cock A device that allows the water heater tank to be drained.

Water hammer A knocking in water pipes caused by a sudden change in pressure after a faucet or water valve shuts off.

Water main A water supply pipe for public use.

Wax ring A wax seal used to seal the base of a toilet so it won't leak.

Wet venting An extension of a waste pipe, receives waste not coming from a toilet or kitchen sink.

Y (wye) fitting A fitting used in drainage systems for connecting branch lines to horizontal drainage lines; also provides cleanouts.

METRIC CONVERSION CHARTS

PIPE FITTINGS

Only fittings for use with copper tube are affected by metrication: metric compression fittings are interchangeable with U.S. in some sizes, but require adapters in others.

Interchangeable Sizes		Sizes Requiring Adapters	
millimeters	inches	millimeters	inches
12	3/8	22	3/4
15	1/2	35	1 1/4
28	1	42	1 1/2
54	2		

Metric capillary (soldered) fittings are not directly interchangeable with U.S. sizes but adapters are available. Pipe fittings that used screwed threads to make the joint remain unchanged. The British Standard Pipe (BSP) thread form has now been accepted internationally and its dimensions will not physically change. These screwed fittings are commonly used for joining iron or steel pipes, for connections on kitchen and bathroom faucet and bath waste outlets and on boilers, radiators, pumps etc. Fittings for use with lead pipe are joined by soldering and for this purpose the metric and inch sizes are interchangeable.

(Information courtesy Metrication Board, Millbank Tower, Millbank, London SW1P 4QU)

METRIC LENGTHS

Lengths Meters	Equivalent Feet and Inches	
1.8m	5'	10 7/8"
2.1m	6'	10 5/8"
2.4m	7'	10 1/2"
2.7m	8'	10 1/4"
3.0m	9'	10 1/8"
3.3m	10'	9 7/8"
3.6m	11'	9 3/4"
3.9m	12'	9 1/2"
4.2m	13'	9 3/8"
4.5m	14'	9 1/3"
4.8m	15'	9"
5.1m	16'	8 3/4"
5.4m	17'	8 5/8"
5.7m	18'	8 3/8"
6.0m	19'	8 1/4"
6.3m	20'	8"
6.6m	21'	7 7/8"
6.9m	22'	7 5/8"
7.2m	23'	7 1/2"
7.5m	24'	7 1/4"
7.8m	25'	7 1/8"

All the dimensions are based on 1 inch = 25 mm

LUMBER

Sizes: Metric cross-sections are so close to their nearest Imperial sizes, as noted below, that for most purposes they may be considered equivalents.

Lengths: Metric lengths are based on a 300mm module, which is slightly shorter in length than an Imperial foot. It will, therefore, be important to check your requirements accurately to the nearest inch and consult the table below to find the metric length required.

Areas: The metric area is a square meter. Use the following conversion factors when converting from Imperial data: 100 sq. feet=9,290 sq. meters.

millimeters	inches		millimeters	inches	
16 x 75	5/8	x 3	44 x 150	1 3/4	x 6
16 x 100	5/8	x 4	44 x 175	1 3/4	x 7
16 x 125	5/8	x 5	44 x 200	1 3/4	x 8
16 x 150	5/8	x 6	44 x 225	1 3/4	x 9
19 x 75	3/4	x 3	44 x 250	1 3/4	x 10
19 x 100	3/4	x 4	44 x 300	1 3/4	x 12
19 x 125	3/4	x 5	50 x 75	2	x 3
19 x 150	3/4	x 6	50 x 100	2	x 4
22 x 75	7/8	x 3	50 x 125	2	x 5
22 x 100	7/8	x 4	50 x 150	2	x 6
22 x 125	7/8	x 5	50 x 175	2	x 7
22 x 150	7/8	x 6	50 x 200	2	x 8
25 x 75	1	x 3	50 x 225	2	x 9
25 x 100	1	x 4	50 x 250	2	x 10
25 x 125	1	x 5	50 x 300	2	x 12
25 x 150	1	x 6	63 x 100	2 1/2	x 4
25 x 175	1	x 7	63 x 125	2 1/2	x 5
25 x 200	1	x 8	63 x 150	2 1/2	x 6
25 x 225	1	x 9	63 x 175	2 1/2	x 7
25 x 250	1	x 10	63 x 200	2 1/2	x 8
25 x 300	1	x 12	63 x 225	2 1/2	x 9
32 x 75	1 1/4	x 3	75 x 100	3	x 4
32 x 100	1 1/4	x 4	75 x 125	3	x 5
32 x 125	1 1/4	x 5	75 x 150	3	x 6
32 x 150	1 1/4	x 6	75 x 175	3	x 7
32 x 175	1 1/4	x 7	75 x 200	3	x 8
32 x 200	1 1/4	x 8	75 x 225	3	x 9
32 x 225	1 1/4	x 9	75 x 250	3	x 10
32 x 250	1 1/4	x 10	75 x 300	3	x 12
32 x 300	1 1/4	x 12	100 x 100	4	x 4
38 x 75	1 1/2	x 3	100 x 150	4	x 6
38 x 100	1 1/2	x 4	100 x 200	4	x 8
38 x 125	1 1/2	x 5	100 x 250	4	x 10
38 x 150	1 1/2	x 6	100 x 300	4	x 12
38 x 175	1 1/2	x 7	150 x 150	6	x 6
38 x 200	1 1/2	x 8	150 x 200	6	x 8
38 x 225	1 1/2	x 9	150 x 300	6	x 12
44 x 75	1 3/4	x 3	200 x 200	8	x 8
44 x 100	1 3/4	x 4	250 x 250	10	x 10
44 x 125	1 3/4	x 5	300 x 300	12	x 12